65
357
15/11/2019
AF622002

Literary Orientalism
A Companion

Literary Orientalism
A Companion

A.R. Kidwai

Viva Books
New Delhi | Mumbai | Chennai | Kolkata | Bangalore | Hyderabad | Kochi | Guwahati

Copyright © Viva Books Private Limited

All rights reserved. No part of this publication may be reproduced, stored in a retrieval system, or transmitted in any form or by any means, electronic, mechanical, photocopying, recording or otherwise, without the prior written permission of the publishers.

First Published 2009
Reprinted 2012

Viva Books Private Limited

4737/23, Ansari Road, Daryaganj, New Delhi 110 002
Tel. 42242200, 23258325, 23283121, Email: vivadelhi@vivagroupindia.net

76, Service Industries, Shirvane, Sector 1, Nerul, Navi Mumbai 400 706
Tel. 27721273, 27721274, Email: vivamumbai@vivagroupindia.net

Jamals Fazal Chambers, 26 Greams Road, Chennai 600 006
Tel. 28294241, 28290304, Email: vivachennai@vivagroupindia.net

B-103, Jindal Towers, 21/1A/3 Darga Road, Kolkata 700 017
Tel. 22816713, Email: vivakolkata@vivagroupindia.net

7, GF, Sovereign Park Aptts., 56-58, K. R. Road, Basavanagudi, Bangalore 560 004
Tel. 26607409, Email: vivabangalore@vivagroupindia.net

101-102, Moghal Marc Apartments, 3-4-637 to 641, Narayanguda,
Hyderabad 500 029, Tel. 27564481, Email: vivahyderabad@vivagroupindia.net

First Floor, Beevi Towers, SRM Road, Kaloor, Kochi - 682 018, Kerala,
Tel. 0484-2403055, 2403056, Email: vivakochi@vivagroupindia.net

232, GNB Road, Beside UCO Bank, Silpukhuri, Guwahati 781 003
Tel. 0361-2666386, Email: vivaguwahati@vivagroupindia.net

www.vivagroupindia.com

ISBN: 978-81-309-1264-6

Published by Vinod Vasishtha for Viva Books Private Limited
4737/23 Ansari Road, Daryaganj, New Delhi 110 002

Printed and bound by Raj Press, R-3, Inderpuri, New Delhi - 110 012.

Dedicated
with gratitude to
Professor Richard Foulkes,
Head, Department of English,
University of Leicester, UK

Contents

Acknowledgements

The help and assistance I got from the following individuals and institutions is gratefully acknowledged:

- University of Leicester, Leicester, UK
- Markfield Institute of Higher Education, Leicester, UK
- Aligarh Muslim University, Aligarh
- Professor Narayan Chandran, Department of English, Central University of Hyderabad
- Mr M. Naved Khan
- Mr Abdul Haleem Kidwai

Sources:

Of the numerous printed and electronic sources used for culling bibliographic information, the following ones deserve particular mention:

- *Annual Bibliography of English Language and Literature*

  Webpage: http://collections.chadwyck.com/marketing/home_abell.jsp
- Smith, B.P., *Islam in English Literature,* New York, 1937
- Masood, Abid, 'Islam in Medieval and Early Modern English Literature', *Islamic Studies,* Islamabad, Pakistan, 49:3, 2005
- *Index Islamicus*

- Hasan, Masoodul, *Sufism and English Literature: Chaucer to the Present Age*, New Delhi, 2007
- Bibliography by Year (Dissertations in English on Arabic-Western Literary Relations)

  Webpage:http://www.libraries.iub.edu/index.php?pageId=2161
- *Index of Islamic Literature* published by the Islamic Foundation, Leicester, UK
- Wazzan, Adnan M., *Taswir al-Islam fi al-Adab al-Inklezi*. Riyadh, Saudi Arabia, 2 Volumes, 2005 (A magisterial survey in Arabic of the image of Islam/ Muslims in the entire history of English literature, from the earliest to present time)

Preface

As a young student of Masters in English Literature at the Aligarh Muslim University, Aligarh, India (1975-7), I was excited to note, for the first time, a few samples of Literary Orientalism in some of the literary texts prescribed for my study: Langland's *Piers the Plowman,* Chaucer's *Prologue to The Canterbury Tales,* Bacon's 'On Boldness', Milton's *Paradise Lost,* Coleridge's 'Kubla Khan' and Eliot's *Wasteland.* Later on, while working on my first doctoral dissertation on the 'Modes of Satiric Consciousness in Lord Byron's Poetry', at the Aligarh Muslim University, it was my great pleasure to study Byron's dabbling with 'the customs of the East' in his 'Beppo' and *Don Juan.* In the 1990s when I embarked upon my second Ph.D. on Byron's Turkish/Oriental Tales at the University of Leicester, UK, I had an opportunity to explore at length this field of English Literature. Generally speaking, however, Literary Orientalism is a largely unacknowledged and little known field of English studies. Notwithstanding the recent appearance of several significant works on its main contours, most of the students of English Literature seem to have a very hazy idea about its history, its existence and its ongoing augmentation. Some are even apt to ask bluntly: What is Literary Orientalism? What does it signify? What are its constituents? Who have been its practitioners? When did it begin? What is its present status? What is its scope and relevance?

This companion to Literary Orientalism, by way of listing and classifying relevant material (bibliographic details of more than 300 critical books, 900 articles and conference presentations and 400 doctoral dissertations) is an attempt to help one find answers to the above questions. Its main objective is to present a conspectus of the tradition of Literary Orientalism, as it brings into sharper light the contribution of 45 select British men of letters with the exception of Poe, from Chaucer (1343–1400) to Doris Lessing (1919–), to this strand of English studies. It specifies their works which are constituted from and draw into focus Oriental material, of which the quantum varies unevenly from one work to another. For example, William Beckford's *Vathek* (1786) abounds in Oriental content and context whereas Shelley's *Revolt of Islam,* notwithstanding its unmistakably Oriental sounding title, has only slight traces of Oriental element. The identification of the critical corpus (books, articles and conference presentations and doctoral dissertations) on each of these 45 writers aims at facilitating literature survey by researches. Apart from its documentary and bibliographic value, this section may help researchers embark upon both fresh and related areas of study, and familiarize them with the latest thrust areas, trends and issues in the field. This companion to Literary Orientalism draws attention also to the pivotal role played by the *Arabian Nights* and Oriental Tales in promoting the tradition of Literary Orientalism.

It will be in order to define at this juncture the key terms, 'Literary Orientalism' and 'Orient' as used in this work. In simple, rather oversimplified words Orientalism represents the fruits of study undertaken by Western scholars of the geographical entity called the 'Orient'. Going by the same rubric, Literary Orientalism stands for the depiction of the Orient/Orientals in Western literary texts. As to the term 'Orient', it refers on one level to a geo-civilizational entity—the lands to the east of the Mediterranean and stretching through Asia, mainly Turkey, Arabia, Persia, China, Japan, India and also covering Africa. On the other level, however, the term 'Orient' has strong and unmistakable religious, socio-cultural and emotional overtones. In this work the Orient specifically stands for Muslim lands. The Orient thus, is inevitably what might be termed as a 'charged topos'. It is worth adding that in Western literary Orientalism, Orientals have been interchangeably labelled down the ages also as 'Saracens/Moors/Easterners/Bedouins/and Mahomeddans'. This companion to Literary Orientalism focuses on the treatment of only Islam and Muslims in Western literary Orientalism, to the exclusion of other religious, ethnic, linguistic or racial groups in the Orient, who otherwise happen to be equally important.

It must be stated that Literary Orientalism as a subfield of English studies had come to the notice of critics and research students much before the publication of Edward Said's *Orientalism* (1978). Said's chief contribution consists in his brilliant analysis of this legacy. What is, nonetheless, significant is that even these pre-1978 critics seem familiar with the tropes of representation, cross-cultural encounter, empathy and of employing the Oriental setting as a pretext for grappling with or interrogating some wider or sensitive issues closer home. For example, as far back as in 1908, Martha P. Conant in her *Oriental Tale in England in the Eighteenth Century,* besides surveying the Oriental Tales of the day, classified these into four distinct groups, which underscore their functional roles:

> The imaginative group...revived...in Beckford's *Vathek.* The moralistic and philosophic groups are prominent in periodical essays from Addison to Dr Johnson... The satiric group is chiefly exemplified by ... Goldsmith's *Citizen of the* World, and by Count Hamilton's entertaining parodies.[1]

Marie de Meester's *Oriental Influences in the English Literature of the Nineteenth Century* (1914) and Edna Osborne's *Oriental Diction and Theme in English Verse, 1740–1840* (1916) stand out as the earliest instances of wide ranging surveys while B.P. Smith's *Islam in English Literature* (1937) as the first well-focussed study of Literary Orientalism. With the passage of this line of enquiry gained much in depth and rootage and critical studies on various eras of English literary history and on individual writers, for example, Chaucer's, Dante's, Shakespeare's, Byron's, and Forster's Orientalism saw the light of the day.[2]

The phenomenon of the cross-cultural encounter, or of the divide between 'us' and 'them', which has been cogently stated by Edward Said, had not gone unnoticed even earlier, in the pre-1978 studies on Literary Orientalism. The Western/European/British image of the Orient/Orientals, representation of the 'Other', with special reference to race, faith group, ethnicity or colour was examined from a variety of angles in several works.[3]

Norman Daniel's *Islam and the West: The Making of An Image* (1962), and Victor J. Tolan's recent works[4] being thorough and substantial study of both the confrontation and interaction between the two major world civilizations – the Islamic and the Western, document the plethora of misconceptions, misperceptions and half-truths that had gained currency in the West up to the medieval period about Islam/Muslims. More significantly, most of these resurface in many specimens of Literary Orientalism – the premise that lies at the core of Said's trenchant critique of select literary texts in his *Orientalism.*

The representation of one group, be it religious, ethnic, linguistic, racial or socio-cultural, by another is liable to err. The history of Literary Orientalism is inevitably shot through with religious and cultural bias. For, it regrettably originated from the clash, both literal and metaphorical, between two major world faiths – Christianity and Islam, which culminated in the Crusades. Little wonder then that the divide between the two is habitually inscribed in literary texts. The material included in this companion to Literary Orientalism, in a sense, both reflects and attempts to bridge the gap between these two great civilizations. Needless to add, such a study has assumed greater relevance and urgency in the post 9/11 world of ours.

After the appearance of Said's *Orientalism* (1978) the nascent field of Literary Orientalism has, no doubt, attracted greater attention. There has been a marked increase in the number of new books and articles, and conference presentations on the subject. More significantly, Literary Orientalism is now being studied in the broader context of its nexus with such rubrics as Feminism/ Mysticism/Post Colonialism/Cultural Studies/Empire/ Politics of Representation/Film and Popular Culture/Self Identity/Exoticism.

Another welcome development is the more active role of young researchers with the Oriental background in their participation in the discourse on Literary Orientalism. Equally impressive has been the recent spurt in the doctoral dissertations in the field. Since 1980, at least 300 doctoral studies have been carried out, delineating its main contours.

Significantly enough, Literary Orientalism has also found its way to the syllabus of several programmers of study/modules at these Universities:

Kingston University, London
MA Module: Representation of Islam
BA Module: English Engagement with Islam
www. kingston.ac.uk/pgenglishma

Middlesex University, London
BA English Literature and Religious Studies
Islam in the Modern World
www.mdx.ac.uk/cnl/ba

Venderbilt University
EMGL 273-01 Islam in English Literature,
BA English: From the Crusades to the War on Terror
www.vanderbilt.edu/english/undergraduate

University of Missouri, St. Louis
Dept of English Literature Courses
Tales of Islamic East 4936

University of York, UK
MA
www. york.ac.uk/depts/engl/pg/ma

Saint Anselm College, US
www. Anselm.edu/depts./English

University of Saskatchewan
www.usak.ca/english/colloqu/courses

Lousiana State University, US

Louisana English Department
American Orientalism
www.english.lsu.edu/

University of Delaware, US
Fiction from and about Islam
EMGL 382-010
www.english.udel.edu/distlist

Umm al-Qura University, Makkah, Saudi Arabia

BA(English)	Islam in English Literature
MA(English)	Islam in English Literature

This points to the steady development of Literary Orientalism as a full-fledged branch of learning in the near future. This companion to Literary Orientalism is a small step towards that big goal.

A bibliographic work of this nature and range is most likely to have some inadvertent omissions and inaccuracies. Suggestions are solicited for the inclusion of entries which escaped my notice, and for ideas about more helpful and reader-friendly classification and labelling of entries.

March 2009
Aligarh Muslim University
Aligarh, India

Abdur Raheem Kidwai
sulaim_05@yahoo.co.in

Notes and References

1. Martha P. Conant, *The Oriental Tale in England in the Eighteenth Century*, New York, 1908, p. xxvi.
2. Illustrative of this are the following:
   - Peter Cochran (Ed.), *Byron and Orientalism*, Cambridge, 2006.
   - John Draper, *Orientalia and Shakespeareana*, New York, 1977.
   - Maria Rosa Menocal, *The Arabic Role in Medieval Literary History: A Forgotten Heritage*, Pennsylvania, 1987.
   - Miguel Asin Palacios, *Islam and the Divine Comedy*, London, 1960.
   - Louis Wann, *The Oriental in Restoration Drama*, Madison, 1918.
   - Arthur Christy's *The Orient in American Transcendentalism*, New York, 1932, points to the existence of an identical tradition in relation to American Literature/the US.
3. Some of these rubrics are reflected at their sharpest in
   - Henri Bandet, *Paradise on Earth: Some Thoughts on European Images of Non-European Man*, New Haven, CT, 1965.
   - Allen Greenberger, *The British Image of India: A Study in the Literature of Imperialism 1880–1960*, New York, 1969.
4. John Victor Tolan (Ed.), *Medieval Christian Perceptions of Islam*, New York, 1995.

   John Victor Tolan (Ed.), *Saracens: Islam in the Medieval European Imagination*, New York, 2007.

   John Victor Tolan, *Son of Ishmael: Muslims through European Eyes*, New York, 2008.

Introduction

> By misapprehension and misrepresentation an idea of the beliefs and practices of one society can pass into the accepted myth of another society in a form so distorted that its relation to the original facts is sometimes barely discernible. Doctrines that are the expressions of the spiritual outlook of any enemy are interpreted ungenerously, and with prejudice, and even facts are modified — and in good faith — to suit interpretation.
>
> (Norman Daniel, *Islam and the West: Making of an Image*, Edinburgh, 1991, p. 22)

The genesis, history and main contours of Literary Orientalism hinge on the encounter between the West/ Europe/Christendom and Islam/Arabs/Muslims in the military, religious, diplomatic, political and socio-cultural domains from the seventh century to this day. It was mostly in terms of religious differences and hostility that Europe first learned about Islam and Muslims. The phenomenal rise and spread of Islam in the seventh century with its military and political repercussions made Europe all the more apprehensive. By the eighth century Islam was entrenched in major parts of Asia, Africa, and was knocking at the very doors of Europe at many points: from the West, through Spain; in the centre, from Sicily to southern Italy; and in the East, into the Balkans and southern Russia. It was resolved to check these threats, and Islam was perceived as a heresy and Muslims were cast in the role of enemy, as a fierce, irrational people given to violence and lust. So far as the knowledge of Islam in the medieval West, R.W. Southern brands the period 700–1100 as the 'Age of Ignorance'.[1] This negative image is reflected in the polemical writings and literary texts of the day, and even of much later date, which constitute the corpus of Literary Orientalism.

Clash of Civilizations

The first real, literally face-to-face, contact between Europe and the Islamic world was, significantly enough by way of military confrontation – the Crusades (1096–1271). Though the Crusading movement was essentially a religious movement, secular tendencies and forces were at work too, including commercial ones. Its cultural and historical significance in forging links between Europe and the Islamic world is immense. As pointed out by Dorothee Metlitzki, the Crusades resulted in the Arab influence on a wide range of Frankish activities – on military techniques, on vocabulary, and on food, clothing and ornamentation.[2]

More fruitful European interaction with the Islamic world flowed, in large measure, from the Muslim conquest of Spain in 711, and the presence of Islamic political power there until 1492: 'As a cultural transplant on European soil, and a natural bridge between East and West ... [Muslim Spain] served as an agent for transmitting basically Eastern ideas.'[3]

Literary Impact of Muslim Spain

This is illustrated best by the influence of the Arabic rhymed verse, which was then a rage in Muslim Spain, on the love poetry of Guillaume IX (1071–1127) in the Provençal language. His love lyrics have little in common with the conventional Latin and Greek poetry or with the ideals of medieval Church. There are unmistakable similarities between the love lyrics of Muslim Spain and the troubadour and trouvere love poetry of Provence. This is acknowledged by the Italian Giammaria Barbieri in his *Dell' Origine della Poesia Rimata* (1571) and reinforced by the Basque author, Estaber Artiaqa and the French writer, Sismondi who affirm:

> The form and content in the new poetry in Europe were introduced by the Arabs in Spain through Provence and especially through Catalonia, where they had established themselves for three long centuries. [4]

Both Dante and Chaucer seem indebted to the troubadour poetry in grappling with intricacies of love. In his University of Sorbonne doctoral thesis on Chaucer, Etienne Sandras provides 'an appendix of thirty pages of "Pieces Justificatives" of trouvere lyrics and their parallels in the works of Chaucer'.[5] Likewise, the concepts of troubadour courtly love find their re-echo in Chaucer's *The Book of Duchess, Franklin's Tale* and *Troilus and Criseyda.* This influence went far beyond Chaucer, as a literary critic points out:

> Dozens of poem in English from Chaucer through to the Romantics... where the sentiment of love, the attitude to women, the *Fin amors* concepts... could be traced back... to Andalusian Arabic poetry.[6]

Cultural Impact

Transmission of learning from the Islamic world, then a centre of a more advanced culture and richer civilization, to Europe is the most remarkable feature of this process. A host of European scholars have attempted to identify the nature and extent of the influence of the Islamic world on Europe in fields as diverse as mathematics, astronomy, medicine, logic, metaphysics, technology, music and other arts and sciences.[7] Through the acquisition of Islamic knowledge there came about what C.H. Haskins calls 'the Renaissance of the Twelfth Century'.[8]

Interaction between Europe and the Ottoman Empire

Another major point of contact between Europe and Islam was of course the Ottoman empire. The Ottoman forays into Europe started in the mid-fourteenth century and ended in 1699 with the Treaty of Karowitz. The feelings against Ottomans in Europe aroused a degree of hatred against Islam and Muslims - a point borne out by their image in Elizabethan literature, to which we will turn later. Notwithstanding frequent military clashes, the conflict contributed greatly to cultural and social exchange and gradually to a better understanding of Islam and Muslims. This aspect is covered thoroughly in Paul Coles' *The Ottoman Impact on Europe.*[9]

Travel Literature

It was by travel, however, that Europe learned a great deal about Islam and the Muslims and English travel literature provides significant clues to the changing image. In the Middle Ages there had been little traffic between England and the Islamic world, but with the establishment of the Levant Company in 1581 the volume of traffic increased considerably. Trade links and diplomatic missions gave rise to a steady flow of visitors, some of the leading figures being Sir Henry Blount, Fynes Moryson, Thomas Coryat, Robert Shirley, George Sandys and William Lithgow. Among the notable religious travellers were William Biddulph, John Cartwright and Rev. Edward Terry. That the travelling gentleman then gradually replaced the traveller indicates that the Islamic world was becoming more easily accessible. Some of the commentators perceived the Bedouin life as an instructive contrast to the artificialities of European existence; others regarded these people as remnants of a primitive race, full of innocence and simplicity; they were seen as abstaining from material possessions which would curtail their freedom. Eyles Irwin published in 1780 his travelogue, *A Series of Adventures in the Course of a Voyage up the Red Sea, on the Coasts of Arabia and Egypt,* which is all admiration for the domestic felicities of the Islamic life; and in 1802 his comic opera 'The Bedouin' was staged in Dublin. In most of the travel writings, the Arabs were depicted as examples of the Noble Savage.

Orientalist Paintings

Next to travel literature there are paintings by the Orientalist painters. Lucas van Leyden's 'Daughters of Lot' of the late fifteenth century is perhaps the first European painting with a distinct Oriental imagery. The fall of Constantinople in 1453 brought the Islamic world deep into the European consciousness. The conquerors' dress, arms and architecture evoked some fascination. Van Dyck painted Sir Robert Shirley as an Oriental with an enormous turban in order to heighten the effect of his being a wealthy person. Franscesco Guardi has to his credit some forty-six paintings on Turkish life. In the eighteenth century, as a ramification of neo-classicism, the Islamic world was generally perceived as the domain of decoration. The image of the Islamic world in these paintings is characterized by eroticism, richness in both customs and splendour, and some remnants of the warrior stereotype. Orientalist paintings in early nineteenth-century England catered for the Romantic feeling for the picturesque and for local colour. Moreover, the Islamic lands stood for a place where sensual desires which could not be indulged in England might easily be satisfied; and finally, these paintings responded to the longing for mystery. A.L. Macfie's observation succinctly sums up the depiction of the Orient in Western paintings:

> Even a cursory examination of the paintings reproduced in such publications as Lynne Thornton, *The Orientalists: Painters – Travellers 1828–1908* (1983), Mary Anne Stevens, *The Orientalists: Delacroix to Matisse* (1984) and Christine Peltre, *Orientalism in Art* (1998) would

> suggest that many of the painters of the Orientalist genre were also frequently inclined ... to create stereotypical images of the 'others as backward, corrupt, irrational and uncontrolled'.[10]

Scholarly Works

A serious interest in Islam is reflected also in the appearance of scholarly volumes on Islamic history, replacing the medieval polemical writings which contain little fact and much fiction. Richard Knolles's *General History of the Turks* (1603) and Simon Ockley's *History of the Saracens* (1708–1718) established this history as an academic discipline. Other notable examples are Pierre Bayle, *A General Dictionary, Historical and Critical (1737–1741)*; Richard Pococke, *A Description of the East (1743–1745)*, and Alexander Russel, *Natural History of Aleppo* (1756).

Early Specimen of Literary Orientalism: A Distorting Mirror

An important and early literary source for studying the image of Islam is provided by the *Chanson de Geste,* the oral poetry of medieval France. These heroic poems, primarily meant for entertaining the public, which are found mostly in twelfth century manuscripts, exercised a great influence on European literature, including of course English literature. The image of Islam in these songs, it is worth clarifying, is the unofficial, unchurchman-like view, in that the Church did not have any role in their composition. Yet, as pointed out by Norman Daniel, 'the Saracen religion in the songs relates to actual facts about Islam in the same way as a distorting mirror twists a real object into an unrecognizable travesty'.[11] They represent Islam as a despicable form of paganism; they denounce the Islamic practice of the segregation of women, polygamy, harems, divorce and ascribe sexual promiscuity to Muslims.[12]

The Middle English romances, as for example *Beues of Hamtoun* or *The Sowdone of Babylone,* are the earliest literary works dealing with the Muslims and their world. However, in the words of Dorothee Metlitzki, 'they are essentially vehicles of fanatical propaganda in which the moral ideal of chivalry is subservient to the requirements of religion, politics and ideology. Pagans are wrong and Christians are right whatever they do ... They are primarily concerned with one basic theme: the war of Christianity against Islam'.[13] Special mention may be made on this count of the Romance *Floris and Blancheflur,* composed in the middle of the thirteenth century. Similar to other Romances of the period, *Floris and Blancheflur* abounds in stereotypes of Muslims and depicts them as irrational pagans and the Prophet Muhammad (peace and blessings be on him) as an imposter. William Langland (c.1330–86) appears to have been swayed by the same prejudices in portraying the Prophet (peace and blessings be on him) in *Piers Plowman* as a Christian heretic abusing the power of the Holy Ghost. Similarly, the second coming in the vision of *Piers Plowman* is preceded by a time deformed by 'Mahomet' (this name, being the generic word for a false god was used for Prophet Muhammad [peace and blessings be on him]).

A note of missionary zeal permeates Chaucer's *Man of Law's Tale,* for Constance, daughter of the emperor of Rome, marries the Sultan of Syria in order to convert him to Christianity: 'That, in destruction of Maumetrye and in encrees of Cristes' lawe dere' (pp. 236–7). The polemical design of the *Tale* is heightened by derisive references to the Qur'an (p. 332) and the Prophet (peace and blessings be on him) (pp. 224, 336 and 340). However, Chaucer speaks admiringly of several Muslim philosophers such as Alchabitius ('Abd al-'Aziz, c. 960) in *Astrolabe* Alocen (Ibn al-Haytham 965–1039) in *The Squire's Tale,* Azrachel (al-Zarqali, 1029–87) in *Astrolabe,* Averroes or Averrois (Ibn Rushd, 1126–98) and Avicenna (Ibn Sina, 980–1037) in 'General Prologue' and *Pardoner's Tale* (823–7) and Aglus or Argus (al-Khwarizmi, 780–850) in *Book of the Duchess, The Miller's Tale* and *Astrolabe*. His *Squire's Tale is* set in the Islamic world; to be precise, it is set at Sarray, a prosperous commercial town founded by the Central Asian ruler, Batu Khan. John Lydgate's 'Fall of Princes' (c.1440), standing out as perhaps the first English literary piece with a detailed account of the Prophet Muhammad (peace and blessings be on him), re-echoes some of the polemical assaults on him in describing him as a magician of low birth who was guilty of leading his followers astray. John Gower's *Confessio Amantis,* however, speaks of Muslims in somewhat conciliatory terms. Nicholas Udall's 'Masque of Turquish Magistrates' performed at the Queen Mary's court in 1555 illustrates how false, tendentious reports gain currency, driven by polemical zeal. Included in this Masque are sixteen 'men turkes maskers' dancing at the feet of sixteen classical goddesses. Idolatry, it goes without saying, has no place in Islam.

Literary Orientalism in the Renaissance Period

To what absurd lengths bigotry prompts one is evidenced also by Christopher Marlowe's *Tamburlaine the Great* which was staged several times after its first performance in 1594. About its glaring anomalies and its negative portrayal of the Orient, Naji B. Ouijan's following comments are worth of considering:

> Marlowe presented to his Elizabethan audience a picture of the East they desired to see, an Orient filled with treachery, cruelty and false doctrine, and Orient that was destroyed by its own rulers... Tamburlaine finally falls dead after bringing death and destruction to East. To make his play popular, Marlowe had to depart widely from history; so he portrays Tamburlaine as anti-Muslim and pro-Christian.

> In Part-I Marlowe has already presented Tamburlaine as a semi-pagan hero who is knowledgeable in classical mythology but in Part-II he becomes a Muslim renouncing his own religion. Bajazeth and Zabina have earlier expressed their doubts about Islam... Marlowe deliberately entertained Elizabethan Christian audience with such false images of the East and its peoples.[14]

A common expression used in the early seventeenth century literature employed mainly for pouring scorn and contempt is 'Turk', used frequently by Shakespeare in *Othello* (II, i, 114), *Hamlet* (III, ii, 275), *King Lear* (III, iv, 91), *Henry IV* (V, ii, 47), *Richard II* (IV, I, 95), *Richard III* (III, v, 40), *The Merchant of Venice* (IV, i, 32) and *Much Ado About Nothing* (III, iv, 56). Bacon also levels a baseless charge against the Prophet Muhammad (peace and blessings be on him), accusing him of being a miracle-monger in his essay 'Of Boldness'.[15] This polemical aspect apart, 'to the minds of most poets [of the day] the country [Arabia] was associated with the images of luxury and wealth'.[16] The gorgeous Oriental life is recounted with some degree of awe in Marlowe's *Jew of Malta* (I, i), John Fletcher's *Bloody Brother* (V, ii), Ben Jonson's *Alchemist* (II, ii, 93–4) and Massinger's *Roman Actor* (II, i).

According to Louis Wann, at least, forty-seven plays by major playwrights were staged in Elizabethan period. More significant is the reason which accounts for such a keen interest in the Orient:

> The production of Oriental plays was not due to the fancy of any one author or group of authors. Wann says: it was due to the interest of the Elizabethan audience in Oriental matters. Two-thirds of these Oriental plays were tragedies because the Elizabethans considered the East as the domain of war, conquest, fratricide, lust and treachery.[17]

This image of the Islamic world, thus, retains some of the old polemical strain, nonetheless it signifies a slight departure from the medieval prejudiced view of Islam and Muslims. It records some positive appreciation for the Islamic life and ways. This had been brought about by closer and first-hand contact. In 1453 Muslims conquered Constantinople, and the centre of Byzantine empire was replaced by the Ottoman empire. Three trading companies had also come up: the Muscovy Company (1555) for trade with Persia; Levant Company (1581) for trade with the predominantly Muslim Near East and the East India Company (1600) for trade with India then under Muslim rule. All this paved the way for more interaction, especially in the fields of diplomacy, trade and travel. How the truth gradually makes its way against prejudices is borne out by Thomas Browne's *Vulgar Errors,* which corrects a misconception, among others originating from the medieval works on Islam, about the Prophet's hanging tomb, reported by Marlowe in *Tambourlaine* 2 (I, I, 137–42) and Beaumont in *The Scornful Lady,* and even at a much later date by Robert Southey in *Roderick* (XXIII, 147–50) and Thomas Moore in *Lalla Rookh.* This medieval report that the Prophet's body hangs in an iron chest in midair in his mosque in Madinah is dismissed by Browne as 'fabulous, and evidently false'.[18]

References to the Islamic world in later seventeenth century literature in general are relatively few and far between, though, for example, Milton is found speaking of the perfumes of Arabia in *Paradise Lost* (IV, 159–64) and Donne using the simile 'like Bejazet encaged' (The Calm), alluding to the popular story that the Turkish Sultan, Bejazet, defeated by Tamerlane in 1407, was paraded publicly in a cage. Dryden's *Don Sebastian,* showing a close thematic affinity with Massinger's *Renegado,* is full of the contrast between Christianity and Islam and is glaringly in favour of the former. In his *Hind and the Panther* (1687) he speaks derisively of Muslims not practising their faith and of their violation of the Islamic prohibition of wine in

'Astraeu Redux' (1660). Of a similar polemical strain are the opening words of the High Marshal of Rhodes in Davenant's first English opera, *The Siege of Rhodes* (1656):

> My sword against produ Solyman I draw,
> His cursed Prophet, and his sensual law.

In the next generation, Pope speaks scoffingly of Islamic laws and of fratricide among Turkish sultans in *The Dunciad* (Book III, 89–90) and *Epistle to Dr. Arbuthnot (198–99)* respectively. In Butler's *Hudibras,* the visage of Bruin, the bear, is as grim 'And rugged as a Saracen/or Turk of Mahomet's own kin' (Part I, 2, 251–2). In Congreve's *Way of the World* the 'Mahometan fools' are derided for their 'heathenish rules', particularly the prohibition of wine in Islam (IV, 1, 404–8). In Goldsmith's *Citizen of the World* there appear some medieval misconceptions about the Muslim paradise, the Islamic belief about the absence of the soul in women, and the Prophet being 'a professed opposer of gaiety' (Letter CXI).

Notwithstanding these traces of the time-worn distorted image of Islam, eighteenth-century literature reflects some tolerance in approaching things Islamic. To this end Gibbon's fairly objective historical account of Islam in his magisterial *History of the Decline and Fall of the Roman Empire* (1776–8) and George Sale's English translation of the Qur'an (1734) – the basic text of Islam – contributed greatly. Above all, the scholarly translations of Islamic works, mainly literary ones, by William Jones paved the way for a better and favourable view of the Islamic world.

Oriental Tales

Another important factor facilitating the spread of Literary Orientalism was the popularity of the *Arabian Nights,* of which the first English translation was published in 1706. As to its reception in England, Muhsin J. Ali aptly remarks: 'Very few books have cast such a spell on the reading public as the *Arabian Nights*'.[19] This contention is corroborated by numerous reprints, complete editions and 'new translations' and 'careful revisions' of the *Arabian Nights* during the century. Its popularity is evidenced also by its serialization over the years in *London News, Churchman's Last Shift, General Magazine, Lady's Magazine, Monthly Extracts* and *Novelist's Magazine.* Addison's response was equally warm in that he published several Oriental pieces in *The Spectator.*

Apart from being a unique amalgam of the informative and the delightful, the *Arabian Nights* was much admired for its exoticism, its depiction of strange social manners, and its machinery of such enthralling figures as jinns, fairies, magicians and talismans. 'These stories', holds E.F. Bleiler, 'appealed ... with a wide range of opportunities, delicacies of style, elaboracies of construction, adventure, eroticism, moralism, sensibility, fantasy, philosophy and irony'.[20] Some of the legends permeating these stories had their parallels in the Celtic, Teutonic and Greek traditions – hence their appeal for a larger readership. Along with their exoticism and the charm of pure adventure, these stories are grounded in solid value systems and deal with such issues as the sinfulness of pride and greed and the vanity of human wishes. Numerous Oriental tales, often pseudo-Oriental imitations and adaptations, appeared in the wake of their popularity, of which a masterly analysis is made by Martha P. Conant. According to her, this phenomenon 'might be called an episode in the development of English Romanticism'.[21]

The beginning of Oriental tales in English literature dates back to the Middle Ages when many Oriental stories had found their way into England through the religio-political, socio-cultural, military and travel contacts with the Islamic lands. The translation of the *Arabian Nights* brought about the full blooming of this genre. As to the vast number of eighteenth-century Oriental tales, Martha P. Conant classifies them into the following four groups – imaginative, moralistic, philosophic and satiric:

> The imaginative group, the earliest, and, at the beginning of the century, the most significant diminished, as the other groups increased in strength, but revived again near the end of our period in Beckford's *Vathek.* The moralistic and philosophic groups are prominent in the periodical essays from Addison to Dr. Johnson. The philosophic group comprises besides *Rasselas* several translations from Voltaire's *contes-philosophiques.* The satiric group is chiefly exemplified by the pseudo-letters culminating in Goldsmith's *Citizen of the World,* and by Count Hamilton's entertaining parodies.[22]

To this list Ros Ballaster perceptively adds the following more categories of Oriental Tales:

> ...the popular mode of the fictional letter written in the voice of an oriental informant, a tradition inaugurated by Giovanni Paolo Marana's *Letters Writ by a Turkish Spy,* translated by William Bradshaw (1687–1694) ... the oriental informant voice is deployed to provide an enlightened rationalist critique of European political and social mores.
>
> Two further examples show the development of the form. Montesquie's *Persian Letters,* translated by Charles Ozell (1722), ... returns to the representation of harem women... as a means of debating the nature and exercise of political authority... Rica's letter serves as a further example of 'reverse ethnography' where a French court lady learns of the comparative and surprising 'freedom' and learning of women in Eastern marriage...
>
> Goldsmith's periodical essays in the voice of a Chinese informant collected under the title *The Citizen of the World* (1762)... expose Europeans as ignorant 'collectors' of fragments of Asian culture who fail to recognize the superior civility and

> philosophical sophistication of Chinese manners. Goldsmith makes the anti-colonial Tory conservative case for scholarly and intellectual – rather than mercantile or missionary – engagement with distant territories.[23]

Along with the *Arabian Nights,* the publication of the *Persian Tales* (1714) translated from French by Ambrose Philips, *Turkish Tales* (1708) rendered by Jacob Tonson and *Mogul Tales* (1736) further strengthened the genre. Another contributing factor was the appearance of Eclogues in the same period, among them those of William Collins, Thomas Chatterton and John Scott. Collin's *Persian Eclogues* came out first in 1757.

Apart from entertaining the readers by way of transporting them to a fanciful, outlandish world 'peopled with talking animals and fairies and jinns' and marked by ostentatious splendour and plentitude, some of the Oriental tales actually served as the means for exploring energetically some of the haunting, disturbing theological, political and socio-cultural issues of the day. Ros Ballaster brings home this point thus:

> Critiques of oriental despotism, absolutism, and religious bigotry in English writings and translations are frequently means of addressing the perceived threat of French absolutism and Catholicism... Particularly popular in translation were those Anglophile French *philosophes* such as Voltaire and Montesquieu, who used oriental examples, history, and cultures as a means of promoting deist or atheist or rationalist principles in France.
>
> ... oriental narrative can be put to use in western political or philosophical critique (as in the case of Joseph Addison's defence of the fable from a number of the *Spectator)* or through the mythic contrast between occidental rationalism and oriental passion in an inset tale, 'The History of

the Christian Eunuch', from Eliza Haywood's novella *Philidore and Placentia.*[24]

Literary Orientalism in the Pre-Romantic Period

Along with the influence of the *Arabian Nights,* the tales of Addison and Johnson had paved the way for the continuation of the tradition of Literary Orientalism in the Romantic period. Like Addison, Johnson wrote Oriental tales mainly for instruction, couched in an amusing style; so that, for example, in his 'Ortogrul of Basra' (*Idler,* 99) the chief character Ortogrul finally realizes the importance of industry. His other contributions 'The History of Almamoulin, the son of Nouradin' *(Rambler,* 190), 'Seged, Emperor of Ethiopia' *(Rambler,* 204–5) – are also concerned, in the main, with moral and ontological issues. Though the characters bear Muslim names and inhabit Muslim countries, these tales have little Oriental colour, and references to famous Oriental places such as Samarcand, Arabia and Abyssinia constitute only a nominal Oriental setting.

Johnson's choice of an Oriental story for his first major work, *Irene* (1736), reflects the vogue of Literary Orientalism in the day. The play has much in common with Massinger's *Renegado* and Dryden's *Don Sebastian* in its denunciation of Oriental despotism. Mahomet, the central character, is an amorous Turkish emperor who falls in love with a Greek captive, Aspasia. Johnson's image of the Islamic world is essentially of the medieval period, betraying hostility towards Islam and Muslims. For example, Johnson repeats the preposterous charge of the medieval detractors of Islam that, according to the Islamic tradition, women do not have souls and are created solely for the pleasure of males *(Irene* I, VII, 15–23).[25]

Johnson appears more at home in writing *Rasselas* (1759) for this work is closer to an essay, a genre in which he undoubtedly excelled. More significantly, it represents his mature outlook on a wide range of subjects and is largely free from any animosity towards Islam and Muslims. Essentially it is philosophical, with the main theme of false expectations in that all the major characters fail to attain any lasting happiness; they continually undergo disappointments. Johnson is mainly concerned with 'the Vanity of Human Wishes', concluding that the gratification of desires does not bring satisfaction, which may be attained only through knowledge, faith and integrity. On the whole, the treatment of the Islamic world is cursory and vague, but it is worth noting that it does not misrepresent it.

Another landmark of pre-Romantic Literary Orientalism is Beckford's *Vathek,* published in Henley's English translation in 1786. Originally it had been written in French. For its supernatural machinery, exotic settings and weird incidents contemporary reviewers related *Vathek* to the *Arabian Nights.* On the one hand, *Vathek* represents the culminating point of the vogue for Oriental tales in eighteenth century England and, on the other, it burlesques this genre by emphasizing the strange and the exotic in terms of its action, plot and imagery. *Vathek* resembles the fiction of Voltaire and Hamilton in its use of wit and satiric techniques and reflects some affinity with Johnson's Oriental tales in its moralizing spirit.

Despite the popularity of Oriental tales in the period, *Vathek* is unprecedented in its coverage and attention to details of Islamic life and customs, both in the text and in Henley's scholarly notes. Beckford's concern for local colour impressed Byron greatly and his homage to Beckford's correctness of costumes is recorded in his note to *The Giaour.*[26]

Notwithstanding the genuinely Oriental setting of and abundant Islamic material in *Vathek* and Beckford's wide familiarity with authentic works on Islam, the themes and spirit of *Vathek* are unmistakably Western – the story of Faust lies at its heart. Like Goethe's Faust, Vathek seeks knowledge, including its forbidden variety, that too, at the price of his soul. Moreover, *Vathek* is not completely free from some misconceptions, though inadvertent ones, about Islamic beliefs and practices. As a result, *Vathek* betrays the Western mindset of its author, especially in portraying Hell and Eblis.

Orientalist Scholarship

To the scholarly contributions of Sir William Jones (1746–94) may be ascribed a major role in preparing the ground for the interest in Islam in the Romantic period for, equipped with a mastery of Arabic, Persian, Hebrew and Sanskrit, Jones produced a number of translations of and commentaries on Oriental literature. In 1772 he brought out an anthology of Arabic and Persian poems rendered into English, among which special mention should be made of his translation of the Arabic poetical masterpiece entitled *Moallakat*. To promote a better understanding of the Islamic world Jones founded the Asiatic Society of Calcutta, India in 1784, the precursor of all Asiatic Societies, and the Society's journal *Asiatic Researches* went a long way in achieving this objective. His writings, containing a wealth of information about things Islamic, served later as a main source for Byron, Southey, Shelley and Moore. His *Persian Grammar* (1771) introduced both Persian literature and language to English literary circles and urged men of letters to benefit from its rich heritage. Jones firmly believed that a study of Oriental works would furnish them 'with a new set of images and similitudes ... and a number of excellent compositions would be brought to light'.[27]

In addition to Jones, a number of other Oriental scholars such as John Richardson (1741–1811), Francis Gladwin (d.c. 1811), Charles Wilkins (c. 1749–1836), William Marsden (1754–1838), William Carey (1761–1838), Daniel Price (1765–1837), John Haddon Marshman (1768–1837), Sir Gore Ouseley (1770–1844), John Leyden (1755–1811),

Matthew Lumsden (1777–1835) and James Atkinson (1780–1852) also helped kindle and sustain public interest in Islam through their scholarly writings on various aspects of Islam.[28]

Travel Literature

The ever-growing body of travel literature too, played an important part in popularizing Literary Orientalism. Wallace C. Brown has already covered this ground in his account of 'The Popularity of English Travel Books about the Near East, 1775–1825',[29]. In view of the continental war, travellers unable to visit Western Europe turned to the Islamic lands, in addition to the large number of those who were genuinely interested in the Islamic world. According to Brown's survey, some seventy travel books about the Islamic world were published in England between 1775 and 1825, and to these may be added numerous pieces on the Islamic world and reviews of travel literature about the Islamic world published in influential periodicals. On the one hand, these writings provided the reading public with useful, at times curious, information and, on the other, they offered much for the inspiration of creative writers. Among the English travellers to the Islamic world, Lady Mary Wortley Montagu (1689–1762) deserves special mention on more than one count: for being one of the very few women travellers to the region, for her representation being singularly free from the binary opposition between the Christian and Islamic worlds as superior/inferior, for her first-hand unconventional account of the harem and for the influence of her *Letters ... written during her travels in Europe, Asia and Africa to persons of distinction* as a literary source for later writings on the Islamic world, as for example, in Byron's '*Turkish Tales*'. She visited Istanbul in 1717 along with her husband Lord Montagu, ambassador of the Levant Company to Turkey. Her *Letters* were, however, published posthumously in 1763.

Since the beginning of relations between the West and the Islamic world, the harem - being the unfamiliar and exotic - had stirred the Western imagination. To this was added the dimension of the Western interest, from the days of its geographical discoveries, in the sexual mores of non-Europeans. For the essential Oriental characteristics of sensuality and violence and its political aspect in terms of the oppression of women, the harem served in the West as a metaphor for tyranny and arbitrary rule in society. Lady Montagu's eyewitness account, however, divests the harem of its mainly sensual, erotic, sensational and promiscuous features. Far from repeating the conventional image of voyeuristic pleasure and sexual fantasy, her account of the harem rather domesticates it and employs it as a suitable setting for drawing comparisons between the Western monogamous and Oriental polygamous forms of sexuality and the position of women in the respective cultures. For example, her letter to Abbe Conti which brings out the comparativeness of the Christian and Islamic codes of womanhood, sexuality and matrimony.

The Islamic concept of sex, completely dissociated from sin, struck Lady Montagu. Moreover, she describes, perhaps for the first time, polygamy positively. Being a woman able to discuss sexual matters freely and intimately with the harem women, Lady Montagu was in a unique position to perceive the Oriental sexuality in a different, broader perspective, and hence formulate her unconventional position on both these matters. The other Western accounts of these subjects tend to be more an exercise in fantasy than a real understanding of the issues involved. It is, therefore, not a surprise to note Lady Montagu's outrage against her predecessors for their ignorance and sensationalization in projecting only a lurid picture of the Islamic world, especially its sex life.

Being able to observe the freedom enjoyed by the veiled harem women granted them by the Islamic law on divorce, inheritance and dower money, Montagu proceeds to contrast and compare their liberty with the Christian and British notions of womanhood and examines, again in a comparative fashion, the two different social and political systems. According to Ros Ballaster, 'Lady Mary challenges the common place representation of Ottoman culture as repressive to women by contrast with Catholic Europe from her own critical position of Protestant Whiggism.'[30]

A highly distinguishable feature of her *Letters* is that it often recounts her rational, meaningful discussions with Turk males on a variety of social, literary and political issues, especially the position of women. What it signifies is the possibility of a purposeful, serious dialogue between the West and the Islamic world. The latter is no longer cast as a barbaric land peopled by those given only to violence and lust.

Lady Montagu's *Letters,* in a sense, anticipate Lord Byron's Orientalism in that both writers make a clear break from the conventionally prejudiced view of Islam, show a fine understanding of Islam helped partly by their eyewitness accounts, rich in genuine local topographical and cultural description and use the Oriental setting for examining a wide range of issues by comparing the Islamic code of life with the traditional Christian/British one, without claiming the latter's moral superiority.

Particular mention should also be made of some other important travel works. James Bruce's *Travels between the Years 1765 and 1773 through Part of Africa, Syria, Egypt and Arabia, into Abyssinia to Discover the Source of Nile* (1790) is, in the main, a record of Bruce's adventures in the Near East as British consul at Algiers (1763–5) and his explorations in Abyssinia (1761–72). Guided by the spirit of genuine inquiry and research, it delves deep into the life and ways of Arabs and regards them as perfect Noble Savages. Bruce's description of the fatal desert storm, Simoom, appears to have fascinated Coleridge, Byron and Southey, for all of them employ it as an effective image.

Alexander Russel's *Natural History of Aleppo* (1758), revised and expanded by his brother Patrick Russel in 1794, relates the observation of these two physicians to the British factory at Aleppo. Though this is essentially a topographical description of Aleppo, it is interlaced with frequent remarks on the creed and life of its inhabitants. This work went a long way in allaying some of the common misconceptions about Islam and Muslims. James Dallaway's *Constantinople, Ancient and Modern* (1797), being an account of Turkey by a chaplain and doctor at the British embassy at the Sublime Port, provides detailed information about Turkish life and customs, while William George Browne's *Travels in Africa, Egypt and Syria from the Year 1792 to 1798* (1799) makes an insightful comparison between the relative happiness of life in the West and in the Islamic lands. Another noteworthy travel book is Edward Daniel Clarke's *Travels in Various Countries of Europe, Asia and Africa* (1810) in six large volumes.

Histories and Journals

Oriental scholarship, set in motion by Sir William Jones and a host of other eminent Orientalists, led to the publication of several histories, including Sir William Ouseley's *The Oriental Collections* (1797). Besides such works, Gibbon's *History of the Decline and Fall of the Roman Empire* (1776–88), containing lengthy sections on Islam and Muslims, deserves special note for its influence on Romantic writers. The period also saw the appearance of a number of specialized journals on the Islamic world, namely, *Oriental Chronicles, Asian Annual Registers, Asiatic Researches* and *Asiatic Review.*

Literary Orientalism in the Romantic Period

Let's now turn to early nineteenth century or the Romantic period to discuss the treatment of Islam, which was promoted and enhanced by certain historical developments and, more importantly, by a general tendency of the age to look at things in a wider, broader context. Of the relevant historical events, special mention should be made of Napoleon's expedition to Egypt (1798), which awakened Englishmen to the strategic military significance of the Islamic lands. Then the War of Independence in Greece (1821–8) put the Islamic world again firmly on the public agenda. Perceived as the struggle of the oppressed against Ottoman despotism, the Greek movement attracted widespread and active sympathy, and Byron in particular responded enthusiastically, devoting considerable energy, time and resources to the cause. The colonization of several Asian and African countries, with its concomitant diplomacy, travel, war and administration, exposed the English to hitherto unknown frontiers and generated an all-round curiosity about distant Islamic lands and their people. Trade grew considerably, resulting in regular and first-hand contacts which called for detailed knowledge. One outcome of this was the appearance of a vast body of literature on Islamic arts, religion, philosophy and culture.

The availability of authentic works on Islam is another distinguishing feature of the Romantic period. The importance of scholarly writings becomes more marked because of the Romantic writers' reliance on them for annotation, not least in the poetical works of Byron, Southey and Moore. Besides, the Islamic world had always its exotic appeal to excite the imagination of creative artists and to kindle the curiosity of the general public. The picturesque scenes of Oriental landscapes, in particular, attracted the Romantics, catering to their urge for a return to primitive nature, while Arabo-Islamic mythology, seen at work in Southey's, Byron's and Moore's writings, furnished them with a new means of grappling with the ultimate reality, and in the case of Moore helped him satirize the contemporary political situation.

Works of all major Romantic poets contain copious allusions to Islam and Muslims. Samuel Taylor Coleridge (1772–1834) provides a convenient starting point. His moving love poem, *Lewti, or the Circassian Love Chaunt* (1798), has its central character, the singer, drawn from the Eastern race. More significantly, it exhibits some possible borrowings from Jones's translation of the Arabic odes, *Moallakat* (1780–1). Coleridge's 'Kubla Khan' employs some images such as the dome and the caves, the damsel and the dulcimer and the flashing eyes and the floating hair which bring to mind its possible Islamic sources. Breyer identifies the Abyssinian maid in 'Kubla Khan' with a houri of the Muslim heaven.[31] The stately dome is a recurrent image in Jones's *The Seven Fountains: An Eastern Allegory.* The image of the damsel and dulcimer suggests the luxury of Oriental palace life, described vividly in the travel literature of the day. Then the dancer with 'flashing eyes', 'floating hair' and 'holy dread' shows a striking similarity to the account of the whirling dervishes – the Muslim mystics who went into a trance in their ecstatic communion with the divine reality. 'Kubla Khan' also draws on Oriental legends about Prophet Muhammad's ascension to and vision about the heavens and the Qur'anic account of the Adite King Shaddad, who is believed to have dreamt of and built an earthly paradise.

Sir Walter Scott's (1771–1832) Oriental material, as reflected in his *Vision of Don Roderick* (1811) and *The Talisman: A Tale of the Crusades* (1825), resurrects some of the medieval conceptions of Islam. Scott is concerned, in the main, in these works with the Muslim conquest of Spain and an account of the Crusades respectively – hence his polemical note.

Shelley's Orientalism

As to the Orientalism of Shelley (1792–1822), it is essentially a means for airing his radical views on the issues confronting Europe in his day. Shelley himself makes this point while relating the Oriental locale of his *Revolt of Islam* (1817) to the intended thrust of the poem:

> The scene is supposed to be laid in Constantinople and modem Greece, but without much attempt at minute delineation of Mahometan manners. It is in fact a tale illustrative of such a Revolution as might be supposed to take place in an European nation.[32]

In Loan and Cythna's revolt and eventual success against the Sultan Othman, Nigel Leask perceives Shelley's 'reaction against the negativity of Tom Moore's 1817 account of Oriental revolution'.[33] Significantly enough, both the Oriental revolutions in *Lalla Rookh* (in 'The Veiled Prophet of Khorassan' and 'Fire-Worshippers') and in Byron's *Bride of Abydos* and *The Corsair* are failed revolutions.

Another distinguishable mark of Shelley's Orientalism is its adherence to convention in depicting a negative view of Islam and, as a result, its endorsement, as in Southey's, of colonialism and evangelism of the day. Despite his dismissal of Christianity as 'an outworn encumbrance' in the context of England, Shelley approved of the missionary work in British India, regarding it as an instrument for bringing about gradual enlightenment and progress. 'He expressed the hope that the zeal of the missionaries for what is called the Christian faith, will produce a beautiful innovation there [in India], even by the application of dogmas and forms of what is here an outworn encumbrance'.[34] For Shelley, both Hinduism and Islam are bereft of any spirituality and pose a threat to civilization. This stance permeates his representation of Islam in *Hellas*. The play glorifies the Greek uprising against Turkish domination and deals with the themes of despotism and redemption. In *Hellas*, the fate of Greece is discussed by Christ, Satan and Mahomet; throughout the play Christianity is symbolized by 'light' and Islam by 'darkness'. It thus brings to the fore once again the medieval, distorted image of Islam, which holds it synonymous with tyranny, lust and fratricide. That *Hellas* may have its negative representation of the Islamic world owing to its classical model is explained thus by Nigel Leask:

> Shelley tells us that *Hellas* is modeled upon Aeschylus' play *The Persians,* identified by Edward Said as the inaugural text of Orientalism in Western culture, in terms of a hellenic power of representation defining itself over against an 'Asiatic Other'. In Shelley's earlier poems, 'Greek' values struggle against 'Asiatic' despotism and priestcraft in a universal metaphysical framework, like the elemental battle between the eagle and the serpent in the first canto of *The Revolt of Islam.*[35]

Among his other works with Islamic material is his first major work, *Queen Mab,* exhibiting as it does the influence of Sir William Jones's *Palace of Fortune* and Southey's *Thalaba* in terms of its scenery, diction and characterization. *Alastor* (1818), too, shows the influence of *Thalaba* both in employing Oriental mythology and in its imperialist tenor. Since Kashmir figures as its prominent locale, Leask thinks that it 'could be read as an unmasking of Britain's desire for its Indian Other'. Shelley's unfinished Gothico-Oriental romance *The Assassins* (1814) offers a critique of some of the social and intellectual concerns of the Assassins, a medieval extremist Muslim group that mercilessly killed its religious and political opponents. The hero and heroine of the romance, Albedir and Khaled, bear Muslim names, yet the Oriental touch is faint. What Shelley ascribes to the Assassins are actually his own views as expressed in his *A Philosophical View of Reform.* Using the pretext of the Assassins' philosophy, Shelley castigates the social order of the day. His poem 'The Indian Serenade' (1821), employs the popular Oriental image of the nightingale. Another relevant piece is 'From the Arabic, an Imitation' (1821), with marked borrowings from the Arabic romance, translated into English by Terrick

Hamilton, entitled *Antar, A Bedoueen Romance* (1819). Michael Rossington discovers in the journey to the Islamic world in both *Alastor* and *Promethus Unbound,* Shelley's response to wider contemporary arguments about the search for 'a cradle of civilization' and in 'The Witch of Atlas' the 'North African location of the Witch's realm, works as a parody of the desire to find in the Islamic world a universal key to all mythologies'.[36] In his concern with the mythologies of the world, his endorsement of colonial and evangelical incursions in the Islamic lands and his cultural narcissism precluding any positive appreciation of the ethnically different, Shelley's Orientalism is akin to Robert Southey's.

The Arab in Wordsworth

Apart from the substantial Literary Orientalism in the works of the above-mentioned Romantic writers, others such as Leigh Hunt, Keats, Crabbe and Landor also make reference to Islam and Muslims. Some allusions to Islam and Muslims occur in Wordsworth's *The Prelude, Ecclesiastical Sonnets,* part I (particularly XXXIV) and 'The Armenian Lady's Love' (1830).

The dream of the Arab in *The Prelude* (V, 86–102) represents a significant change in Literary Orientalism in the Romantic period. Unlike Pope, who in *The Dunciad* had portrayed Arabs as an ignorant people opposed to learning and accused them of burning libraries, Wordsworth acknowledges the great Arab intellectual tradition and its contribution to world knowledge. The Arab is made to appear with a stone and shell, standing respectively for the books of science and poetry; so doing, Wordsworth acknowledges the Arab preservation and transmission of knowledge which helped retrieve Greek ideas. Far from the conventional 'Noble Savage', Wordsworth's Arab stands out as a culture-hero. More importantly, the Arab in *The Prelude* has answers to the dreamer's questions, signifying the opening of doors for dialogue and communication between the West and the Islamic world. Wordsworth is perhaps the first writer to grant this equal status to an Arab, who is no more conventionally cast in the role of a warrior or an enemy.

Similarly, the Arab's shell denotes a book of poetry, or in Yousef Tarawreh's view, 'the *Arabian Nights* [is] a possible source of Wordsworth's conception of the shell, especially in view of these tales' frequent references to genies or genii and efreets being held within shells'. Again, according to Tarawreh, 'the subtle significations of stone and shell ... are related to the Oriental invention of the alphabets ... and the invention of paper'.[37] Wordsworth's treatment of the Islamic world in *The Prelude* is markedly positive.

Leigh Hunt's 'Mahmoud' (1823) celebrates the justice of Mahmud Ghaznavi, a Muslim ruler, who ordered a criminal to be executed in the dark and explained that he had the light put out lest the accused might be his own son. 'Cambus Khan' (1823) is quite close to the *Arabian Nights* in its description of luxuries and gorgeousness. The poem relates at length the Khan's feast and the fabulous gifts presented to him by the neighbouring, overawed kings. Hunt's other works with streaks of Literary Orientalism are: 'Abou Ben Adham', 'Jaffar', 'The Bitter Gourd' 'Abraham and the Fire-Worshipper' and 'The Trumpets of Doolkarnein'.

Landor's *Count Julian,* revolving around the theme of the Muslim conquest of Spain, contains few references to the Islamic world. George Crabbe draws heavily on the *Arabian Nights* for his tale 'The Confidant' (1818) in order to bring home a moral point about sin and atonement.

Keats's works testify to his familiarity with the *Arabian Nights* and Beckford's *Vathek.* In one of his letters to Fanny Brawne of July 1819 he makes a pointed reference to the story of 'The Man who Laughed Not' in the *Arabian*

Nights.'[38] In *Endymion* some fables are apparently taken from the *Arabian Nights, Vathek* and *Thalaba.* For example, regarding the story of Glaucus who was destined to live for a thousand years, Sidney Colvin observes: '[It] inevitably reminds us of such stories as that of the fisherman in the *Arabian Nights*, and of the spell laid by Suleiman upon the rebellious Djinn, whom he imprisoned for a thousand and eight hundred years in a bottle until Fisherman released him.'[39] According to Forman, in writing 'Aye, even as dead still as a marble man/Frozen in that old tale Arabian' *Endymion* (1,405–6) Keats had in mind the eldest lady's story in 'The Porter and the Three Ladies of Baghdad' of the *Arabian Nights.*[40] On Keats's Orientalism Colvin makes this insightful remark: 'The scenery, indeed, is often not merely of a Gothic vastness and intricacy: there is something of Oriental bewilderment - an *Arabian Nights* jugglery with space and time'.[41] Douglas Bush lists the *Arabian Nights* and *Vathek* as possible sources for Keats's mythology in *Hyperion.*[42] In sum, although Keats's Orientalism is peripheral, it does point to the strong influence of particular texts.

Political Aspect of Orientalism in the Romantic Period

The British expansion eastwards or imperialism with all the related implications lie at the heart of the Romantic discourse. Nigel Leask accounts thus for the Orientalism of the day:

> The sheer demand for Orientalism, the proliferation of Orientalist styles and narratives in the arts of the Romantic period: the eighteenth-century vogue for Chinoiserie is diversified into a demand for Egyptian, Ottoman, Mughal and Hindu motifs, components of what John Barrell calls, 'the imagery of an early but well-established imperialist culture'. Demand and desire are rationalized in terms of an (always risky) analogy with the imperial triumphs of the classical works.

> For the Orientalist poet Tom Medwin, English Romantic literature found a precedent and alibi in the Athenian practice of incorporating the imagery of its subjugated people into its own culture ... the products of an imperial heraldry which incorporated the symbols of the conquered with its own coats of arms.[43]

Moreover, one should not lose sight of the palpable political aspect of this discourse, arising out of the consolidation of British political and military power in the Islamic world, once again most notably in India. For a negative perception of the Islamic world, especially of its decayed institutions and decadent social fabric, underlined an urgent need for some remedial action on the part of the British, which was deemed as God's will or a moral duty. This generated support for the civilizing mission and evangelical work which would bring about reform and enlightenment in the colonies. What was good for the West must be better for them. To this ongoing socio-political debate the Romantics responded in their own, obviously varied, ways. This trend appears at its sharpest in the products of what Marilyn Butler brands 'a school of new powerful politicised poetry'.[44] Some of the works illustrative of this are Southey's epics namely, *Thalaba* (1801), *Madoc* (1805), and *The Curse of Kehama* (1801), Mary Shelley's novel *The Last Man* (1824), Shelley's *Revolt of Islam* (1818), *Prometheus Unbound* (1820) and *Hellas* (1821), Thomas Moore's *Lalla Rookh* (1817) and, to a considerably less extent, Byron's '*Turkish Tales*' (1813–16) and his play *Sardanaplus* (1821).

Most of these works depict revolutions, though mostly failed ones, aiming at the overthrow of some despotic Oriental ruler. What is significant is the close parallelism between these Oriental and contemporary tyrannical European regimes. Written in the wake of the French Revolution they pulsate with allusions to this event. Nonetheless, their concern with the imperialism, colonialism and evangelism of the day is much more distinct. Embedded in the discourse are responses to the following contemporary historical events: Napoleon's invasion of Syria and Egypt in 1798; the growing French role in the affairs of Persia and Afghanistan; wide-ranging discussion in both parliament and press on the British management of Indian affairs, especially administering its educational system and the pressing evangelical campaign by the Clapham Sect calling for the Parliament's approval for their conversion mission in India. Charles Grant's *Observations on the State of Society among the Asiatic Subjects of Great Britain* (1813), an official field study, advocated strongly Christian proselytism in India. The Indian society, it argued, reeling under oppressive and cruel Hinduism was 'a classic instance of unreformed despotism, precisely the type of the old regime the French were now rationally sweeping away'.[45] Eventually, the evangelists won their case in that the Parliament amended the East India Act in 1813, permitting proselytisation.

Swayed by negative representations of India, Southey and Shelley appear to have joined the call for the civilizing mission or indirectly the imperialism project. At the other end of the scale, Byron's '*Turkish Tales*', however, seem to question the validity of assumptions underlying this project.

Let us now recapitulate the distinguishing features of Literary Orientalism in the Romantic period as we have so far witnessed it. It represents a significant advance in both the range and quality of attention and use. It is neither tethered to religious and theological concerns as in earlier periods, nor does it betray paucity of authentic information as in the pre-Romantic period. Far from being merely exotic or employed simply as a pretext for moralizing or satirizing, it often reflects a genuine interest in the Islamic world, which is articulated creatively and imaginatively. Writers of this period appear on sure grounds about their knowledge of Islam and Muslims, partly owing to the availability of a large body of relevant literature and partly because of greater and easier first-hand access to the Islamic lands.

Literary Orientalism in the Victorian Period

Little wonder then that Literary Orientalism grew in depth and rootage in the Victorian period, as a host of historians, men of letters and academicians specializing in the study of the Orient focused their interest on things Oriental. 'The Matter of Araby' turned somewhat into the spirit of the age. Take the following substantial historical works as illustrative: Major David Price's *Chronological Retrospect or Memoirs of then Principal Events of Muhammedan History* (1811–21); John Malcom's *History of Persia* (1815); William Muir's *Life of Mahomet and History of Islam* (1856–61) and *The Caliphate* (1891). Thomas Carlyle (1795–1881) broadened the prospects of Literary Orientalism, especially the idea of the Arab-Islamic Orient, with his study *Heroes and Hero Worship* (1840) which is premised on philosophical concepts of history and heroism. According to Muahmmad A. al-Dami,

> Inseparable as they are, history and heroism shaped the framework within he tackled the Arab Islamic past... Carlyle seems to have been especially attracted to this prophetic life-pattern of suffering, revelation and salvation within Middle Eastern settings, hence the recurrent images of the wanderer, the nomadic Bedu, the Sahara or the hajj.[46]

As opposed to this, Cardinal Newman (1801–90), in his *Historical Sketches: The Turks in their Relation to Europe* 'presents the history of Islamic Orient not only to implement his Catholic approach to the past, but also to envision a new world order in which a spiritually reformed Europe guides and governs and essential barbarian East.'[47]

The travel writings of Richard Burton (1821–90), Gifford Palgrave (1826–88), Wilfrid Scawen Blunt (1840–

1922) and Charles M. Doughty (1843–1926) stand out as varied responses to the lure of the Orient. Burton heaps praise on Arabs, especially their character and conduct and their contributions to knowledge. He speaks highly of the educational institutions, libraries and hospitals flourishing in the medieval Muslim world. Palgrave appears at the other end of the scale in his loathing of the Bedouin. In his *Narrative* Palgrave tries his level best to remove popoular notions in the Europe about the Bedouin's nobility, generosity and hospitality. He, nonetheless, admires the lifestyle and conduct of the settled Arabs of Najd, and acclaims Arabs as a master race. Unlike Palgrave, Blunt was a Bedouinphile. He was struck by the simplicity of Bedouin religion. As to Doughty as an Arabist, Kathryn Tidrick informs:

> His experiences were determined by his uncompromising profession of Christiantity... His hatred of Islam was worthy of the most vituperative medieval bigot... He never forgot his experience of Arabian humanity and in later life wrote movingly in his poetry of the charity of poor folk.[48]

Among the Victorian men of letters, the Oriental element is markedly present in Tennyson's poetry. His 'Expedition of Nadir Shah into Hindostan' (1827) records his denunciation of Oriental despotism while his 'Written by an Exile of Bassorah While Sailing down the Euphrates' (1827) expresses the nostalgia on the part of the exiled Noureddain. His 'Recollection of the Arabian Nights' (1830) stands out as a testimony to the keen European interest in the *Arabian Nights* as it seeks to recapture the splendour of Baghdad. His *Akbar's Dream* represents his endorsement of the syncretic faith as practised by the Mughal king Akbar. He, nonetheless, equates it with the Christian moral code. As it was written in the heyday of British rule over India, its religio-political overtones assume greater significance. Robert Browning's *Mulekeh* (1880) brings to mind the narrative form of Arabian tale. Its Oriental colour is light yet it underscores Browning's familiarity with the tradition of Literary Orientalism. Arnold extended further the range of this tradition. His *Sohrab and Rustum,* of which the source is John Malcolm's *History of Persia* recreates the epic story lying at the core of the Persian masterpiece, Firdausi's *Shahnameh.* It is rich in Oriental costume, diction and local colour. According to Arnold, his *Persian Passion Play* compares the Christian dramatic performance, called the Ammergan passion play, with 'something...produced in the wonderful East from which, whatever airs of superiority Europe may justly give itself, all our religion has come'.[49] Throughout, Arnold's focus is on the devotion of Muslims engaged in the mourning rituals commemorating the martyrdom of the Prophet's grandson, Hussain, in order to underscore the lack of spiritual fervour among Europeans.

With the phenomenal increase in the twentieth century in the interaction between the Orient and the West at every level, it is not surprising to note frequent references to the Orient not only in literature but also in cinema, popular fiction and in electronic media. The quantum of representation is too vast to be covered in this brief survey. Nonetheless, mention should be made of the unmistakable Oriental elements in the works of Rudyard Kipling, E.M. Forster, W.B. Yeats, T.S. Eliot and Doris Lessing.

Orientalism in Film

On the depiction of the Orient in Hollywood movies, Ziauddin Sardar's comments are worth-considering:

> We find on the silver screen all the age-old stereotypes recycled, revived, refreshed and reinvested.... The ferociously evil oriental, remains consistent: the Arab terrorists of *Exodus* (1960); the deranged Mahdi of *Khartoum* (1966); the evil and dangerous Chinese of *The Face of Fu Munchu* (1965); the sadistic and inhuman Turks of *Midnight Express* (1978); the mad terrorists of *The Ambassador*

> (1984), and equally mad hostage-takers of the 'fundamental state' in *Iron Eagle* (1985); the China town mobsters of the *Year of the Dragon* (1985); the devious Arab villains of *Jewel of the Nile* (1985); the Palestinian terrorists of *Delta Force* (1986); the power-mad leader of the Crimson Jihad in *True Lies* (1994); the Algerian Terrorists in *Executive Decision* (1996) and the Arab terrorists of *the Siege* (1998).[50]

Orientalism in Popular Fiction

In popular fiction, especially of our times, Muslims appear mostly in dark colours – fanatical in their religion, tyrannical in their socio-political life, particularly in relation to women and given to lust and violence in both private and public domains. This tendency is evident at its sharpest in Jean P. Sasson's two best sellers *Princess* and *Princess Sultana's Daughters* published by Bantam Books, New York, in 1993 and 1994 respectively. Her denunciation of Muslim/Saudi Arabian society reflects an extreme configuration of antagonism towards, and caveat against any cross-cultural sympathy. For her the Western tradition is the norm and those outside it are perceived as loathsome. What strikes one first on this count is the tantalizing pictures of veiled Muslim harem women on the title pages of both works. Harem has been widely perceived in Western Literary Orientalism, travel literature and Orientalist paintings as a heaven for flagrantly gratifying all sexual desires. In the first edition of *Roget's Thesaurus* (1852) harem is grouped together with synonyms for 'brothel'. Sasson adroitly exploits this emotive image as a visual image, lending as it does massive titillating appeal, and in turn, a bigger market for her works. Like the missioned practitioners of Crusade progaganda, Sasson is committed to the sinister goal of redeeming Muslims who are perceived as the ones steeped in pitch darkness – religious, spiritual, socio-cultural and political.

According to the 'Preface', Sultana, the Muslim heroine, unable to articulate her tragic story herself related it to Sasson for a wider and appropriate presentation. This at once indicates the binary opposition between the superior Westerner and inferior Muslim, which is ingrained deeply on Sasson's mind. For her, a Muslim is not capable of even speaking for himself/herself. Only an intellectually superior and linguistically competent Westerner knows how to communicate. Moreover, it establishes the latter's superiority in the sense the he/she possesses the enviable skill of entering the mind of others. It is worth mentioning in this context that very few Muslim characters in the whole corpus of Literary Orientalism have ever been granted a voice to express themselves; they depend upon superior Westerners for both their existence and for their description. Religiously following this centuries-old tradition of stifling and gagging the Muslim voice, Sasson does not let any male Muslim, especially the representatives of the ruling and religious classes, speak for themselves. They are at the mercy of the narrator for their description which, needless to add, is always maliciously contrived to project them in the worst possible light.

That violence is an ineluctable part of Islam is set forth in great detail and with much relish. While medieval writers used to exert themselves in portraying Muslims as bloodthirsty in relation to their enemy, Sasson goes a step further in describing that violence is embedded deep even in their family life (*The Princess,* p. 77 and *Daughters,* p. 99). She is faithfully true to the polemical tradition in her account of polygamy, reflecting as it does the pious horror of a Westerner about the provision for polygamy in Islamic law.

That Islam is shorn of any spirituality is another fairly common charge of polemical Western writers down the ages. Sasson picks up the same thread in dismissing the Hajj as no more than a slave market in that Sultana's father is seen throughout the Hajj period as buying 'new slave children' (p. 30). Her crude attempt to divest Hajj of its religious halo and spiritual beauty continues in *Princess Sultana's Daughters* by referring, in a refrain-like manner, to it as a 'chaotic affair', and 'pandemonium' (p. 78), and to 'the dreaded effects of four million frenzied worshippers bent on trampling, crushing and killing fellow pilgrims in the dangerous religious ceremony' (pp. 81, 83 and 84).

As in other polemical works, the binary contrast between Muslim and Western societies, biased in the latter's favour, is also evident in Sasson's work. What is more pernicious is that the Muslim characters, especially women, are shown abandoning their faith on witnessing the West's all-round superiority. In the same vein, Western characters appear throughout as saviours, be they the British nurse, American pilot or British doctor (*Daughters,* pp. 249, 71 and 74), liberating the hapless Muslim woman reeling under her father's and her husband's oppression. Small wonder then that Sultana's mindset soon turns completely Western. In coping with the trauma of her mother's death she finds no comfort or consolation in the Qur'an or any other Islamic mode; instead she turns to 'the wise' Christian poet-philosopher Kahil Gibran for solace (pp. 97–8). Maha, Sultana's daughter representing the next generation of Muslim women, logically goes a step further by disowning Islam altogether and by blaspheming against all that is sacred in Islam (*Daughters,* pp. 196 and 221). Sasson twists her knife in the wound by tracing the plight of foreign working women in Saudi Arabia to the Quranic command. According to her, 'Muslims consider any women who is not Muslim as a prostitute' (p. 136). Such malicious generalizations painting Muslims as devils undoubtedly render Sasson's novels as an abhorrent instance of 'hate literature'.[51]

Definition of and Current Debates on Orientalism

Needless to, add, it was Edward Said's *Orientalism* (1978) which set in motion a lively debate on the Western tradition of Orientalism, Ziauddin Sardar paraphrases Said's definitions of Orientalism thus:

1. The classical tradition of studying a region by means of its languages and writings; thus anyone who teaches, researches or writes about the Orient is an Orientalist. It is in this form that Orientalism lives on through its doctrines and theses, with expert Orientalist as its main authority.
2. A way of coming to terms with the Orient that is based on the Orient's special place in European Western experience.
3. An overarching style of thought, with a history going back to antiquity, based on an ontological and epistemological distinction made between the 'Orient' and 'the Occident'.
4. A Western style for dominating, restructuring, and having authority over the Orient.
5. A library or archive of information commonly and, in some of its aspects, unanimously held. What bound the archive together was a family of ideas and a unifying set of values proven in various ways to be effective. These ideas explained the behavior of the Orientals; they supplied the Orientals with a mentality, a genealogy, an atmosphere; most important, they allowed the Europeans to deal with and even to see Orientals as a phenomenon possessing regular characteristics.
6. A system of representations framed by a whole set of forces that brought the Orient into Western learning, Western consciousness, and later, Western Empire.
7. The western 'corporate institution' responsible for dealing with the Orient: describing it, containing it, controlling it, teaching and learning about it, making statements about it, authorizing views of it and ruling over it by these and other means.[52]

Said's above thesis has evoked varied responses from a host of scholars. A.L. Macife offers the following critique on their main contours:

> What is striking about the debate regarding Orientalism inspired by the critique of the subject, mounted by Abdel-Malek, Tibawi, Said and Turner in the decades following the end of the Second World War, is the extent to which it fails to divide its participants on the basis of ethnic, racial, national, cultural, philosophical and religious affiliation. Abdel-Malek (Egyptian, Coptic) and Turner (English), both leading critics of Orientalism, adopt a rigorously Marxist (materialist) approach to the subject, whereas Tibawi (Palestinian), a convinced Muslim, adopts a Muslim-humanist approach, and Said (Palestinian, Christian) adopts a post-modernist approach, based on the Foucauldian concepts of epistemic field, power-knowledge and discourse, and the Gramscian concept of cultural hegemony. Bernard Lewis (British-American), all leading critics of Said's *Orientalism*, adopt a traditional (realist) approach to the subject - though MacKenize claims an awareness of post-modernist theory - while Ahmad (Indian), also a leading critic of Said's *Orientalism*, adopts a Marxist (materialist) approach, similar to the approaches adopted by Abdel-Malek and Turner. Pollock (American), a supporter of Said, sees German orientalism as an example of the power-knowledge relationship identified by Foucault, while Richardson (English) adopts a philosophical-analytical approach, and al'Azm (Arab) criticized Said for being non-scientific. Moore-Gilbert (English), Rendall (British) and Gemie (Arab) adopt a severely empiricist approach, while Hildreth (American) defends Said against the attack mounted on him by MacKenzie, calling up in Said's defence the philosophical approach advocated by Husserl, the German philosopher. Inden (American) and King (British) seek to analyze British views of Indian history from

> Saidian, representational point of view, while Majeed (Indian) sees them as the product of English utilitarianism. Finally, Mackenize and Kabbani (Arab) both employ post-modernist methods of analysis to deconstruct nineteenth-century Orientalist art, arriving in the process at radically different conclusions. If a consistent division of sorts can be identified between the participants in the debate regarding Orientalism, its is the division between Said's representational view of knowledge and the traditional (realist-Marxist) view taken by many of his principal critics.[53]

This companion to Literary Orientalism seeks to extend the above debate on the various facets of Literary Orientalism by way of identifying the relevant material on the subject.

Notes and References

1. R.W. Southern, *Western Views of Islam in the Middle Ages,* Cambridge, MA, 1978, p. 14.
2. Dorothee Metlitzki, *The Matter of Araby in Medieval England,* New Haven, CT, 1977, p. 4.
3. Anwar Chejne, 'The Role of al-Andalus in the Movement of Ideas between Islam and the West' in *Islam and the Medieval West: Aspects of Intercultural Relations,* ed., Khalil L Semaan, Albany, NY, 1980, pp. 114–15.
4. Abdul Wahid Lulua, 'Andalusian and English Lyrical Poetry: Probable Influence Through the Troubadours', in Jalal Uddin Khan and Adraian E. Hare (Eds.), *English and Islam: Creative Encounters 96,* Kuala Lumpur, IIUM, 1998, p. 4
5. Ibid., p. 12
6. Ibid., p. 18

The following works shed valuable light on the literary influence of Muslim Spain on Europe:

- Roger Boase, 'Arab Influences on European Love Poetry' in Salma K. Jayyusi (Ed.), *The Legacy of Muslim Spain,* Leiden, E.J. Brill, 1992.
- A.J. Denomy, '*Fin Amors:* The Pure Love of the Troubadours: Its Amorality and Possible Sources', *Medieval Studies,* 7, 1945.
- Etienne G. Sandras, *Etude sur G. Chaucer considere comme Imitateur des Trouveres,* Paris, Augueste Durad, 1859.
- H.J. Chaytor, *The Troubadours and England* Cambridge, CUP, 1923.
- J. Audiau, *Les Trubadours et L' Angletrre,* Paris, 1920.

7. Some of these works are: Thomas Arnold and A. Guillame, (Eds.), *The Legacy of Islam,* Oxford, 1931; Donald Campbell, *Arabian Medicine and its Influence on the Middle Ages,* London, 1926; Paul Coles, *The Ottoman Impact on Europe,* London: 1968; D.M. Dunlop, *The Arabic Science in the West,* Karachi, 1958; H.G. Farmer, *Historical Facts for the Arabian Musical Influence,* London, 1930; R.A. Jairazbhoy, *Oriental Influences in Western Art,* New York, 1965 and J.T. Monroe, *Islam and the Arabs in Spanish Scholarship,* Leiden, 1970.
8. C.H. Haskin, The *Renaissance of the Twelfth Century: Studies in the History of Medieval Science,* Cambridge, MA, 1927, p. 80.
9. Paul Coles, *The Ottoman Impact on Europe,* London, 1968.
10. A.L. Macfie, *Orientalism,* London, Longman, 2002, pp. 59–60.
11. Norman Daniel, *Heroes and Saracens: A Reinterpretation of the 'Chanson de Geste',* Edinburgh, 1984, p. 4.
12. Apart from in Norman Daniel's excellent works, the image of Islam in the *Chanson de Geste* is examined also in C.M. Jones, 'The Conventional Saracens of the Songs of Geste', *Speculum,* 17, 1942, pp. 201–25.
13. Dorothee Metlitzki, *The Matter of Araby in Medieval England,* p. 160.
14. Naji B. Oueijan, *The Progress of an Image: The East in English Literature,* New York, Peter Lang, 1996, p. 19. Little wonder then that the following Elizabethan plays are marred by a distorted description of Islamic faith and practices: Philip Massinger's *Renegado* (1624), Thomas Kyd's *Soliman and Perseda* (1588) Fulke Greville's *Mustapha (1606)* and *Alham* (1632) and Thomas Geoffe's *The Raging Turk* (1627).
15. Francis Bacon, *The Essays of Bacon,* London, 1903, p. 81.

16. Samuel C. Chew, *The Crescent and the Rose: Islam and England during the Renaissance,* New York, 1937, p. 432.
17. Naji B. Oueijan, *The Progress of an Image: The East in English Literature,* New York, Peter Lang, 1996, p. 15.
18. *Sir Thomas Browne's Pseudodxia Eplidemica, ed.,* Robbin Robbins, Oxford, 1981, vol, 1, p. 107.
19. Muhsin Jassim Ali, *Scheherazade in England: A Study of Nineteenth Century English Criticism of the Arabian Nights,* Washington, D.C, 1981, p. 3.
20. E.F. Bleiler, *Three Gothic Novels,* New York, 1966, p. xxviii.
21. Martha P. Conant, *The Oriental Tale in England in the Eighteenth Century,* New York, 1908, p. viii.
22. Ibid., p. xxvi.
23. Ros Ballaster, *Fables of the East: Selected Tales 1622–1785.* Oxford, Oxford University Press, pp. 10 and 11.
24. Ibid., pp. 7 and 9.
25. *The Poems of Samuel Johnson* (Eds.), D.N. Smith and E.L. McAdam, Oxford, 1941, p. 276.
26. *The Works of Lord Byron: Poetry,* ed., E.H. Coleridge, London, 1922, vol. II, p. 145.
27. William Jones, *Works,* (Ed.), Lord Teignmouth, London, 1807, vol. X, p. 360.
28. A.J. Arberry, *British Orientalists,* London, 1943.
29. W.C. Brown, 'The Popularity of Engllsh Travel Books about the Near East, 1775–1825', *Philological Quarterly,* 15, 1936, pp. 70–80.
30. Ros Ballaster, op. cit., p. 10.
31. B.R. Breyer, 'Towards an Interpretation of *Kubla Khan*' in *English Studies in Honour of James Southal Wilson,* (Ed.), Fredson Bowers, Virginia, 1951, pp. 227–90.

32. Frederick 1. Jones, ed., *Collected Letters of P.B. Shelley,* Oxford, 1964, vol. I, pp. 563–4.
33. Nigel Leask, *British Romantic Writers and the East: Anxieties of Empire,* Cambridge, 1992, p. 110.
34. Donald H. Reiman, (Ed.), *Shelley and His Circle* Cambridge, MA, 1973, vol. IV, p. 987.
35. Nigel Leask, *British Romantic Writers and the East,* p. 72.
36. Michael Rossington, 'Shelley and the Orient', *Keats-Shelley Review, 5,* Autumn 1991, p. 20.
37. For this discussion on *The Prelude,* I have drawn on Yousef Tarawreh's 'Islamic Reflections: Revisionist Portrayals of Arab Civilization with Particular Reference to Wordsworth, Pope, Cervantes, and Dante' in *International Journal of Islamic and Arabic Studies,* 4, 1987, pp. 62–3.
38. H. Buxton Forman, (Ed.), *The Poetical Works and Other Writings of John Keats,* New York, 1938, vol. VIII, p. 13.
39. Sidney Colvin, *John Keats: His Life and Poetry. His Friends. Critics and After-Fame,* London, 1920, p. 191.
40. H. Buxton Forman, *The Poetical Works... of John Keats,* vol. II, p. 1.
41. Sidney Colvin, *John Keats: His Life,* p. 173.
42. Douglas Bush, *Mythology and the Romantic Tradition in English Poetry,* Cambridge, MA, 1969, p. 116.
43. Nigel Leask, *British Romantic Writers,* p. 8.
44. Marilyn Butler, 'Byron and the Empire in the East', in Andrew Rutherford (Ed.), *Byron: Augustan and Romantic,* London, 1990, p. 68.
45. Ibid., p. 71.
46. Muhammad A. al-Dami, *Arabian Mirrors and Western Soothsayers: Nineteenth Century Approaches to Arab-Islamic History.* New York, Peter Lang, 2002, pp. 65–6.

47. Ibid., p. 99.

48. Kathryn Tidrick, *Heart Beguiling Araby: The English Romance with Arabia.* London, I.B. Tauris, 1981, pp. 142 and 151.

49. Matthew Arnold, 'A Persian Passion Play' in *The Works of Matthew Arnold,* vol. III, London, Macmillan, 1903, pp. 246–7.

50. Ziauddin Sardar, *Orientalism,* Buckingham, Open University Press, 1999, pp. 95–6.

51. For a detailed review on Sasson's bestsellers, see A. R. Kidwai, 'Pulp Fiction or Hate Literature', in A. R. Kidwai (Ed.), *Stranger than Fiction: Images of Islam and Muslims in English Fiction,* New Delhi, APH, 2000, pp. 86–98.

52. Ziauddin Sardar, op. cit., p. 68.

53. A.L. Macfie, *Orientalism,* London, Longman, 2002, pp. 216–17.

1

Samples of Literary Orientalism: Writers, Works and Critical Studies

Joseph Addison
(1672–1719)

- *Observations by Four Indian Kings*, **Spectator**, 50, 27 April 1711.
- *Mahomet's Journey to the Seven Heavens and the Adventures of the Sultan of Egypt*, **Spectator**, 94, 18 June 1711.
- *The Vision of Mirza*, **Spectator**, 159, 1 September 1711.
- *Story of Sick King*, **Spectator**, 195, 13 October 1711.
- *Story of the Dervish*, **Spectator**, 289, 31 January 1711–1712.
- *Persian Fable of a Drop of Water Which Became a Pearl*, **Spectator**, 293, 5 February 1711–1712.
- *Story of Courageous Muli Moluc, Emperor of Morocco*, **Spectator**, 349, 10 April, 1712.
- *Story of Alnaschar*, **Spectator**, 535, 13 November 1712.
- *Story of Helim and Abdullah*, **Guardian**, 167, 22 September 1713.
- *Letter to the King of Bantam*, **Spectator**, 557, 21 June 1714.
- *Story of Hilpa, Harpath and Shalum*, **Spectator**, 584 and 585, 23 and 25 August 1714.
- *Persian Emperor's Riddle*, **Freeholder**, 17, 17 February 1716.

Article/s

Ascari, Maurizio, 'The Role of Addison's Dream Visions and Oriental Tales in the Nascent Poetics of Short Fiction', *Textus*, 18:1, 2005, 11–23.

Matthew Arnold

(1822–88)

- *Sohrab and Rustum*
- *The Sick King in Bokhara*
- *A Persian Passion Play*

Article/s

Haddad, Emily A., 'Matthew Arnold in Bukhara: Nature in the Middle Eastern City', in Emily A. Haddad, *Oriental Poetics*, Aldershort, UK, Ashgate, 2002, 141–6.

Jarrett-Kerr and Martin, William R., 'Arnold Versus the Orient: Some Footnotes to a Disenchantment', *Comparative Literature Studies*, 12, 1975, 129–46.

Musawi, Muhsin J., 'Waiting for the "Liberal Saints": An Assessment of Matthew Arnold's Last Political Essays', *Arab Journal for the Humanities*, 9:35, 1989, 321–37.

Shurbutt, Sylvia Bailey, 'The Poetry of Matthew Arnold: Nature and the Oriental Wisdom', *University of Dayton Review*, 13:3, 1985–6, 41–8.

Woodford, 'The Sick King in Bokhara: Arnold and the Sublime of Suffering', in Robert Giddings (Ed.), *Matthew Arnold: Between Two Worlds*, London, Vision, 1986, 100–20.

Doctoral Dissertation/s

MacNeill, Jennie E., 'The Orient in Matthew Arnold's Poetry', University of Toronto, 1935.

Zaidi, Syed Faiz, 'Image of the Orient in Victorian Poetry with Special Reference to Tennyson, Browning and Arnold', Aligarh Muslim University, Aligarh, India, 2003.

William Beckford
(1759–1844)

- *Vathek*

Book/s

Graham, Kenneth W. (Ed.), *Vathek and the Escape from Time: Bicentenary Revaluations*, New York, AMS Press, 1990.

Graham, Kenneth and Berland, Kevin, *William Beckford and the New Millenium*, New York, AMS Press, 2004.

Moussa, Mahmoud F. (Ed.), *William Beckford of Fonthill, 1760–1844: Bicentenary Essays*, Cairo, Dar al-Marifah, 1960.

Article/s

Alexander, B., 'The Decay of Beckford's Genius' in Fatma Mahmoud, Moussa (Ed.), *William Beckford of Fonthill, 1760–1844*, Cairo, Dar al-Marifah, 1960.

Anon, 'William Beckford and Islam', *Connoisseur*, 191, 1976, 250–3.

Baker, Ernest, 'The Oriental Tale from *Rasselas* to *Vathek*', in Ernest Baker (Ed.), *History of English Novel*, 5, 55–76.

Bullough, G., 'Beckford's Early Travels and His "Dream of Delusion"' in Fatma Mahmoud Moussa (Ed.), *William Beckford of Fonthill, 1760–1844*, Cairo, Dar al-Marifah, 1960.

Cass, Jeffrey, 'Homoerotics and Orientalism in William Beckford's *Vathek*: Liberalism and the Problem of Pederasty', in Diane Long Hoeveler and Jeffrey Cass (Eds.), *Interrogating Orientalism: Contextual Approaches and Pedagogical Perspectives*, Columbus, Ohio State University Press, 2006, 107–20.

Conger, S. M., 'Maternal Negotiations with the Underworld: Origins and Ends in William Beckford's *Vathek* and Mary Shelley's *Proserpine*', in Werner Schneiders, Jane Godden (et al.) (Eds.), *Transactions of the Ninth International Congress on the Enlightenment Münster ... 1995*, vol. I, Oxford: Voltaire Foundation, 1996, 448–51.

Folsom, James K., 'Beckford's *Vathek* and the Tradition of Oriental Satire', *Criticism*, 6, 1964, 53–69.

Frank, Frederick, 'A Checklist of *Vathek* Criticism', in Kenneth W. Graham (Ed.), *Vathek and the Escape from Time: Bicentenary Revaluations*, New York, AMS Press, 1990, 247–68.

Garber, Frederick, 'Beckford, Delacroix and Byronic Orientalism', *Comparative Literature Studies*, 18, 1981, 321–32.

Garrett, J., 'Beckford's Amorality: Deconstructing the House of Faith', in *Transactions of the Ninth International Congress on the Enlightenment*, Münster ... 1995, vol. I, Oxford: Voltaire Foundation, 1996, 455–8.

Gill, R.B., 'The Enlightened Occultist: Beckford's Presence in *Vathek*', in Kenneth W. Graham (Ed.), *Vathek and the Escape from Time: Bicentenary Revaluations*, New York, AMS, 1990, 131–43.

Graham, Kenneth W., 'Beckford's Adaptation of the Oriental Tale in *Vathek*', *Enlightenment Essays,* 5:1, 1974, 24–33.

Graham, Kenneth W., 'Perverse Interactions of the Gothic, Enlightened, and Oriental: William Beckford's *Vathek*; with, *The Episodes of Vathek*', in Kenneth W. Graham and Kevin Berland (Eds.), *William Beckford and the New Millennium*, New York, AMS Press, 2004, 119–30.

Hussain, Imdad, 'Beckford, Wainwright, De Quincey and Oriental Exoticism', *Venture*, 1, September 1960, 234–48.

Jack, M., 'William Beckford: The Poor Arabian Story-Teller', *Transactions of the Ninth International Congress on the Enlightenment,* Münster ... 1995. vol. I Oxford: Voltaire Foundation, 1996, 451–4.

Knox-Shaw, Peter, '*Vathek* and The Seven Fountains by Sir William Jones', *Notes and Queries*, 240, New Series 42:1, March 1995, 75–6.

Liu, Alan, 'Toward a Theory of Common Sense Beckford's *Vathek* and Johnson's *Rasselas*', *Texas Studies in Literature and Language*, 26, 1984, 183–217.

Moussa, Mahmoud Fatma, 'Orientals in Picaresque: A Chapter in the History of the Oriental Tale in England', *Cairo Studies in English*, 1961–2, 145–188.

Manzalaoui, Mahmoud, 'Pseudo-Orientalism in Transition: the Age of *Vathek*' in Fatima Mahmoud Moussa (Ed.), *William Beckford of Fonthill 1770–1844*, Cairo Studies in English, 1960, 123–50.

Moussa, Mahmoud F., 'Beckford, Vathek and the Oriental Tale', in Fatima Mahmoud Moussa (Ed.), *William Beckford of Fonthill, 1960–1844: Bicentenary Essays*, Cairo, 1960, 63–121.

Musawi, Muhsin J., 'Beckford's *Vathek*, as an Arabian Tale', *Orientalism*, 3, 1989, 3–16.

Parreaux, A., 'The Caliph and the Swinish Multitude' in Fatma Mahmoud Moussa (Ed.), *William Beckford of Fonthill, 1760–1844*, Cairo, 1960.

Saglia, Diego, 'William Beckford's 'Sparks of Orientalism' and the Material-Discursive Orient of British Romanticism', *Textual Practice*, 16:1, 2002, 75–92.

Sergheni, El Habib Benrahal, 'William Beckford's Symbolic Appropriation of the Oriental Context', in C.C. Barfoot and Theo D'haen (Eds.), *Oriental Prospects: Western Literature and the Lure of the East*, Amsterdam, GA, Rodopi, 1998, 43–64.

Sherwani, Sherin, 'Muslim Characters in Beckford's *Vathek*' in A.R. Kidwai (Ed.), *Stranger Than Fiction: Images of Islam and Muslims in English Fiction*, Delhi, A.P.H., 2000, 15–48.

Svilpis, J.E., 'Orientalism, Fantasy, and Vathek', in Kenneth W. Graham (Ed.), *Vathek and the Escape from Time: Bicentenary Revaluations*, New York, AMS, 1990, 49–72.

Thompson, K.F., 'Beckford and Henley', *Etudes Anglaises*, 41, July-September 1961, 225–8.

Thompson, K.F., 'Henley's Share in *Vathek*', *Philological Quarterly*, 31, 1952, 75–80.

Tintner, A.R., 'Fire of the Heart in 'Al Aaraaf': Beckford and Byron as Source', *Poe Studies*, 22, December 1989, 47–8.

Wahba, M., 'Beckford, Portugal and "Childish Error"' in Fatma Mahmoud Moussa (Ed.), *William Beckford of Fonthill, 1760–1844*, Cairo, 1960.

Doctoral Dissertation/s

Benrahhal-Serghini, el-Habib, 'The Road to Istakhar: A Critical Study of the Text and Context of William Beckford's "Vathek" and the "Episodes", 1760–1844', Belguim, Universitaire Instelling Antwerpen, 1994.

Shervani, Shirin, 'A Critical Study of William Beckford's *Vathek*: *An Arabian Tale* (1786)', Aligarh Muslim University, Aligarh, India, 2000.

Taipei, 'Chang, Tom Tung-p'ing, 'Dialectic of Reason and Imagination in William Beckford's *Vathek, An Arabian Tale*', Tamkang University, 1993.

William Blake

(1757–1827)

- *To Thomas Butts*
- *The Sea of Being*
- *Auguries of Innocence*
- *The Songs of Los, 6, 1–6*
- *The Marriage of Heaven and Hell*

Book/s

Clark, Steve and Suzuki, Masashi (Eds.), *The Reception of Blake in the Orient*, London, New York, Continuum, 2006.

Hage el-, George Nicolas, *William Blake and Kahlil Gibran: Poets of Prophetic Vision*, State University of New York at Binghamton, 1981.

Weir, David, *Brahma in the West: William Blake and the Oriental Renaissance*, Albany, New York State University Press, 2003.

Article/s

Ali, Salah Salim, '*Ishraqi* Themes in the Poetry and Prose of William Blake and William B. Yeats', *Hamdard Islamicus*, 16:iii, 1993, 37–61.

Fallon, David, '"That Angel Who Rides on the Whirlwind": William Blake's Oriental Apotheosis of

William Pitt', *Eighteenth-Century Life*, 31:2, 2007, 1–28.

Larrissy, Edward, 'Blake's Orient', *Romanticism*, 11:1, 2005, 1–13.

Robert Browning

(1812–80)

- *The Return of the Druses*
- *A Camel Driver*
- *Solomon and Bilkis*
- *Abbas Shah*
- *Mihrab Shah*
- *Muleykeh*

Article/s

Khattab, Ezzat, 'Browning in Arabic', *Arab Studies Quarterly*, 5:2, 1983, 113–18.

Doctoral Dissertation/s

Archer, Frederick, 'Orientalism in Browning', University of North Carolina at Chapel Hill, 1904.

Warren, Mary Keith, 'Orientalism in Browning', Boston University, 1930.

Zaidi, Syed Faiz, 'Image of the Orient in Victorian Poetry with Special Reference to Tennyson, Browning and Arnold', Aligarh Muslim University, Aligarh, India, 2003.

Richard F. Burton

(1821–90)

- *The Qasidah of Abdu Al-Yezdi*
- *Sindh, and the Races that Inhabit the Valley of the Indus*
- *Falconry in the Valley of the Indus*
- *Personal Narrative of a Pilgrimage to Al-Madinah and Meccah*
- *First Footsetps in East Africa*
- *Zanzibar: City, Island and Coast*
- *A Plain and Literal Translation of the Arabian Nights Entertainments*

Book/s

Jutzi, Alan H. (Ed.), *In Search of Sir Richard Burton: Papers from a Huntington Library Symposium*, San Mariono, CA, Huntington Library, 1993.

Article/s

Godsall, Jon R., 'Fact and Fiction in Richard Burton's *Personal Narrative of a Pilgrimage to Al-Madinah and Meccah*', 1855–6', *IRAS*, Series 3, 3, 1993, 331–51.

Marle, Hans van, 'Conrad and Richard Burton on Islam', *Conradiana*, 17:2, 1985, 137–42.

Rosenthal, Melinda M., 'Burton's Literary Uroburos: *The Arabian Nights* as Self-Reflexive Narrative', *Pacific Coast Philology*, 25:1–2, 1990, 116–25.

Roy, Parama, 'Oriental Exhibits: Englishmen and Natives in Burton's *Personal Narrative of a Pilgrimage to al-Madinah & Meccah'*, *Boundary*, 2, 22:1, 1995, 186–210.

Tidrick, Kathryn, 'Richard Burton', in Kathryn Tidrick, *Heart Beguiling Araby: The English Romance with Arabia*, London, I.B. Tauris, 1989, 57–83.

Wasti, Syed Munir, 'A Study of Sir Burton's [Sic] English "Kasidah"' *Ariel (A Research Journal of English Language and Literature)*, 18, 1992–3, 49–53.

Doctoral Dissertation/s

Assad, Thomas J., 'The Near East and the Late Victorians: An Approach to Sir Richard Francis Burton, Wilfrid Scawen Blunt, and Charles Montagu Doughty', University of Wisconsin - Madison, 1954.

Davies, Robert, 'Warriors and Gentlemen: The Occidental Context of the Arabian Travel Narratives of Burton, Blunt and Lawrence', University of Technology, Loughborough, 1991.

Grant, B. J., 'Burton/Empire: Strategies of Appropriation', University of Kent, 2005.

Issa, W., 'Aspects of Orientalism: Four English Writers; Burton, Blunt, Flecker and T.E. Lawrence', University of Reading, 1986.

Ma'at, Y.S., 'Sir Richard Burton: A Study of His Literary Works relating to the Arab World and Islam', University of St. Andrews, 1978.

Mohd, Jamal A.I., 'A Critical Study of Richard F. Burton's Tales from 1001 *Arabian Nights*', Aligarh Muslim University, Aligarh, India, 1999.

Nichols, Pamela Catherine, 'Force and Charm in the Desert: Manly Adventure and Gentlemanly Behaviour in the Middle Eastern Travel Writings of Richard and Isabel Burton and Wilfrid Scawen and Anne Blunt', New York University, 1994.

Pandit, Pallavi, 'Orientalist Discourse and Its Literary Representations in the Works of Four British Travel Writers: James Morier, Alexander Kinglake, Richard Burton, and Gertrude Bell', Pennsylvania State University, 1990.

Rogers, William Norris, 'Arabian Involvement: A Study of Five Victorian Travel Narratives', University of California, Berkeley, 1972.

Sampson, Kathryn Ann, 'The Romantic Literary Pilgrimage to the Orient: Byron, Scott, and Burton', University of Texas at Austin, 1999.

Sulaiman, J.Y., 'Victorian Travellers' Attitudes to the Arab World', University of Wales, Bangor, 1991.

Taha Al-, M., 'The Orient and Three Victorian Travellers: Kinglake, Burton and Palgrave', University of Leicester, 1989.

Zane, Kathleen J.C., 'Paradigms of Place in Travel Literature: The Oriental Voyages of Nerval, Burton, Kinglake, and Chateaubriand', City University of New York, 1984.

Lord Byron
(1788–1824)

- *Childe Harold Cantos I and II*
- *The Giaour*
- *The Bride of Abydos*
- *The Corsair*
- *Lara*
- *The Siege of Corinth*
- *Beppo*
- *Don Juan*
- *Tale of Calil*

Book/s

Cochran, Peter (Ed.), *Byron and Orientalism*, Cambridge, Cambridge Scholars, 2006.

Deneau, Daniel P., *Byron's Narrative Poems of 1813: Two Essays*, Salzburg, 1975.

Franklin, Caroline, *Byron's Heroines*, Oxford University Press, 1992.

Kidwai, A.R., *Orientalism in Lord Byron's 'Turkish Tales'*, Lewiston, USA, Mellen University Press, 1995.

Melikian, Anahid, *Byron and the East*, Beirut, American University, 1977.

Oueijan, Naji B., *A Compendium of Eastern Elements in Byron's Oriental Tales*, New York, Lang, 1999.

Prochazka, Martin (Ed.), *Byron: East and West*, Prague, Univerzita Karjova, 2000.

Raizis, M.B. (Ed.), *Byron and the Mediterranean World*, Athens, Hellenic Byron Society, 1995.

Watkins, Daniel P., *Social Relations in Byron's Eastern Tales*, London, Associated University Presses, 1987.

Yokota-Murakami, Takayuki, *Don Juan East/West: On the Problematics of Comparative Literature*, Albany, New York State University Press, 1998.

Article/s

Aycock, Roy E., 'Lord Byron and Bayle's *Dictionary*', *Year Book of English Studies*, 1975, 142–52.

Beatty, Bernard, 'Calvin in Islam: A Reading of Lara and *The Giaour*', *Romanticism*, 5:1, 1999, 70–86.

Blackstone, Bernard, 'Byron and Islam: The Triple Eros', *Journal of European Studies*, 4, 1974, 325–63.

Brown, Wallace C., 'Byron and English Interest in the Near East', *Studies in Philology*, 34, 1937, 55–64.

Butler, Marilyn, 'Byron and the Empire in the East', in Andrew Rutherford (Ed.), *Byron: Augustan and Romantic*, London, 1990, 63–81.

Butler, Marilyn, 'Plotting the Revolution: The Political Narratives of Romantic Poetry and Criticism', in Kenneth R. Johnston (et al.) (Eds.), *Romantic Revolutions: Criticism and Theory*, Bloomington, 1990, 133–57.

Butler, Marilyn, 'The Orientalism of Byron's *Giaour*', in Bernard Beatty and Vincent Newey (Eds.), *Byron and the Limits of Fiction*, Liverpool, 1988, 78–96.

Cardwell, Richard A., 'Byron and the Orient: Appropriation or Speculation', in Peter Cochran (Ed.), *Byron and Orientalism*, Cambridge, Cambridge Scholars, 2006, 152–74.

Christensen, Jerome, 'Perversion, Parody and Cultural Hegemony: Lord Byron's Oriental Tales', *South Atlantic Quarterly*, 88, Summer 1989, 570–603.

Cochran, Peter, 'Byron's and 'Tully's *Tripoli*'', *Byron Journal*, 20, 1992, 77–88.

Cochran, Peter, 'Byron's Orientalism', in Peter Cochran (Ed.), *Byron and Orientalism*, Cambridge, Cambridge Scholars, 2006, 1–33.

Cochran, Peter, 'Harold Goes to Hell: The Orientalism of *Childe Harold's Pilgrimage*', in Peter Cochran (Ed.), *Byron and Orientalism*, Cambridge, Cambridge Scholars, 2006, 34–66.

Cochran, Peter, 'Studies of Byron's Orientalism', in Peter Cochran (Ed.), *Byron and Orientalism*, Cambridge, Cambridge Scholars, 2006, 67–151.

Daffron, Eric, 'Disorienting the Self: The Figure of the White European Man in Byron's Oriental Tales and Travels', in Jay Losey and William D. Brewer (Eds.), *Mapping Male Sexuality: Nineteenth-Century England*, Madison, NJ, Fairleigh Dickinson University Press, 2001, 69–90.

Demata, Massimiliano, 'A Bibliography of Byron's Oriental Reading: Addenda and Corrections', *Notes and Queries*, 46:1, 1999, 39–41.

Franklin, Caroline, 'Juan's Sea Changes: Class, Race and Gender in Byron's *Don Juan*' in Nigel Wood (Ed.), *Don Juan, Theory in Practice Series,* London, Open University Press, 1993, 56–89.

Franklin, Caroline, 'Quiet Cruising o'er the Ocean Woman": Byron's *Don Juan* and the Woman Question, *Studies in Romanticism,* 29:4, Winter 1990, 603–31.

Franklin, Caroline, '"Some Samples of the Finest Orientalism": Byronic Philhellenism and Proto-Zionism at the time of the Congress of Vienna', in Tim Fulford (Ed.), *Romanticism and Colonialism: Writing and Empire, 1780–1830,* Cambridge, Cambridge University Press, 1998, 221–42.

Franklin, Michael J., 'The Building of Empire and the Building of Babel: Sir William Jones, Lord Byron, and their Productions of the Orient', in Martin Prochazka (Ed.), *Byron East and West,* Prague, Charles University, 2000, 63–78.

Garber, Frederick, 'Beckford, Delacroix and Byronic Orientalism', *Comparative Literature Studies,* 18, 1981, 321–32.

Garber, Frederick, 'Byron's *Giaour* and the Mark of Cain', *Etudes Anglaises,* 26, April-June 1973, 150–9.

Giuliano, Cheryl Fallon, 'Gulnare/Kaled's 'Untold' Feminization of Byron's Oriental Tales', *Studies in English Literature 1500–1900,* 33:4, 1993, 785–807.

Griffith, Ben W. Jr., '*The Revolt of Islam* and Byron's *The Corsair*', *Notes and Queries,* 201, June 1956, 265.

Haddad, Emily A., 'Out of the Desert: Byron's *Turkish Tales*', in Emily A. Haddad, *Oriental Poetics*, Aldershort, UK, Ashgate, 2002, 136–40.

Herz, N., 'Byron's *Bride of Abydos*', *Notes and Queries*, 10th Series, 11, June 1909, 445.

Hossain, Mary, 'Women and Paradise', *Journal of European Studies*, 19, 1989, 293–310.

Hull, Gloria T., 'The Byronic Heroine and Byron's *The Corsair*', *Ariel*, 8, 1978, 71–83.

Johnson, Lee, 'Delacroix and *the Bride of Abydos*', *Burlington Magazine*, 114, September 1972, 579–85.

Jordan, Hoover H., 'Byron and Moore', *Modern Language Quarterly*, 9, December 1948, 429–39.

Kelsall, Malcolm, ''Once Did She Hold the Gorgeous East in Fee ...': Byron's Venice and Oriental Empire', in Tim Fulford (Ed.), *Romanticism and Colonialism: Writing and Empire, 1780–1830*, Cambridge, Cambridge University Press, 1998, 243–60.

Kelsall, Malcolm, 'Byron and the Women of the Harem', in Alice Levine and Robert N. Keane (Eds.), *Rereading Byron: Essays Selected from Hofstra University's Byron Bicentennial Conference*, New York, Garland, 1993, 165–73.

Kidwai, A.R., 'A Bibliography of Byron's Oriental Reading', *Notes and Queries*, 237, June 1992, 167–8.

Kidwai, A.R., 'A Vulgar Error': Byron on Women and Paradise, *Byron Journal*, 21, 1993, 87–8.

Kidwai A.R., 'Oriental Heroines in Lord Byron's *Turkish Tales*', *The Aligarh Journal of English Studies,* 20:1, 1998, 51–77.

Kidwai, A.R., 'Samples of the Finest Orientalism: Image of the Orient in Lord Byron's '*Turkish Tales*', *Aligarh Critical Miscellany,* 9:1, 1996, 65–84.

Kidwai, A.R., 'Byron's Allusion to Zuleika: A Note', *Byron Journal,* 19, 1999, 149.

Kidwai, A.R., 'The Tale of Calil' in A.R. Kidwai, *Orientalism in Lord Byron's Turkish Tales,* Lewiston, Mellen University Press, 1995, 259–65.

Klimova, Svetlana, 'Byron's *Turkish Tales* and Russian Byronism: Pushkin and the Early Nineteenth-Century Russian Reception of Byron', *Byron Journal,* 33:2, 2005, 117–25.

Klinger, H., 'The Tale of Calil', *Times Literary Supplement,* 2 August 1985, 851.

Knox-Shaw, Peter, '*Persuasion,* Byron, and the *Turkish Tale*', *Review of English Studies,* 44:173, 1993, 47–69.

Leask, Nigel, 'Byron and the Eastern Mediterranean: Childe Harold II and the Polemic of Ottoman Greece', in Drummond Bone (Ed.), *The Cambridge Companion to Byron,* Cambridge University Press, 2005.

Leask, Nigel, 'Byron Turns Turk: Orientalism and the Eastern Tales', in Nigel Leask, *British Romantic Writers and the East: Anxieties of Empire,* Cambridge, Cambridge University Press, 1993, 13–67.

Leask, Nigel, 'Resolving the Corsair: Lara and The Island', in Jane Stabler (Ed.), *Byron: A Critical Reader*, London, Longmans 1998.

Lew, Joseph W., 'The Necessary Orientalist? *The Gioaur* and Nineteenth Century Imperialist Misogyny', in Alan Richardson and Sonia Hofkosh (Eds.), *Romanticism, Race, and Imperial Culture, 1780–1834*, Bloomington, IN, Indiana University Press, 1996, 173–202.

Makdisi, Saree, 'Versions of the East: Byron, Shelley, and the Orient', in Alan Richardson and Sonia Hofkosh (Eds.), in *Romanticism, Race, and Imperial Culture, 1780–1834*, Bloomington, Indiana University Press, 1996, 203–36.

Manning, Peter J., 'Tales and Politics: The *Corsair, Lara* and *The White Doe of Rylstone*', in Peter J., Manning, *Reading Romantics*, New York, 1990, 195–215.

Manning, Peter J., 'The Home-ing of Byron's *Corsair*' in Peter J. Manning, *Reading Romantics*, New York, 1990, 216–37.

Marandi, Seyed Mohammed, 'Byron's Infidel and the Muslim Fisherman', *Keats-Shelley Review*, 20, 2006, 133–55.

Marandi, Seyed Mohammed, 'The Bride of The East', in Peter Cochran (Ed.), *Byron and Orientalism*, Cambridge, Cambridge Scholars, 2006, 215-31.

Marshall, W.H., 'The Accretive Structure of Byron's *The Giaour*', *Modern Language Notes*, 76, 1961, 502–9.

McColl, Robert, '"Best Success were Sacrilege": Investigating Antitheses in *The Seige*', in Peter Cochran (Ed.), *Byron and Orientalism*, Cambridge, Cambridge Scholars, 2006, 232–45.

Meyer, Eric, '"I Know Thee Not, I Loath Thy Race": Romantic Orientalism in the Eye of the Other', *ELH*, 58, 1991, 657–99.

Ogle, Robert B., 'The Metamorphosis of Selim: Ovidian Myth in *The Bride of Abydos*', *Studies in Romanticism*, 20, 1981, 21–31.

Oueijan, Naji B., 'Western Exoticism and Byron's Orientalism', *Prism(s): Essays in Romanticism*, 6, 1998, 27–39.

Oueijan, Naji B., 'Byron's Eastern Literary Portraits' in M.B. Raizis (Ed.), *Byron and the Mediterranean World*, Athens, Hellenic Byron Society, 1995, 93–103.

Oueijan, Naji B., Byron, 'Delacroix and the Oriental Sublime', *Revue de l'Université de Moncton*, Numéro hors série, 2005, 115–25.

Oueijan, Naji B., 'Byron's Eastern Quests: A Liberation of the Spirit', *Palma Journal*, Beirut: Notre Dame University Press, 8, 2002, 83–96.

Platt, Jas, 'Pronunciation of *Giaour*', *Notes and Queries*, 8th Series, 9, May, 1896, 368.

Rapf, Joanna, 'The Byronic Heroine: Incest and the Creative Process', *Studies in English Literature*, 21, 1918, 637–45.

Richardson, Alan, 'Astarte: Byron's *Manfred* and Montesquieu's *Letters Persanes*', *Keats-Shelley Journal*, 40, 1991, 19–22.

Richardson, Alan, 'Escape from the Seraglio: Cultural Transvestism in *Don Juan*', in Alice Levine and Robert N. Keane (Eds.), *Rereading Byron: Essays Selected from Hofstra University's Byron Bicentennial Conference*, New York, Garland, 1993, 175–85.

Rishmawi, G. K., 'The Muslim East in Byron's *Don Juan*', *Papers on Language & Literature*, 35:3, 1999, 227–43.

Rishmawi, G.K., 'Islam and Muslims in Byron's *The Corsair*', *International Journal of Arabic-English Studies*, 1:2, 2000, 299–312.

Schneider, Jeffrey L., 'Secret Sins of the Orient: Creating a (Homo)textual Context for Reading Byron's *The Giaour*', *College English*, 65:1, 2002, 81–95.

Seed, David, '"Disjointed Fragments": Concealment and Revelation in *The Giaour*', *Byron Journal*, 18, 1990, 14–27.

Stauffer, Andrew, 'The Hero in the Harem: Byron's Debt to Medieval Romance in *Don Juan*', *European Romantic Review*, 10:1, Winter 1999, 84–97.

Thomas, Gordon K., 'Finest Orientalism, Western Sentimentalism, Proto-Zionism: The Muses of Byron's *Hebrew Melodies*', *Prism(s)*, 1, 1993, 51–66.

Tintner, A.R., 'Fire of the Heart in "Al Aaraaf": Beckford and Byron as Source', *Poe Studies*, 22, December 1989, 47–8.

Vitale, Marina, 'The Domesticated Heroine in Byron's *Corsair* and William Hone's Prose

Adaptation', *Literature and History*, 10, Spring 1984, 72–94.

Warden, J.S., 'Siege of Corinth', *Notes and Queries*, 5 June, 1852, 534.

Waterman, David F., 'Byron's Reflexive Orientalism in Cantos V and VI of *Don Juan*', *Etudes Anglaises*, 49:1, Winter 1996, 29–39.

Watkins, D.P., 'Social Relations in Byron's *The Giaour*', *Journal of English Literary History*, 52, Winter 1985, 873–92.

Wiener, H.S.L., 'Byron and the East: Literary Sources of the "*Turkish Tales*"', in Herbert John Davis (Ed.), *Nineteenth Century Studies in Honour of C.S. Northup*, New York, 1968, 89–128.

Wolfson, S.J., 'Couplets, Self and *The Corsair*', *Studies in Romanticism*, 27, 1988, 491–513.

Doctoral Dissertation/s

Asfour, Mohammad Hassan, 'The Crescent and the Cross: Islam and the Muslims in English Literature from Johnson to Byron', Indiana University, 1973.

Bagabas, Omar Abdullah, 'Byron's Representation of the Orient in "*Childe Harold's Pilgrimage*" "*Don Juan*" and "The Oriental Tales"', University of Essex, 1993.

Bazei al-, Saad Abdulrahman, 'Literary Orientalism in Nineteenth-Century Anglo-American Literature: Its Formation and Continuity', Purdue University, 1983.

Hejazi al-, Ali Ahmad Ali, 'Arabo-Islamic Mythology in English Poetry, 1755–1825', University of Wisconsin–Milwaukee, 1979.

Husain, I., 'The Oriental Elements in English Poetry (1784–1859)', University of Edinburgh, 1934.

Kidwai, A. R., '"Samples of the Finest Orientalism": A Study of the Orient in Lord Byron's "*Turkish Tales*"', University of Leicester, 1993.

Liassis, N., 'Lord Byron's Attitudes to the Near East in the Oriental Tales', University of Reading, 1997.

Marandi, Seyed Mohammed, 'Lord Byron, His Critics and Orientalism', University of Birmingham, 2003.

Melikian, Anahid, 'Byron and the Near East', University of Wisconsin-Madison, 1954.

Orman, Thomas Joseph, '"Something Which Is Not Us": Self, Place, and Otherness in Byron's Poetry', University of Toronto, 1992.

Osborne, Edna Pearle, 'The Orientalism of Byron', University of Kansas, 1914.

Oueijan, Naji Boulos, 'A Compendium of Eastern Elements in Byron's Oriental Tales', Baylor University, 1985.

Rishmawi, George K., 'Oriental Element in English Romantic Poetry: Shelley and Byron', State University of New York at Buffalo, 1983.

Rose, Dallen J., 'A Classical Orient : Orientalism and Greece in John Cam Hobhouse's *A Journey Through Albania – During the Years 1809 and 1810*', Washington State University, 2004.

Sampson, Kathryn Ann, 'The Romantic Literary Pilgrimage to the Orient: Byron, Scott, and Burton', University of Texas at Austin, 1999.

Sharafuddin, M. A., 'Islam and Romanticism: A Study of Orientalism in English Verse Narrative, 1798–1817', University of York, 1988.

Siddiqui, Shahzad Ahmad, 'The Oriental Content and Context in Byron's *Don Juan*', Aligarh Muslim University, Aligarh, India, 2008.

Stavrou, Stavros, 'Seeking the Exotic Romantic Orientalism in Keats, Shelley, and Byron', Dalhousie University, 1991.

Sultana, Fehmida, 'Romantic Orientalism and Islam: Southey, Shelley, Moore, and Byron', Tufts University, 1989.

Tageldin, Shaden M., '"Mahomet's Bride" and the "Moral North": The Poetic Politics of European Spatial, Social, and Sexual "Orient-ation" in Don Juan's Byronic Near East', Harvard University, 1992.

Tezla, Albert, 'Byron's Oriental Tales: A Critical Study', University of Chicago, 1952.

Wiener, Harold S.L., 'The Eastern Background of Byron's Turkish Tales', Yale University, 1938.

Zughoul, Mohammed Said, 'A Comparative Study of Islamic Allusions in Lord Byron's Poetry and Prose', Indiana University of Pennsylvania, 1992.

Thomas Carlyle
(1795–1881)

- *On Heroes, Hero–Worship and the Heroic in History*

Article/s

ApRoberts, Ruth, 'Mahomet, or Turning to the East', in Ruth ApRoberts, *The Ancient Dialect: Thomas Carlyle and Comparative Religion*, Berkeley, University of California Press, 1988, 87–101.

Da'mi al-Muhammed A., 'Arab Heroism for Victorian Britian: Carlyle's Contrasts of Faith and Doubt', in Muhammed A. al-Da'mi, *Arabian Mirrors and Western Soothsayers*, New York, Lang, 2002, 65–98.

Da'mi Al-, Muhammed A, 'On Carlyle's Concept of the Arab-Islamic Orient: A Study in "The Hero as Prophet"', in Muhsin Al-Musawi (Ed.), *Orientalism*, 2, Baghdad, Cultural Affairs, 1987, 62–86.

Pionke, Albert D., 'Beyond "The Hero as Prophet": A Survey of Images of Islam in Carlyle's Works', *Literature and Belief*, 25:1/2, 2005, 496–511.

Watt, Montgomery, 'Carlyle on Muhammed', *Hibbert Journal*, 53, 1954–5, 247–54.

Doctoral Dissertation/s

Mohamed, Donna Fahimah, 'Western Biographies of Muhammad and the Question of Orientalism', University of North Carolina at Chapel Hill, 1994.

Paull, Michael Ray, 'The Figure of Mahomet in Middle English Literature', University of North Carolina at Chapel Hill, 1969.

Geoffrey Chaucer

(1343–1400)

- *The Man of Law's Tale*
- *The Knight's Tale*
- *The Squire's Tale*
- *Astrolabe*

Book/s

Bryan, W.F. and Dempster, G. (Eds.), *Sources and Analogues of Chaucer's Canterbury Tales*, Chicago, University of Chicago Press, 1941.

Heffernan, Carol F., *The Orient in Chaucer and Medieval Romance*, Woodbridge, Suffolk, Rochester, NY, Brewer, 2003.

Metlitzke, Dorothee, *The Matter of Araby in Medieval England*, New Haven, Yale University Press, 1977.

Schildgen, Brenda Deen, *Pagans, Tartars, Moslems and Jews in Chaucer's Canterbury Tales*, Gainesville, University Press of Florida, 2001.

Article/s and Conference Presentations

Birns, Nicholas, 'Christian-Islamic Relations in Dante and Chaucer: Reflections on Recent Criticism', in Joan E. Hallisey and Mary-Ann Vetterling (Eds.), *Proceedings: Northeast Regional Meeting of the Conference on Christianity and Literature*, Weston, MA, Regis College, 1996.

Bleeth, Kenneth A., 'Orientalism and the Critical History of Chaucer's *Squire's Tale*', in Kathryn L. Lynch (Ed.), *Chaucer's Cultural Geography*, New York and London, Routledge, 2002.

Delany, Sheila, 'Chaucer's Orientalism in the Legend', Presented at the 'New York Medieval Club Conference', 1995.

Delany, Sheila, 'Chaucer's Prioress, the Jews and the Muslims', *Medieval Encounters*, 5: 2, 1999, 198–213.

Delany, Sheila, 'Geographies of Desire: Orientalism in the *Legend of Good Women*', *Chaucer Yearbook: A Journal of Late Medieval Studies*, 1, 1992, 1–32.

Finkelstein, Dorothee, '"The Code of Chaucer's Secree of Secrees": Arabic Alchemical Terminology in the Canon's *Yeoman's Tale*', *Archiv fur das Studium der Neueren Sprachen und Literaturn*, 207, 1970, 260–76.

Gittes, Katherine Slater, '*The Canterbury Tales* and the Arabic Frame Tradition', *PMLA*, 98:2, 1983, 238–51.

Grudin, Michaela Paasche, 'Credulity and the Rhetoric of Heterodoxy: From Averroes to Chaucer', *The Chaucer Review*, 35: 2, 2000, 204–22.

Kelly, Henry Ansgar, 'Jews and Saracens in Chaucer's England: A Review of the Evidence', *Studies in the Age of Chaucer*, 27, 2005, 129–69.

Lynch, K. L., 'East Meets West in Chaucer's Squire's and Franklin's Tales', *Speculum*, 70:3, 1995, 530–51.

Lynch, K.L., 'Storytelling, Exchange and Constancy: East and West in Chaucer's *Man of Law's Tale*', *The Chaucer Review*, 33: 4, 1999, 409–22.

Mead, Jenna, 'Reading by Said's Lantern: Orientalism and Chaucer's *Treatise on the Astralobe*', *Medieval Encounters: Jewish, Christian and Muslim Dialogues and Culture*, 5: 3, 2000, 350–7.

Schibanoff, Susan, 'Worlds Apart: Orientalism, Antifeminism, and Heresy in Chaucer's *Man of Law's Tale*', *Exemplaria*, 8:1, 1996, 59–96.

Schildgen, Brenda Deen, 'Heathenesse in the *Canterbury Tales*: Christian versus Islamic and Pagan Space in the *Man of Law's Tale*', in Brenda Deen Schildgen, *Pagans, Tartars, Moslems and Jews in Chaucer's Canterbury Tales*, Gainsville, FL, University Press of Florida, 2001, 48–68.

Walker, Warren S., 'Extant Analogues of '*Franklin's Tale*' in Turkish Oral Tradition', *The Chaucer Review*, 33:4, 1999, 432–8.

Wood, Marjorie Elizabeth, 'The Sultaness, Donegild, and Fourteenth-Century Female Merchants: Intersecting Discourses of Gender, Economy, and Orientalism in Chaucer's *Man of Law's Tale*', *Comitatus*, 37, 2006, 65–85.

Doctoral Dissertation/s

Aloni, Gila, 'Islamic Ideology in Chaucer's *Man of Law's Tale*', University of Paris, 2008.

Halaby, Raouf Jamil, 'Arabic Influences on Chaucer: Speculative Essay on a Study of a Literary

Relationship', East Texas State University, 1973.

Howell, Margaret J., 'Oriental Influences in Chaucer's *Squire's Tale*', Indiana University, 1970.

Saigh, E. J. S., 'Eastern Influences in Chaucer with Special Reference to the Arabs', University of London, 1946.

S.T. Coleridge

(1772–1834)

- *Muhammad*
- *Egypt: Hats over Turbans*
- *Kubla Khan*
- *Lewti or the Circassian Love Chaunt*
- *The Fall of Robespierre*
- *Malta, Egypt etc.*

Book/s

Schneider, Elisabeth, *Coleridge, Opium and 'Kubla Khan'*, Chicago, 1953.

Article/s

Hussain, Imdad, 'Orientalism and Coleridge', *Venture*, 1 and 2, 1960, 33–46 and 1961, 44–55.

Kidwai, A.R. and Newey, Vincent, 'The Outline of Coleridge's and Southey's "Muhammad", *Notes and Queries*, 238, March 1993, 38–9.

Leask, Nigel, 'Kubla Khan and Orientalism: The Road to Xanadu Revisited', *Romanticism*, 4:1, 1998, 1–21.

Milligan, Barry, 'Opium smoking and the Oriental infection of British identity', in Sue Vice (Ed.), *Beyond the Pleasure Dome: Writing and Addiction from the Romantics*, Sheffield, Sheffield Academic Press, 1994, 93–100.

Ober, W.U., '"Muhammad": The Outline of a Proposed Poem by Coleridge and Southey', *Notes and Queries*, New Series, 5, 1958, 448.

Pettit, Henry, 'Coleridge's Mount Abora', *MLN*, 54, 1941, 376.

Shaffer, E.S., 'The Oriental Idyll', in E.S. Shaffer, *'Kubla Khan' and the Fall of Jerusalem: The Mythological School in Biblical Criticism and Secular Literature, 1770–1880,* Cambridge, Cambridge University Press, 1975, 96–144.

Doctoral Dissertation/s

Ahmad, M., 'Oriental Influence in English Poetry of the Romantic Period', University of Birmingham, 1959–60.

Asfour, Mohammad Hassan, 'The Crescent and the Cross: Islam and the Muslims in English Literature from Johnson to Byron', Indiana University, 1973.

Barker, C., 'The Stone and the Shell: The Image of the Arab and the Romantic Sublime in the Poetry of Wordsworth and Coleridge', University of Exeter, 2006.

Milligan, Barry, 'Pleasures and Pains: Opium and the Orient in Nineteenth-Century English Culture', Duke University, 1992.

William Congreve
(1670–1729)

- *Way of the World IV, 1, 404–8.*
- *The Mourning Bride*

Article/s

Berkaoui, Khalid, 'Colonial Irony: The Andalusian Moor in Congreve's *The Mourning Bride*', in Mohamed Dahbi, Mohamed Ezroura and Lahcen Haddad (Eds.), *Cultural Studies, Interdisciplinarity, and the University*, Rabat, Faculty of Letters and Human Sciences, 1996, 167–73.

Joseph Conrad

(1857–1924)

- *An Outcast of the Island*
- *Lord Jim*
- *Rescue*
- *Almayer's Folly*
- *The Shadow Line*

Book/s

Hampson, Robert, *Cross-Cultural Encounters in Joseph Conrad's Malay Fiction*, Basingstoke, Palgrave, 2000.

Article/s

Bowen, Roger, 'Investing in Conrad, Investing in the Orient: Margaret Drabble's *The Gates of Ivory*', *Twentieth Century Literature*, 45:3, 1999, 278–98.

Hampson, Robert G., 'Conrad, Guthrie, and "*The Arabian Nights*"', *Conradiana: A Journal of Joseph Conrad Studies*, 18, 1986, 141–3.

Idris, Farhad, 'The Native Returns: Conrad and Orientalism in V. S. Naipaul's *An Area of Darkness*', *South Carolina Review*, 32:2, 2000, 43–53.

Lester, John, 'Conrad and Islam', *Conradiana*, 13:3, 1981, 163–79.

Marle, Hans van, 'Conrad and Richard Burton on Islam', *Conradiana*, 17:2, 1985, 137–42.

Weryho, Jan, 'Under Eastern Eyes: The Relevance of Edward Said's Study of Joseph Conrad to His Critique of Orientalism', *Conradiana*, 1992, 57–65.

Doctoral Dissertation/s

Bancroft, Nicholas M., 'Constructing the Self and the Other: An Analysis of Joseph Conrad's *Heart of Darkness*', Northern Michigan University, 2003.

Mattar, O. M. S., 'Themes in the Early Tales of Joseph Conrad and their Presentation to Arab Students', University of London, Institute of Education, 1975.

Shoukany, Muhammed Nasser, 'Orientalism and the Arab Literary Responses: Studies in Ahmad Faris Al-Shidyaq, Charles M. Doughty, Joseph Conrad, Jabra I. Jabra and Tawfiq Yusuf Awwad', University of Texas at Austin, 1990.

Daniel Defoe

(1659–1731)

- *Robinson Crusoe*

Book/s

Fausett, D., *The Strange Surprizing Sources of Robinson Crusoe*, Amsterdam, Rodopi, 1994.

Article/s

Attar, Samar, 'Serving God or Mammon? Echoes from Hayy Ibn Yaqzan and Sindbad the Sailor in *Robinson Crusoe*', in Brian Stimpson. (Ed.), *Robinson Crusoe: Myths and Metamorphoses*, London, Macmillan, 1996, 78–97.

Ekhtiar, Shelly, 'Hayy ibn Yaqzan: The Eighteenth Century Reception of an Oriental Self-taught Philospher', *Studies on Voltaire and the Eighteenth Century*, 302, 1992, 217–45.

Irimia, Michaela, 'Defoe and Cantemir: Eighteenth-Century Explorers, West and East', in Kevin L. Cope and Laura Morrow (Eds.), *1650–1850: Ideas, Aesthetics, and Inquiries in the Early Modern Era*, New York, AMS Press, 3, 1997, 239–49.

Merrett, Robert, 'Daniel Defoe and Islam', *Lumen*, 24, 2005, 19–34.

Trumpener, Katie, 'Rewriting Roxanne: Orientalism and Intertextuality in Montesquieu's *Lettres Persanes* and Defoe's *The Fortunate Mistress*', *Stanford French Review*, 11, 1987, 177–91.

Doctoral Dissertation/s

Baeshen, Lamia Mohamed Saleh, '"Robinson Crusoe" and "Hayy Bin Yaqzan": A Comparative Study', University of Arizona, 1986.

Shaw, Sheila G., 'The Influence of the *Arabian Nights* on Early Eighteenth Century English Literature, with Special Reference to *Robinson Crusoe* and *Gulliver's Travels*', Bryn Mawr College, 1959.

Yaghmour, F.E., 'Some Oriental Elements in Restoration Tragedy', University of Sheffield, 1977.

John Dryden

(1631–1700)

- *Astrae Redux*
- *Almanzor and Almahide: or the Conquest of Granada*
- *Aureng-Zebe*
- *Don Sebastian*
- *The Hind and the Panther*
- *An Evening's Love*

Book/s

Wann, Louis, *The Oriental in Restoration Drama,* Madison, University of Wisconsin Press, 1918.

Article/s

Bhattacharya, N., 'Ethnopolitical Dynamics and the Language of Gendering in Dryden's *Aureng-Zebe*', *Cultural Critique,* 25, 1993, 152–76.

Kirsch, Arthur C., 'The Significance of Dryden's *Aureng-Zebe*', *English Literary History,* 29: 2, 1962, 160–74.

Matar, Nabil, 'The First Turks and Moors in England', in Randolph Vigne and Charles Littleton (Eds.), *From Strangers to Citizens,* Brighton, Portland, The Huguenot Society of Great Britain and Ireland, 2001, 261–8.

Yaghmour, Fakhry, 'Renegades in Heroic Plays', *Dirasat*, Amman, Jordan, 12: 3, 1985, 39–55.

Doctoral Dissertation/s

Orr, Bridget Erica, 'Theatrical Voyages and Conquests: The Colonial Discourse of Restoration Drama, 1660–1696', Cornell University, 1995.

Rawashdeh, Moh'd, 'England in Disguise: The Orient on Restoration and Eighteenth-Century Stage', Purdue University, 2001.

Saab, H., 'Restoration Orientalism: The Representation of the Turk in Serious Drama', University of Swansea, 1999.

Zubaydi Al-, S.J., 'Dryden's *Almanzor and Almahide* or *the Conquest of Granada*: A Study of Its Sources and Meaning', M.A. University of Birmingham, 1974–5.

T.S. Eliot

(1888–1965)

- *Burnt Norton (the Rose Garden)*
- *Ash-Wednesday (the Rose Garden)*

Book/s

Fleissner, Robert F., *T. S. Eliot and the Heritage of Africa: the Magus and the Moor as Metaphor*, New York, Lang, 1992.

Article/s

Perna, Floriana, 'Between Orient and Occident: T. S. Eliot's Encounter with Alterity', in Agostino Lombardo (Ed.), *Presenza di T. S. Eliot*, Rome, Bulzoni, 2001, 71–82.

Raizada, Harish, 'T.S. Eliot and the Wisdom of the East' in Harish Raizada, *Literary Studies*, Aligarh, India, Three Men's Publications, 1968, 81–158.

Trivedi, Harish, 'T.S. Eliot, English Literature and India', in Harish Trivedi, *Colonial Transactions: English Literature and India*, Manchester, Manchester University Press, 1993, 15–22.

Doctoral Dissertation/s

Bluck, R.N., 'Oriental and Christian religion in the Work of T.S. Eliot, Up to "Ash-Wednesday"', University of Leeds, 1983.

J.E. Flecker

(1884–1915)

- *The Gates of Damascus*
- *The Golden Journey to Samarkand*
- *Yasmin*
- *Mansour*
- *The Bus in Stanboul*
- *Hassan*

Article/s

Bosworth, C.E., 'James Elroy Flecker: Poet, Diplomat, Orientalist', *Bulletin of the John Rylands University Library of Manchester*, 69, 1987, 359–78.

Siegrist, Mary, 'A Poet of the Orient, J.E. Flecker', *New York Times Book Review*, 30 July, 1922, 8–24.

Doctoral Dissertation/s

Issa, W., 'Aspects of Orientalism: Four English Writers; Burton, Blunt, Flecker and T.E. Lawrence', University of Reading, 1986.

Rahal, I., 'A Critical Apparatus for an Edition of James Elroy Flecker's *Hassan*', M.A., University of Leicester, 1978.

E.M. Forster

(1879-1970)

- *Abinger Harvest*
- *A Passage to India*
- *The Hill of Devi*

Book/s

Bose, S., *Attitudes to Imperialism: Kipling, Forster and Paul Scott*, Delhi, Amar Prakashan, 1990.

Chakravorty, D.K., *A Passage to the Orient*, Delhi, Amar Prakashan, 1988.

Das, G.K., *E.M. Forster's India*, London, Macmillan, 1977.

Jeffreys, Peter, *Eastern Questions: Hellenism and Orientalism in the Writings of E. M. Forster and C. P. Cavafy*, Greensboro, NC, ELT Press, 2005.

Mukherjee, Sujit, *Forster and Further: The Tradition of Anglo-Indian Fiction*, Hyderabad: Orient Longman, 1993.

Parry, Benita, *Delusions and Discoveries: Studies on India in the British Imagination*, Berkeley, University of California Press, 1972.

Sahni, Chaman L., *Forster's A Passage to India: The Religious Dimension*, New Jersy, Humanities Press, 1981.

Shahane, V.A., *Perspectives on E.M. Forster's A Passage to India: A Collection of Critical Essays*, New York, Barnes and Noble, 1968.

Article/s

Hambly, Gavin R.G., 'Muslims in English-Language Fiction', in Robin W. Winks and James R. Rush (Eds.), *Asia in Western Fiction*, Manchester, Manchester University Press, 1990, 35–52.

Inden, R., 'Orientalist Constructions of India', *Modern Asian Studies*, 20:3, 1986, 401–48.

Kazmi, Syed Nasir Raza, 'E.M. Foster and Anita Desai: Portraits of Indian Muslims in English Fiction', in Jalal Uddin Khan and Adrian E. Hare (Eds.), *English and Islam: Creative Encounters 96*, Kuala Lampur, Malaysia, International Islamic University, 1996, 161–71.

Lowe, Lisa, 'Orientalism as Literary Criticism: Reception of E.M. Forster's *A Passage to India*', in Lisa Lowe, *Critical Terrains: French and British Orientalisms*, Ithaca, Cornell University Press, 1991, 102–35.

Meyers, J., 'The Politics of *A Passage to India*', *Journal of Modern Literature*, 1:3, 1971.

Phillips, K.J., 'Hindu Avatars, Moslem Martyrs, and Primitive Dying Gods in E.M. Forster's *A Passage to India*', *Journal of Modern Literature*, 15:1, Summer 1988, 121–40.

Pirbhai, Mariam, 'Against the Oriental(ist) Current: Homosexuality and Empire in E. M. Forster's *The Other Boat*', *Dalhousie Review*, 86:3, 2006, 345–58.

Rizvi, Simi, 'Muslim Characters in E.M. Forster's *A Passage to India*', in A.R. Kidwai (Ed.), *Stranger than Fiction: Images of Islam and Muslims in English Fiction*, Delhi, A.P.H., 2000, 49–85.

Sahni, Chaman L., 'E.M. Forster's *A Passage to India*: The Islamic Dimension', *Cahiers Victoriens Et edouardiens*, 17 April 1983, 73–88.

Shaheen, Mohammad, 'Forester's Salute to Egypt', *Twentieth Century Literature*, 39, 1993, 32–47.

Shaheen, Mohammad, 'Forster's Alexandria, The Transitional Journey', in G.K. Das and John Beer (Eds.), *E.M. Forster: A Human Exploration: Centenary Essays*, New York, New York University Press, 1979, 78–89.

Shaheen, Mohammad, 'Forster's Orientalism', *Arab Journal for the Humanities*, 6:24, 1986, 324–45.

Suleri, Sara, 'Forster's Imperial Erotic', in Sara Suleri, *The Rhetoric of English India*, Chicago, University of Chicago Press, 1992, 132–48.

Thumboo, Edwin, 'E.M. Forster's *A Passage to India*: from Caves to Court', *Southern Review*, 10:4, 1978.

Doctoral Dissertation/s

Basu, Sriparna, 'Overlapping Terrains: Orientalism, Indian Nationalism and the Erotics of Cross-Cultural Contact', University of Illinois at Urbana-Champaign, 1999.

Doll, Robert, G., 'From Alexandria to Aziz: Sources of E.M. Forster's Eastern Protagonist', University of California, San Diego, 1992.

Durdana, Benazir, 'Muslim India in Anglo-Indian Fiction', Ohio State University, 1997.

Ganguly, A.P., 'E.M. Forster's *A Passage to India*: A Detailed Study of his Treatment of India's Landscape, History, Social Anthropology and Religion', University of London, 1984.

Jeffreys, Peter G., 'Hellenism and Orientalism in the Work of E.M. Forster and Constantine Cavafy: A Parallel Reading', University of Toronto, 1999.

Khan, A.B., 'The Indian Vision of E.M. Forster', Oxford University, 1982.

Kobor, Kelli Michele, 'Orientalism, the Construction of Race, and the Politics of Identity in British India, 1800–1930', Duke University, 1998.

Ray, Amit, 'Negotiating the Modern: Orientalism and "Indianess" in the Anglophone World', University of Michigan, 2004.

Rizvi, Simi, 'The Oriental Content and Context in E.M. Forster's Novels and Essays', Aligarh Muslim University, Aligarh, India, 2001.

Saleh, T.A., 'The Foreign Milieu in E.M. Forster's Works', M.A., University of Exeter, 1964–5.

Turk, Jo Audrey Mastrud, 'E.M. Forster's Double Vision: The Split in *A Passage to India*', University of Florida, 1977.

Oliver Goldsmith

(1730–74)

- *Citizen of the World Letter LXXI*
- *Citizen of the World Letter XCIX*
- *Citizen of the World Letter CXI*
- *Asem, an Eastern Tale*
- *Zobeida*

Article/s

Baker, Ernest, 'The Oriental Tale from *Rasselas* to *Vathek*', in Ernest Baker (Ed.), *History of English Novel*, 5, 55–76.

Brooks, Christopher: 'Goldsmith's *Citizen of the World*: Knowledge and the Imposture of "Orientalism"', *Texas Studies in Literature and Language*, 35:1, 1993, 124–44.

Woods, Samuel H., 'Images of the Orient: Goldsmith and the Philosophers', *Studies in Eighteenth-Century Culture*, 15, 1986, 257–70.

Zhijian, Tao, 'Citizen of Whose World? Goldsmith's Orientalism', *Comparative Literature Studies*, 33:1, 1996, 15–34.

Doctoral Dissertation/s

Hurley, James Luke, 'Orientalism in Johnson and Goldsmith', DePaul University, 1939.

Leigh Hunt

(1810-73)

- *Mahmoud*
- *Abou ben Adhem and the Angel*
- *Jaffar*
- *The Bitter Gourd*
- *The Trumpets of Doolkarnein*

Article/s

Jones, Russell, 'Leigh Hunt's Oriental Motifs – 'Abou Ben Adhem', *Journal of the Royal Asiatic Society,* 7:iii, 1997, 389–97.

Kidwai, A.R. and Newey, Vincent, 'Leigh Hunt's 'Abraham and the Fire Worshipper' - A Possible Source', *Notes and Queries,* 241, March, 1996, 44–5.

Wasti, Syed Munir, 'Eastern Elements in the Works of Leigh Hunt', *Ariel (A Research Journal of English Language and Literature),* 19, 1993–4, 72–6.

Samuel Johnson

(1709–1784)

- *Irene*
- *Rasselas*
- *History of Abdullah and Zoraide*
- *Obaidah and the Hermit,* ***Rambler****, 65, October 1750*
- *Hamet and Raschid,* ***Rambler****, 38, 28 July 1750*
- *Nouradin the Merchant and his son Almamoulin,* ***Rambler****, 120, May 1751*
- *Morad the son of Hanuth and his son Abounzaid,* ***Rambler****, 190, 11 January 1752*
- *Seged, the Emperor of Ethiopia,* ***Rambler****, 204 and 205, 29 February and 3 March, 1752*
- *Gelaleddin of Bassora* ***Idler****, 75, 22 September 1759*
- *Ortogral of Basra* ***Idler****, 99, 8 March 1760*
- *Omar son of Hassan,* ***Idler****, 101, 22 March 1760*
- *The History of Abu Zaid,* ***Rambler****, 38*

Article/s

Abdelwahed, Said T., 'Samuel Johnson's *Rasselas* and the Culture of the East', *Annals of the Faculty of Arts, Ain Shams University*, 24:ii, 1996–7, 69–78.

Ali, Muhsin Jassim, '*Rasselas* as a Colonial Discourse', *Central Institute of English & Foreign Languages Bulletin*, 8:1, 1996, 47–60.

Baker, Ernest, 'The Oriental Tale from *Rasselas* to *Vathek*', in Ernest Baker (Ed.), *History of English Novel*, 5, 55–76.

Basker, James G., 'Multicultural Perspectives: Johnson, Race and Gender', in Philip Smallwood (Ed.), *Johnson Re-Visioned: Looking Before and After*, Lewisburg, Bucknell University Press, 2001, 64–79.

Campbell, Charles, 'Johnson's Arab: Anti-Orientalism in *Rasselas*', *Abhath al-Yarmouk Literature & Linguistics*, 12:1, 1994, 51–66.

Eversole, Richard, 'Imlac and the Poets of Persia and Arabia', *Philological Quarterly*, 58, 1979, 155–70.

Fleck, Richard F, 'Samuel Johson's *Rasselas*: A Perspective on Islam', *Weber Studies*, 10:1, Winter 1993, 50–7.

Hudson, Nicholar, 'Open and Enclosed Readings of *Rasselas*', *The Eighteenth Century: Theory and Interpretation*, 31:1, 1990, 48–56.

Kolba, Gwin, J., 'The Paradise in Abyssinia and the Happy Valley in *Rasselas*', *Modern Philology*, 16, 1958, 10–16.

Leask, Nigel, 'Wandering Through Eblis: Absorption and Containment in Romantic Exoticism', in Tim Fulford and P.J. Kitson (Eds.), *Romanticism and Colonialism: Writing and Empire*, Cambridge, Cambridge University Press, 1998, 165–88.

Le Gallienne, Richard, 'A Day with Dr Johnson at the Turk's Head', *Literary Digest International Book Review*, July 1923, 1:8, 25–7.

Liu, Alan, 'Toward a Theory of Common Sense' Beckford's *Vathek* and Johnson's *Rasselas*', *Texas Studies in Literature and Language*, 26, 1984, 183–217.

Musawi, Muhsin J., 'Possible Arabic Sources for Imlac's Poetics in Johnson's *Rasselas*', *Orientalism*, 1, Jan. 1987, 5–34.

Musawi, Muhsin J., 'The Arabic Context of Johnson's *Rasselas*', *Orientalism*, 2 February 1987, 5–61.

Oueijan, Naji B., 'The Orient in Dr. Johnson's Rasselas', *Dirasat*, 22, 1987, 41–8.

Power, Stephen S., 'Through the Lens of Orientalism: Samuel Johnson's *Rasselas*', *West Virginia University Philological Papers*, 40, 1994, 6–10.

Scherwatzky, Steven, 'Johson, *Rasselas* and the Politics of Empire', *Eighteenth-Century Life*, 16, 1992, 103–13.

Thomas, Donald, 'Samuel Johnson's Arabia', *Journal of English*, 15, 1987, 1–14.

Tillotson, Geoffrey, '*Rasselas* and the Persian Tales', *Times Literary Supplement*, 29 August 1935.

Versluis, Arthur, 'From Transcendentalism to Universal Religion: Samuel Johnson's Orientalism', *American Transcendental Quarterly*, 5:2, 1991, 109–14.

Weitzman, A.J., 'More Light on *Rasselas*: The Background of the Egyptian Episodes', *Philological Quarterly*, 48, 1969, 42–58.

Doctoral Dissertation/s

Asfour, Mohammad Hassan, 'The Crescent and the Cross: Islam and the Muslims in English Literature from Johnson to Byron', Indiana University, 1973.

Avery, Elizabeth Christina, 'The Oriental Tale in England and France: With Special Reference to Dr. Johnson and Voltaire', State University of New York at Buffalo, 1932.

Florschuetz, Timothy Jon, 'An Examination of the Nile River in Samuel Johnson's *The History of Rasselas, Prince of Abyssinia*', Arizona State University, 1991.

Hurley, James Luke, 'Orientalism in Johnson and Goldsmith', DePaul University, 1939.

Nassir, Ghazi Q., 'A History and Criticism of Samuel Johnson's Oriental Tales', Florida Sate University, 1989.

Sir William Jones

(1746–94)

- *From the Persian Poem of Hatifi*
- *To Lady Jones: From the Arabic*
- *A Hymn of Camdeo*
- *A Hymn of Ganga*
- *A Hymn of Indra*
- *A Hymn of Lacshmi*
- *A Hymn of Narayena*
- *A Hymn of Sereswaty*
- *A Hymn of Surya*
- *Two Hymns to Pracriti*
- *A Hymn to Bhavani*
- *A Hymn to Durga*
- *Ode Arabica*
- *An Ode of Jami: In the Persian Form and Measure*
- *Ode Persica*
- *The Palace of Fortune: An Indian Tale*
- *A Persian Song of Hafiz*
- *The Seven Fountains: An Eastern Allegory*
- *Solima: An Arabian Eclogue*
- *A Song from the Persian*
- *A Turkish Ode of Masihi*
- *Sacontala*
- *Gitagovinda*
- *Essay on the Life and Writings of Ferdosi*
- *Moallakat*

Book/s

Arberry, A.J., *Asiatic Jones*, London, 1946.

Cannon, Garland Hampton and Brine, Kevin R. (Eds.), *Objects of Enquiry: The Life, Contribution, and Influences of Sir William Jones, 1746–1794*, New York, New York University Press, 1995.

Cannon, Garland Hampton, *Sir William Jones, Orientalist, and Annotated Bibliography of His Works*, Honolulu, University of Hawaii Press, 1952.

Cannon, Garland Hampton, *The Life and Mind of Oriental Jones: Sir William Jones, the Father of Modern Linguistics*, Cambridge, Cambridge University Press, 1990.

Drew, John, *India and the Romantic Imagination*, Delhi, Oxford University Press, 1987.

Kaul, R.K., *Studies in William Jones: An Interpreter of Oriental Literature*, Shimla, India, IIAS, 1995.

Franklin, Michael J., *Sir William Jones: A Critical Biography*, Cardiff, University of Wales Press, 1995.

Franklin, Michael J., *Sir William Jones: Selected Poetical and Prose Works*, Cardiff, University of Wales Press, 1995.

Mukherjee, S.N., *Sir William Jones: A Study in 19th-Century British Attitudes to India*, London, Sangam Books, 1968.

Murray, Alexander (Ed.), *Sir William Jones, 1746–1794: A Commemoration*, Oxford, Oxford University Press, 1998.

Pachori, Satya S. (Ed.), *Sir William Jones–A Reader*, New Delhi, Oxford University Press, 1993.

Article/s

Arberry, Arthur John, 'Persian Jones', *Asiatic Review*, 40, 1944, 186–96.

Arberry, Arthur John, 'Oriental Pearls at Random Strung', *Bulletin of the School of Oriental and African Studies*, 11, 1946, 699–712.

Cannon, Garland H., 'Orientalism and Sir William Jones', *Michigan Alumnus Quarterly Review*, 62:10, 1955, 70–8.

Cannon, Garland H., 'Sir William Jones and Literary Orientalism', in C.C. Barfoot and Theo D'haen (Eds.), *Oriental Perspectives: Western Literature and the Lure of the East*, Amsterdam, Rodopi, 1998, 27–41.

Cannon, Garland H., 'The Construction of the European Image of the Orient: A Bicentenary Reappraisal of Sir William Jones as Poet and Translator', *Comparative Criticism*, 8, 1986, 167–88.

Cannon, Garland, 'Jones's Founding and Directing of the Asiatic Society', *British Library India Office Library and Records Report for 1984–85*, 11–28.

Cannon, Garland, 'Sir William Jones's Persian Linguistics', *Journal of the American Oriental Society*, 78, 1958, 262–73.

Franklin, Michael J., 'Accessing India: Orientalism, anti-'Indianism', and the Rhetoric of Jones and Burke', in Tim Fulford (Ed.), *Romanticism and Colonialism: Writing and Empire, 1780–1830*, Cambridge, Cambridge University Press, 1998, 48–66.

Franklin, Michael J., '"And the Celt Knew the Indian": Sir William Jones, Oriental Renaissance and Celtic Revival', in Gerard Carruthers and Alan Rawes (Eds.), *English Romanticism and the Celtic World* , Cambridge, University of Cambridge Press, 2003, 20–37.

Franklin, Michael J., 'Cultural Possession, Imperial Control, and Comparative Religion: The Calcutta Perspectives of Sir William Jones and Nathaniel Brassey Halhed', *Yearbook of English Studies*, 32, 2002, 1–18.

Franklin, Michael J., '"I Burn with a desire of seeing Shiraz": A New Letter from Sir William Jones to Harford Jones', *Review of English Studies,* N.S. 56:227, 2005, 748–56.

Franklin, Michael J., 'Sir William Jones and Asiatic Society of Bengal', in Jaina C. Sanga (Ed.), *South Asian Literature in English: An Encyclopaedia',* Westport, Conn., and London, Greenwood, 2004, 18–19, 176–8.

Franklin, Michael J., 'The Building of Empire and the Building of Babel: Sir William Jones, Lord Byron, and their Productions of the Orient', in Martin Prochazka (Ed.), *Byron East and West,* Prague, Charles University, 2000, 63–78.

Hasnat, A.B. Abul, 'Some Aspects of the Impact of Sir William Jones's Persian Studies on English Romantic Poetry', *Indo-Iranica,* 41, 1988, 72–90.

Hilles, F.W., 'Self Portrait of the Great Orientalist', *Yale Review,* 60, 1971, 259–67.

Kaul, R.K., 'Jones on Persian Poetry', in R.K. Kaul, *Studies in William Jones: An Interpreter of Oriental Literature*, Shimla, India, IIAS, 1995, 48–82.

Kaul, R.K., 'Orientalism and William Jones', in R.K. Kaul, *Studies in William Jones: An Interpreter of Oriental Literature*, Shimla, India, IIAS, 1995, 1–27.

Kaul, R.K., 'The Seven Odes: Jones on Arabic Poetry', in R.K. Kaul, *Studies in William Jones: An Interpreter of Oriental Literature*, Shimla, India, IIAS, 1995, 28–47.

Knox-Shaw, Peter, '*Vathek* and The Seven Fountains by Sir William Jones', *Notes and Queries*, 240, New Series 42:1, March 1995, 75–6.

Mojumder, Abu Taher, 'Orientalism and Sir William Jones', *Journal of the Asiatic Society*, Calcutta, India, 36:3, 1994, 123–6.

Momma, Haruko, 'A Man on the Cusp: Sir William Jones's 'Philology' and 'Oriental Studies'', *Texas Studies in Literature and Language*, 41:2, 1999, 160–79.

Palit, Chittabrata, 'Orientalism, William Jones and Oriental Studies', *Journal of the Asiatic Society*, Calcutta, India, 36:3, 1994, 131–40.

Rowse, A.L., 'Welsh Orientalist: Sir William Jones', *History Today*, 21, 1971, 57–64.

Tritton, A.S., 'The Student of Arabic', *Bulletin of the School of Oriental and African Studies*, 11, 1946, 695–8.

Doctoral Dissertation/s

Cannon, Garland Hampton, 'Oriental Jones: A Biography', University of Texas at Austin, 1955.

Minikes, Madeline, 'The Contribution of Sir William Jones's Orientalism to Nineteenth Century Occidental Thought', Sarah Lawrence College, 1965.

James Joyce

(1882–1941)

- *Finnegans Wake*

Article/s

Atherton, J.S., 'Islam and the Koran in *Finnegans Wake*' *Comparative Literature*, 1954, 240–55.

Bringhurst, Robert, 'The Koran, the Wake, and Atherton', *Wake Newsletter*, December 1973, 92–3.

Caraher, Brian G., 'A "Ruin of all Space, Shattered Glass and Toppling Masonry": Joyce's Orientalism in the Context of 11 September 2001 and 1922', *Textual Practice*, 18:4, 2004, 497–520.

Kershner, R. Brandon, '*Ulysses* and the Orient', *James Joyce Quarterly*, 35:2/3, 1998, 273–96.

Peternel, Joan, 'Laurel Sicks, Rag Words, and James Joyce: Crossroads of East and West', *James Joyce Quarterly*, 34:1/2, 1996/7, 135–43.

Power, Henriette Lazaridis, '"Shahrazade, Turko the Terrible, and Shem: The Reader as Voyeur" in *Finnegans Wake*', in Morris Beja and Shari Benstock (Eds.), *Coping with Joyce: Essays from the Copenhagen Symposium*, Columbus, Ohio State University Press, 1989, 248–61.

Shloss, Carol Loeb, '"Behind the Veil": James Joyce and the Colonial Harem', *James Joyce Quarterly*, 35, 1998, 333–47.

Shloss, Carol Loeb, 'Joyce in the Context of Irish Orientalism', *James Joyce Quarterly*, 35:2/3, 1998, 264–71.

Somers, Leonard H., 'Islam and Creation Myths: A Reading of Page five of *Finnegans Wake*', in Troy Gottlib Gaiser (Ed.), *International Perspectives of James Joyce*, New York, Whitston, 1986, 153–60.

Yared, Aida, '"In the Name of Annah": Islam and Salam in Joyce's *Finnegans Wake*', *James Joyce Quarterly*, 35:2/3, 1998, 401–38.

Doctoral Dissertation/s

Choudhry, Z.A., 'Some Eastern Aspects of *Finnegans Wake*', University of Reading, 1994.

Lonnquist, Barbara Christian, 'James Joyce and Virginia Woolf, Two-Tongue Common Readers: Egypt and the Rites of Allusion in "*Finnegans Wake*" and "Between the Acts"', University of Pennsylvania, 1995.

Power, Henriette Lazaridis, 'Shahrazade's Wake: The *Arabian Nights* and the Narrative Dynamics of Charles Dickens and James Joyce', University of Pennsylvania, 1988.

John Keats
(1795–1821)

- *Endymion I, 405–6*
- *Hyperion*
- *The Cap and Bells*

Article/s

Wassil, Gregory, 'Keats's Orientalism', *Studies in Romanticism*, 39:3, 2000, 419–47.

Doctoral Dissertation/s

Stavrou, Stavros, 'Seeking the Exotic Romantic Orientalism in Keats, Shelley, and Byron', Dalhousie University, 1991.

Rudyard Kipling
(1865-1936)

- *Certain Maxims of Hafiz*
- *Akbar's Bridge*
- *Amir's Homily*
- *Bride Progress*
- *The Eye of Allah*
- *The City of Dreadful Night*
- *The Killing of Hatim Tai*
- *Naulakha: A Story of West and East*
- *The City of Brass*
- *Kim*

Book/s

Bose, S., *Attitudes to Imperialism: Kipling, Forster and Paul Scott*, Delhi, Amar Prakashan, 1990.

Hopkirk, Peter, *Quest for Kim: In Search of Kipling's Great Game*, Oxford, Oxford University Press, 2001.

Moore-Gilbert, B. J., *Kipling and Orientalism*, London, Croom Helm, 1986.

Parry, Benita, *Delusions and Discoveries: Studies on India in the British Imagination*, Berkeley, University of California Press, 1972.

Wurgaft, Lewis D., *The Imperial Imagination: Magic and Myth in Kipling's India*, Middletown, CT, Wesleyan University Press, 1983.

Article/s

Baneth, Émilienne, '"Ship Me Somewhere East of Suez": Rudyard Kipling's Strange Exile from Himself', *Jouvert*, 6:1–2, 2001.

Islam, Shamsul, 'The Islamic Tradition in Kipling's Work', *Kipling Journal*, 37:174, 1970, 10–14.

Islam, Shamul, 'Kipling's use of Indo-Pakistani Languages', *Kipling Journal*, 37:171, 1969, 15–19.

Macfie, Alexander Lyon, 'Kipling and Orientalism', *Kipling Journal*, 80:317, 2006, 46–53.

McBratney, John, 'Images of Women in Rudyard Kipling: A Case of Doubling Discourse', *Inscriptions*, 3–4, 1988, 28–56.

Mohanty, S.P., 'Kipling's Children and the Colour Line', *Race and Class*', 31, 1989, 16–22.

Parry, Benita, 'The Contents and Discontents of Kipling's Imperialism', *New Formations*, 6, 1988, 49–63.

Said, Edward, '*Kim*': The Pleasures of Imperialism', *Raritan*, 2, 1987, 20–30.

Suleri, Sara, 'The Adolescence of Kim' in Sara Suleri, *The Rhetoric of English India*, Chicago, University of Chicago Press, 1992, 111–13.

Doctoral Dissertation/s

Kaufman, Ester, 'The Use of Oriental Material by James Thomson, Oscar Wilde, and Rudyard Kipling', Cornell University, 1947.

W.S. Landor

(1775-1864)

- *Soliman and Mufti*
- *Mahomet and Serguis*
- *Count Julian*
- *The Nightingale and Rose*
- *Poems from the Arabic and Persian*
- *Gebir*

Article/s

Haddad, Emily A., 'Nightingales and Roses I: Walter Savage Landor and Oriental Literature', in Emily A. Haddad, *Oriental Poetics*, Aldershort, UK, Ashgate, 2002, 171–4.

Kestner, Joseph, 'The Genre of Landor's *Gebir*', *The Wordsworth Circle*, 5:1, 1974, 41–9.

Richardson, Alan, 'Epic Ambivalence: Imperial Politics and Romantic Deflection in Williams's *Peru* and Landor's *Gebir*', in Alan Richardson and Sonia Hofkosh (Eds.), *Romanticism, Race and Imperial Culture, 1780–1834*, Bloomington, Indiana University Press, 1996, 265–82.

Vitoux, Pierre, '*Gebir* as an Heroic Poem', *Wordsworth Circle*, 7:1, 1976, 51–7.

Wasti, Syed Munir, 'The Exotic East in the Poetry of Walter Savage Landor', *Ariel (A Research Journal of English Language and Literature)*, 39–46.

Doris Lessing

(1919 - --)

- *Four Gated City*
- *Learning How to live*
- *Briefing for Descent into Hell*
- *Shikasta*
- *The Marriages between Zones Three, Four and Five*

Book/s

Galin, Muge, *Between East and West: Sufism in the Novels of Doris Lessing*, Albany, New York State University Press, 1997.

Hasan, Masoodul, *Sufism and English Literature: Chaucer to the Present Age*, Delhi, Adam Publisher, 2007, 268–71.

Article/s

Martin, Joe, 'Doris Lessing's Alchemy: Fusing Sufism and Fiction', *Sufi*, 39, 1998, 38–49.

Doctoral Dissertation/s

Galin, Muge N., 'The Path of Love: Sufism in the Novels of Doris Lessing', Ohio State University, 1992.

Christopher Marlowe

(1564–93)

- *The Jew of Malta*
- *Tamburlaine*

Book/s

Brown, John Russell (Ed.), *Marlowe: Tamburlaine the Great Edward the Second and the Jew of Malta,* London, Macmillan, 1982.

Bartels, Emily C., *Spectacles of Strangeness: Imperialism, Alienation and Marlowe,* Philadelphia, University of Pennsylvania Press, 1993.

Article/s and Conference Presentation/s

Araci, Emre, '"Turkish" Imagery in Elizabethan Drama', *RNL,* 4, 1973, 82–98.

Bakay, Gönül, '21st Century Reflections on Images of the Turk in the Renaissance Literature of England', Presented at the Conference '1453 to 1699: Cultural Encounters between East and West', Institute of English Studies, London, 5–7 December 2002.

Bartels, Emily C., 'Malta, the Jew, and the Fictions of Difference: Colonialist Discourse in Marlowe's

The Jew of Malta', *English Literary Renaissance*, 20, 1990, 1–16.

Bartels, Emily C., 'The Double Vision of the East: Imperialist Self-Construction in Marlowe's *Tmburlaine*', *Renaissance Drama*, 23, 1992, 3–24.

Battenhouse, Roy W., 'Tamburlaine's Passions', in Clifford Leech (Ed.), *Marlowe: A Collection of Critical Essays*, New Jersey, Prentice-Hall, Inc., 1964, 57–68.

Boerth, Robert, 'The Mediterranean and the Mediterranean World on the Stage of Marlowe and Shakespeare', *Journal of Theatre and Drama*, 2, 1996, 35–58.

Brown, William J., 'Marlowe's Debasement of Bajazet: Foxe's *Actes and Monuments* and *Tamberlaine*, Part I', *Renaissance Quarterly*, 24, 1971, 38–48.

Burton, Jonathan H., 'Anglo-Ottoman Relations and the Image of the Turk in *Tamburlaine*', *Journal of Medieval and Early Modern Studies*, 30:1, 2000, 125–56.

Cunninghan, J.S. and Warren, Roger, 'Tamburlaine the Great Rediscovered (1978)', in John Russell Brown (Ed.), *Marlowe: Tamburlaine the Great Edward the Second and the Jew of Malta*, London, Macmillan, 1982, 139.

Dombrowsk, Rosemarie, 'Amalgamated Otherness: Caliban and the Colonialist Agenda of Elizabethan Travel Literature and Ethnography', Presented at the 'Rocky Mountain Medieval Renaissance Association Conference',

University of Nevada, Las Vegas, 23–5 May 2002.

Euridge, Gareth M., 'Before Orientalism: The Allure of Islam in Renaissance England', Presented at Modern Language Association, Chicago, 27–9 December 1995.

Hawamdeh, Mufeed F., 'Marlovian Turkophobia: A Study of the Image and Role of Turks in *Tamburlaine the Great,* Parts 1 and 2', *Damascus University Journal for the Arts and Human and Educational Sciences,* 4:ii , 1998, 47–71.

Hodges, Kenneth, 'Green Turks and English Knights: Sir Gawain, the Green Knight, and the Islamic al-Khidr', Presented at the 'Fortieth International Conference on Medieval Studies', 5–8 May 2005 at Western Michigan University.

Hoenselaars, A. J., 'The Elizabethans and Turks at Constantinople', *Cahiers Elisabethians,* 47, 1995, 29–42.

Hutchings, Mark, 'In Thrace; Brought up in Arabia: The Jew of Malta, II.iii.131', *Notes and Queries,* 47: 245, 2000, 428–30.

Ibrahim, Carleen, '"By the Pen and that Which They Write": A Muslim Perspective of Marlowe's Use of the Holy Quran in *Tamburlaine* I and II', in *English and Islam: Creative Encounters 96,* Kuala Lumpur, Malaysia, International Islamic University, 1996, 33–51.

Khalaf, Elias Mustafa, 'Islam in Marlowe's *Tamburlaine the Great', Al-Balqa',* 4:i, 1996, 61–88.

Khattab, Ezzat, 'Muhammad in Marlowe's *Tamburlaine*', *Majallat Kulliyat al-Adab*, 1, 1970, 41–52.

Knight, Sarah, '"So Rich a Prize as This": Persia in Marlowe's *Tamburlaine the Great*', Paper presented at the Conference '1453 to 1699: Cultural Encounters between East and West', Institute of English Studies, London, 5–7 December 2002.

Knobler, Adam, 'Timur the (Terrible/Tartar) Trope: A Case of Repositioning in Popular Literature and History', *Medieval Encounters*, 7:i, 2001, 101–12.

Knowlton, E.C., 'Indian Moors' and *Doctor Faustus*', *Cahiers Elisabethains*, 23, 1983, 93–7.

Mahood, M.M., 'Marlowe's Heroes', in R.J. Kaufmann (Ed.), *Elizabethan Drama: Modern Essays in Criticism*, New York, Oxford University Press, 1961, 95–122.

Ribner, Irving, 'The Idea of History in Marlowe's Tamburlaine', in R.J. Kaufmann (Ed.), *Elizabethan Drama: Modern Essays in Criticism*, New York, Oxford University Press, 1961, 81–94.

Shepherd, Simon, 'Turks and Fathers', in Simon Shepherd, *Marlowe and the Politics of Elizabethan Theatre*, New York, St. Martin's Press, 1986, 142–77.

Vitkus, Daniel, 'Turks and Jews in Marlowe's *The Jew of Malta*', in Sullivan, Garrett A., Jr. (et al.) (Eds.), *Early Modern English Drama: A Critical Companion*, Oxford, Oxford University Press, 2006, 61–72.

Waith, Eugene M., 'Marlowe's Herculean Hero', in John Russell Brown (Ed.), *Marlowe: Tamburlaine the Great Edward the Second and the Jew of Malta*, London, Macmillan, 1982, 85–127.

Waith, Eugene M., 'Tamburlaine', in Clifford Leech (Ed.), *Marlowe: A Collection of Critical Essays*, New Jersey, Prentice-Hall, Inc., 1964, 68–91.

Wann, Louis, 'The Oriental in Elizabethan Drama', *Modern Philology*, 12, January 1915, 163–87.

Doctoral Dissertation/s

Abu Baker, Mohamed Hassan, 'Representations of Islam and Muslims in Early Modern English Drama from Marlowe to Massinger', University of Glasgow, 1997.

Beshti el-, Bashir Mahmud, 'The Displacement Towards the East: The Oriental in English Renaissance Literature and Culture', University of California, Berkeley, 1989.

Boerth, Robert John, 'Disorientations: The Matter of the East in English Renaissance Drama', University of California, Irvine, 1995.

Burton, Jonathan, '"Turn'd Turk": Islam and English Drama, 1579–1624', City University of New York, 1999.

Farhan, I.H., 'Traces of Averroistic Influence on Christopher Marlowe', M.Litt., University of Strathclyde, 1978.

Mugawar, Fahd M.T.S., 'The Oriental Element in the Elizabethan Drama with Special Reference to Marlowe, Shakespeare and Ben Jonson', Aligarh Muslim University, Aligarh, India, 2004.

Peernajmodin, H., 'Orientalist Representations of Persia in the Works of Spenser, Marlowe, Milton, Moore and Morier', University of Birmingham, 2002.

Rais, Mahmoud, 'The Representation of the Turk in English Renaissance Drama, Cornell University', 1973.

Philip Massinger

(1583–1640)

- *The Renegado*

Article/s and Conference Presentation/s

Degenhardt, Jane, 'Catholic Martyrdom in Dekker and Massinger's *The Virgin Martir* and the Early Modern Threat of "Turning Turk"', *ELH*, 73:1, 2006, 83–117.

Degenhardt, Jane, 'From Body to Symbol, (or Castration to Re-virgination): The Limits of Faith in Massinger's "*The Renegado*"', Paper presented at the Conference '1453 to 1699: Cultural Encounters between East and West', Institute of English Studies, London, 5–7 December 2002.

Dombrowsk, Rosemarie, 'Amalgamated Otherness: Caliban and the Colonialist Agenda of Elizabethan Travel Literature and Ethnography', Presented at the 'Rocky Mountain Medieval Renaissance Association Conference', University of Nevada, Las Vegas, 23–5 May 2002.

Euridge, Gareth M., 'Before Orientalism: The Allure of Islam in Renaissance England', Presented at Modern Language Association, Chicago, 27–9 December 1995.

Euridge, Gareth M., 'The Renegade in English Seventeenth-Century Imagination', *Studies in English Literature,* 33, 1993, 489–505.

Floyd-Wilson, Mary, 'Moors, Race, and the Study of English Renaissance Literature; A Brief Retrospective', *Literature Compass,* 3 July 2006, Online.

Holmberg, Rachel, 'Ravished: *The Renegado* and Anxieties of Conversion', Presented at the Group for Early Modern Cultural Studies Conference, 2002.

Malieckal, Bindu, '"Wanton Irreligious Madness": Conversion and Castration in Massinger's *The Renegado*', *Essays in Arts and Sciences,* 31, 2002, 25–43.

Matar, Nabil, 'The First Turks and Moors in England', in Randolph Vigne and Charles Littleton (Eds.), *From Strangers to Citizens,* Brighton, Portland, The Huguenot Society of Great Britain and Ireland, 2001, 261–8.

Phialas, Peter G., 'The Source of Massinger's *Emperour of the East*', *Publication of Modern Language Association,* 65: 4, 1950, 473–82.

Rice, Warner G., 'The Sources of Massinger's '*The Renegado*'', *Philological Quarterly,* 11, 1932, 65–75.

Robinson, Benedict, '"Strange Commodities": Commerce and Conversion in *The Renegado*', Paper presented at the Conference '1453 to 1699: Cultural Encounters between East and West', Institute of English Studies, London, 5–7 December 2002.

Wann, Louis, 'The Oriental in Elizabethan Drama', *Modern Philology*, 12, January 1915, 163–87.

Doctoral Dissertation/s

Abu Baker, Mohamed Hassan, 'Representations of Islam and Muslims in Early Modern English Drama from Marlowe to Massinger', University of Glasgow, 1997.

Artemel, S.S., 'The Idea of Turkey in the Elizabethan Period and in the Early Seventeenth Century, with Special Reference to Drama', University of Durham, 1965–6.

Beshti el-, Bashir Mahmud, 'The Displacement Towards the East: The Oriental in English Renaissance Literature and Culture', University of California, Berkeley, 1989.

Boerth, Robert John, 'Disorientations: The Matter of the East in English Renaissance Drama', University of California, Irvine, 1995.

Burton, Jonathan, '"Turn'd Turk": Islam and English Drama, 1579-1624', City University of New York, 1999.

Degenhardt, Jane Hwang, 'Faith, Embodiment and Turning Turk: Islamic Conversion on the Early Modern Stage and the Production of Religious and Racial Identity', University of Pennsylvania, 2005.

Rais, Mahmoud, 'The Representation of the Turk in English Renaissance Drama', Cornell University, 1973.

Rice, Warner G., 'Turk, Moor, and Persian in English Literature from 1550 to 1660, with Particular Reference to the Drama', University of Harvard, 1931.

John Milton

(1608–74)

- *Paradise Lost II, 2*
- *Paradise Lost IV, 159*
- *Paradise Lost X, 432*

Book/s

Cawley, Robert Ralston, *Milton and the Literature of Travel*, Princeton, Princeton University Press, 1951.

Dahiyat, Eid, *John Milton and the Arab-Islamic Culture*, Amman, Shukayr and Akasheh, 1987.

Lim, Walter S. H., *The Arts of Empire: The Poetics of Colonialism from Raleigh to Milton*, Newark, University of Delaware Press, 1998.

Robinson, Benedict Scott, *Islam and Early Modern English Literature : The Politics of Romance from Spenser to Milton*, New York , Palgrave Macmillan, 2007.

Article/s

Banerjee, Pompa, 'Milton's India and *Paradise Lost*', *Milton Studies*, 37, 1999, 142–65.

Cass, Jeffrey, 'Miltonic Orientalism: Jane Eyre and the two Dalilas', *Dickens Studies Annual*, 33, 2003, 191–213.

Draper, John W., 'Milton's Ormus', *Modern Language Review*, 20, 1925, 323–7.

Lim, Walter S. H., 'Epic, Colonialism, Empire: A Reading of Milton's *Paradise Lost* and *Paradise Regained*', in Robert Young, Ban Kah Choon and Robbie Goh (Eds.), *The Silent Word: Textual Meaning and the Unwritten*, Singapore, Singapore University Press and World Scientific Publishing, 1998, 45–57.

MacLean, Geralad M., 'Milton, Islam and the Ottomans', in Sharon Achinstein and Elizabeth Sauer (Eds.), *Milton and Toleration*, Oxford, Oxford University Press, 2007.

Siddiqui, M. N., 'Milton and the Orient', *Osmania Journal of English Studies*, 2, 1962, 37–47.

Doctoral Dissertation/s

Kang, Nae Heui, 'The Renaissance Representation of the Other: Travel Literature, Spenser, Shakespeare, and Milton', Marquette University, 1986.

Kenton, William G., 'English Liberty and Turkish Tyranny: The Symbolic Function of the East in Milton's Poetry and Prose', New York University, 2005.

Peernajmodin, H., 'Orientalist Representations of Persia in the Works of Spenser, Marlowe, Milton, Moore and Morier', University of Birmingham, 2002.

Robinson, Benedict, 'The Romance of the East: Islam and English Literature after the Reformation (Edmund Spenser, William Shakespeare, John Milton)', Columbia University, 2002.

Lady Mary Wortley Montagu

(1689–1762)

- *Turkish Embassy Letters*

Book/s

Grundy, Isobel, *Lady Mary Wortley Montagu*, Oxford, Oxford University Press, 1999.

Lewis, Reina, *Rethinking Orientalism: Women, Travel, and the Ottoman Harem*, New Brunswick, NJ, Rutgers University Press, 2004.

Article/s and Conference Presentation/s

Ahmed, Leila, 'Western Ethnocentrism and Perceptions of the Harem', *Feminist Studies*, 8:3, 1982, 524–5.

Allen, M.D., 'The New Path: English Women Travelers in the Middle East', *West Virginia University Philological Papers*, 40, 1994, 1–5.

Andrea, Bernadette, '"She that Spake to the Great Turk": Early Modern English Women in the Ottoman Empire', Presented at the 'Comparative Literature Colloquia', Green College, University of British Columbia, 2 November 1995.

Andrea, Bernadette, 'Women and their Rights: Fethullah Gulen's Gloss on Lady Montagu's *Embassy* to the Ottoman Empire', in Robert A. Hunt and Yuksel A. Aslandogan (Eds.), *Muslim Citizens of the Globalized World: Contributions of the Gulen Movement*, Somerset, NJ, The Light and IID Press, 2006, 137–54.

Aravamudan, Srinivas, 'Lady Mary Worley Montagu in the *Hammam:* Masquerade, Womanliness, and Levantinization', *English Literature History*, 62, 1995, 69–104.

Bohls, Elizabeth A., 'Aesthetics and Orientalism in Lady Mary Wortley Montagu's *Letters*', *Studies in Eighteenth-Century Culture*, 23, 1994, 179–205.

DelPlato, Joan, 'A English 'Feminist' in the Turkish Harem: A Portrait of Lady Mary Wortley Montagu', in Frederick M. Keener and Susan E. Lorsch (Eds.), *Eighteenth-Century Women and the Arts*, Greenwood, Ill, 1988, 163–78.

Dubino, Jeanne, 'Turkish Tales: Mary Wortley Montagu's *Turkish Embassy Letters* and Virginia Woolf's *Orlando*', *Selected Papers from the Annual Conference on Virginia Woolf*, 12, 2003.

Fernea, Elizabeth Warnock, 'An Early Ethnographer of Middle Eastern Women: Lady Mary Wortley Montagu (1689–1762)', *Journal of Near Eastern Studies*, 40, 1981, 329–38.

Foster, Shirley, 'Colonialism and Gender in the East: Representations of the Harem in the Writings of Women Travellers', *Yearbook of English Studies*, 34, 2004, 6–17.

Grundy, Isobel, ''The Barbarous Character We Give Them': White Women Travellers Report on Other

Races', *Studies in Eighteenth-Century Culture*, 23, 1993, 73–86.

Heffernan, Teresa, 'Feminism Against the East/West Divide: Lady Mary's *Turkish Embassy Letters'*, *Eighteenth-Century Studies*, 33:2, 2000, 201–15.

Horwath, Peter, 'Why did the Turks Meet the Wortley Montagus at "Betsko" (1717)', *English Language Notes*, 29, 1992, 24–6.

Koundoura, Maria, 'Between Orientalism and Philhellenism: Lady Mary Wortley Montagu's "Real" Greeks', *Eighteenth Century*, 45:3, 2004, 249–264.

Lew, Joseph W., 'Lady Mary's Portable Seraglio', *Eighteenth-Century Studies*, 24:4, Summer 1991, 432–50.

Logan, Deborah A., 'Harem Life, West and East', *Women's Studies*, 26:3/4, 1997, 449–74.

Lowe, Lisa, 'Travel Narratives and Orientalism: Montagu and Montesquieu', in Lisa Lowe, *Critical Terrains: French and British Orientalisms*, Ithaca, Cornell University Press, 1991, 30–74.

Richon, Olivier, 'Representation, the Harem and the Despot', *Block*, 10, 1985, 34–41.

Roberts, Mary, 'Contested Terrains: Women Orientalists and the Colonial Harem', in Jill Beaulieu and Mary Roberts (Eds.), *Orientalism's Interlocutors: Paintings, Architecture, Photographs*, Durham, NC, Duke University Press, 2002, 179–204.

Weitzman, Arthur J., 'Voyeurism and Aesthetics in the Turkish Bath: Lady Mary's School of Female

Beauty', *Comparative Literature Studies*, 39:iv, 2002, 347–59.

Wood, A.C., 'The English Embassy at Constantinople: 1660–1762', *English Historical Review*, 40: 160, 1925, 533–61.

Yegenoglu, Meyda, 'Supplementing the Orientalist Lack: European Ladies in the Harem', in Mahmut Mutman and Meyda Yegenoglu (Eds.), *Orientalism and Cultural Differences*, Santa Cruz, University of California at Santa Cruz, 1992, 45–80.

Doctoral Dissertation/s

Melissinos, Joyce Mitchell, 'The Stuff of Fable: Accounts of Embassies from England and Russia to the Middle East and the Far East in the Eighteenth Century: an Overlooked Dimension of Voyage and Travel Literature', University of Rochester, 1995.

Meloccaro, Lynne, 'Orientalism and the Oriental Tale: Gender, Genre, and Cultural Identity in Eighteenth-Century England', Rutgers University, 1992.

Thomas Moore

(1779–1852)

- *From Abdullah, in London, to Mohassan, in Ispahan*
- *From the High Priest of Apollo to a Virgin of Delhi*
- *Lalla Rookh*
- *Cashmerian*
- *Maharatta*
- *Ode to the Sublime Porte*
- *Gazel*
- *The Tale of the Blanket*
- *The Epicurean*

Book/s

Gwynn, Stephen, *Thomas Moore,* London, 1905.

Lennon, Joseph, *Irish Orientalism: A Literary and Intellectual History,* Syracuse, NY, Syracuse University Press, 2004.

Mansoor, M., *The Story of Irish Orientalism,* London, Longmans, Green and Co., Ltd., 1944.

Article/s

Asfour, Mohammad, 'Thomas Moore and the Pitfalls of Orientalism', *International Journal of Islamic and Arabic Studies,* Indiana, 4, 1, 1987, 1–12.

Brown, Wallace C., 'Thomas Moore and English Interest in the East', *Studies in Philology,* 34, 1937, 578–88.

Gregory, Allan, 'Thomas Moore's Orientalism', in Peter Cochran (Ed.), *Byron and Orientalism*, Cambridge, Cambridge Scholars, 2006, 173–82.

Haddad, Emily A., 'Nightingales and Roses II: Moore and the Orient as an Ideal', in Emily A. Haddad, *Oriental Poetics*, Aldershort, UK, Ashgate, 2002, 175–7.

Haddad, Emily A., 'Truth in Illustrating Robert Southey and Thomas Moore', in Emily A. Haddad, *Oriental Poetics*, Aldershort, UK, Ashgate, 2002, 113–17.

Jordan, Hoover H., 'Byron and Moore', *Modern Language Quarterly*, 9 December 1948, 429–39.

Kidwai, A.R., 'A Bibliography of Moore's Oriental Reading' in A.R. Kidwai, *Orientalism in Lord Byron's Turkish Tales*, Lewiston, Mellen University Press, 1995, 275–80.

Repplier, Agnes, 'When Lalla Rookh was Young', *Atlantic Monthly*, 100, 1907, 807–12.

Wickens, G.M., '*Lalla Rookh* and the Romantic Tradition of Islamic Literature in English', *Year Book of Comparative and General Literature*, 20, 1971, 61–6.

Doctoral Dissertation/s

Asfour, Mohammad Hassan, 'The Crescent and the Cross: Islam and the Muslims in English Literature from Johnson to Byron', Indiana University, 1973.

Hejazi al-, Ali Ahmad Ali, 'Arabo-Islamic Mythology in English Poetry, 1755–1825', University of Wisconsin-Milwaukee, 1979.

Husain, I., 'The Oriental Elements in English Poetry (1784–1859)', University of Edinburgh, 1934.

Lennon, Joseph Allen, 'The Celt and the Oriental: The Narratives of Irish Orientalism', University of Connecticut, 2001.

Meagher, Shelley, 'Islam in Irish Poetry', University of Oxford, 2006.

Peernajmodin, H., 'Orientalist Representations of Persia in the Works of Spenser, Marlowe, Milton, Moore and Morier', University of Birmingham, 2002.

Sultana, Fehmida, 'Romantic Orientalism and Islam: Southey, Shelley, Moore, and Byron', Tufts University, 1989.

Sharafuddin, M. A., 'Islam and Romanticism: A Study of Orientalism in English Verse Narrative, 1798–1817', University of York, 1988.

Towey, P., '"The New Orientalism": Representations of Islam and its Effects in Ireland', Dublin, University College, 2004.

Yaqub, Huma, 'A Critical Study of Thomas Moore's *Lalla Rookh*, "The Loves of the Angels" and "Ghazals"', Aligarh Muslim University, Aligarh, India, 2000.

George Peele

(1556–96)

- *The Battle of Alcazar*

Article/s and Conference Presentation/s

Dimmock, Matthew, 'Swapping the "Geneua Bible" for the "Turkish Alcoran": *The Battle of Alcazar* and Early English Representations of the Ottoman Turk', Paper presented at the 'Early Modern/ Renaissance Postgraduate Conference', University of Newcastle upon Tyne, 5–6 April 2001.

Edelman, Charles, '*The Battle of Alcazar,* Muly Mollocco, and Shakespeare's *2 and 3 Henry VI*', *Notes and Queries,* 2002, 196–7.

Hyland, Peter. 'Moors, Villainy and *The Battle of Alcazar*', *Parergon,* 16:2, 1999, 85–99.

Larsen, Thorlief, 'The Historical and Legendary Background of Peele's *Battle of Alcazar*', *Transactions of the Royal Society of Canada,* 2, 1939, 185–97.

Rice, W.G., 'A Principal Source of *The Battle of Alcazar*', *Modern Language Notes,* 58, 1943, 428–31.

Viguers, Susan T., 'Peele's *The Battle of Alcazar*', *Explicator,* 43, 1985, 9–12.

Edgar Allan Poe
(1809–49)

- *Tales of the Grotesque and Arabesque*
- *Ligeia*
- *Al-Araf*
- *Tamerlane*
- *Israfel*
- *The Thousand-and-Second Tale of Scheherazade*

Article/s

Denuccio, Jerome D., 'Fact, Fiction, Fatality: Poe's "The Thousand-and-Second Tale of Scheherazade", *Studies in Short Fiction*, 27, 1990, 365–70.

Gruesser, John C., '"*Ligeia*' and Orientalism", *Studies in Short Fiction*, 26:2, Spring 1989, 145–9.

Kidwai, A.R. and Newey, Vincent, 'The Burning Heart in Poe's 'Al-Aaraf': Another Possible Source', *Notes and Queries*, 242, March 1997, 365–6.

Schueller, Malini Johar, 'Harems, Orientalist Subversions, and the Crisis of Nationalism: The Case of Edgar Allan Poe and "Ligeia", *Criticism*, 37, 1995, 601–23.

Tintner, A.R., 'Fire of the Heart in 'Al Aaraaf': Beckford and Byron as Source', *Poe Studies*, 22, December 1989, 47–8.

Wasti, Syed Munir, Eastern Influences on the Work of Edgar Allen Poe, *Ariel: A Research Journal of English Language and Literature*, 21, 1995–6, 65–9.

Doctoral Dissertation/s

Almansour, Ahmed Nidal, 'The Middle East in Antebellum America: The Cases of Ralph Waldo Emerson, Nathaniel Hawthorne, and Edgar Allan Poe', Ohio State University, 2005.

Kleitz, Dorsey Rodney, 'Orientalism and the American Romantic Imagination: The Middle East in the Works of Irving, Poe, Emerson, and Melville', University of New Hampshire, 1988.

Smith, Patricia Clark, 'Novel Conceptions, Unusual Combinations: The Arabesque in Poe', Yale University, 1970.

Alexander Pope

(1688–1744)

- *The Dunciad III, 79–82*
- *Epistle to Arbuthnot 197–8*
- *Essay on Man*
- *Fable of the Traveller and Adder*

Article/s

Bradham, JoAllen, 'An Ass Charged with Books: Pope's *Dunciad* and the *Koran*', *South Atlantic Review*, 60:1, 1995, 1–15.

Tarawreh, Yousef, 'Islamic Reflections: Revisionist Portrayals of Arab Civilization with Particular Reference to Wordsworth, Pope, Cervantes, and Dante', *International Journal of Islamic and Arabic Studies*, 4, 1987, 55–74.

Sir Walter Scott

(1771–1832)

- *Talisman, Chapter 3*
- *The Surgeon's Daughter, Chapter 10*
- *Vision of Don Roderick*
- *The Search after Happiness or the Quest of Sultana Solomaun*

Article/s

Pelckmans, Paul, 'Walter Scott's Orient: *The Talisman*' in C.C. Barfoot and Theo D'haen (Eds.), *Oriental Prospects: Western Literature and the Lure of the East*, Amsterdam, Rodopi, 1998, 97–109.

Watt, James, 'Scott, the Scottish Enlightenment, and Romantic Orientalism', in Leith Davis (et al.) (Eds.), *Scotland and the Borders of Romanticism*, Cambridge, Cambridge University Press, 2004, 94–119.

Youngkin, Molly, '"Into the Woof, a Little Thibet Wool": Orientalism and Representing "Reality" in Walter Scott's *The Surgeon's Daughter*', *Scottish Studies Review*, 3:1, 2003, 33–57.

Doctoral Dissertation/s

Azouqa, Aida O., 'Sir Walter Scott and British Orientalism: 1800–1825', University of Chicago, 1993.

Sampson, Kathryn Ann, 'The Romantic Literary Pilgrimage to the Orient : Byron, Scott, and Burton', University of Texas at Austin, 1999.

William Shakespeare

(1564–1616)

- *Comedy of Errors IV, I, 103–4*
- *Coriolanus IV, ii, 24*
- *Cymbeline III, iii, 2*
- *Hamlet III, ii, 275–92*
- *2 Henry IV, III, ii, 334*
- *2 Henry IV, V, ii, 47*
- *1 Henry VI, I, ii, 140–7*
- *King Lear III, iv, 84*
- *King Lear III, iv, 91*
- *King Lear III, iv, 148*
- *Macbeth II, I, 1*
- *Macbeth V, I, 56*
- *Merchant of Venice II, i, 25–6*
- *Merchant of Venice II, vi, 41*
- *Merchant of Venice II, vii, 1–77*
- *Merchant of Venice IV, i, 30–1*
- *Much Ado About Nothing III, iv, 56*
- *Othello I, iii, 48–9*
- *Othello II, i, 114*
- *Othello II, iii, 175*
- *Othello V, ii, 349*
- *Richard II, IV, I, 39*
- *Richard III, III, v, 40*
- *Tempest I, ii, 263*
- *Twelfth Night III, iv, 310*
- *Taming of the Shrew II, i, 349–53*

Book/s

Draper, John, *Orientalia and Shakespeareana*, New York, Vantage Press, 1977.

Fujita, Minoru and Pronko, Leonard (Eds.), *Shakespeare East and West*, New York, St Martin's Press, 1996.

Gillies, John, *Shakespeare and the Geography of Difference*, Cambridge, Cambridge University Press, 1994.

Habib, Imtiaz, *Shakespeare and Race: Postcolonial Praxis in the Early Modern Period*, Lanham, MD, University Press of America, 2000.

Hoenselaars, A.J., *Images of Englishmen and Foreigners in the Drama of Shakespeare and His Contemporaries; A Study of Stage Characters and National Identity in English Renaissance Drama, 1558–1642*, London, Associated University Presses, 1992.

Jones, Eldered, *Othello's Countrymen: Africans in English Renaissance Drama*, Oxford, Oxford University Press, 1965.

Kishi, Tetsuo and Pringle, Roger and Wells, Stanley (Eds.), *Shakespeare and Cultural Traditions: The Selected Proceedings of the International Shakespeare Association World Congress, Tokyo, 1991*, Newark, Delaware University Press, 1994.

Loomba, Ania, *Shakespeare, Race and Colonialism*, Oxford, Oxford University Press, 2002.

Malieckal, Bindu, *'Bondslaves and Pagans Shall Our Statesmen Be': Moors, Turks, and Venetians in Othello*, Shakespeare Association of America, San Francisco, California, April 1999.

Mishima, Toshiko, *Shakespeare and the Orient*, 1959.

Article/s and Conference Presentation/s

Alshetawi, Mahmoud F., 'Shakespeare's Journey into the Arab World: An Initial Bibliography', *Shakespeare Yearbook*, 13, 2002, 442–99.

Araci, Emre, '"Turkish" Imagery in Elizabethan Drama', *RNL*, 4, 1973, 82–98.

Bakay, Gönül, '21st Century Reflections on Images of the Turk in the Renaissance Literature of England', Presented at the Conference '1453 to 1699: Cultural Encounters between East and West', Institute of English Studies, London, 5–7 December 2002.

Barbour, Richmond, '"There is Our Commission": Writing and Authority in *Measure for Measure* and the London East India Company', *Journal of English and Germanic Philology*, 99:2, 2000, 193–214.

Bartels, Emily C., 'Making More of the Moor: Aaron, Othello and Renaissance Refashioning of Race', *Shakespeare Quarterly*, 41, 1990, 433–54.

Bartels, Emily C., 'Othello and the Moor', in Garrett A. Jr Sullivan, Patrick Cheney and, Andrew Hadfield (Eds.), *Early Modern English Drama: A Critical Companion*, Oxford, Oxford University Press, 2006, 140–151.

Bartholomeusz, Dennis, 'Shakespeare Imagines the Orient: The Orient Imagines Shakespeare', in Tetsuo Kishi (et al.) (Ed.), *Shakespeare and Cultural Traditions: The Selected Proceedings of the International Shakespeare Association World*

Congress, Tokyo, 1991, London, Associated University Presses, 1994, 188–204.

Bate, Jonathan, '*Othello* and the Other; or, Turning Turk: The Subtleties of Shakespeare's Treatment of Islam', *Times Literary Supplement*, 19 October 2001, 14–15.

Bell, Millicent, 'Shakespeare's Moor', *Raritan*, 21:4, 2002, 1–14.

Boerth, Robert, 'The Mediterranean and the Mediterranean World on the Stage of Marlowe and Shakespeare', *Journal of Theatre and Drama*, 2, 1996, 35–58.

Brotton, Jerry, '"This Tunis, Sir, was Carthage": Contesting Colonialism in *The Tempest*', in Ania Loomba and Martin Orkin (Eds.), *Post-Colonial Shakespeare*, London, Routledge, 1998, 23–42.

Brotton, Jerry, 'Carthage and Tunis:, *The Tempest* and Tapestries', in Peter Hulme and William H. Sherman (Eds.), *'The Tempest' and Its Travels*, Philadelphia, University of Pennsylvania Press, 2000, 132–7.

Burton, Jonathan H., '"A Most Wily Bird", Leo Africanus, *Othello* and the Trafficking in Difference', in Ania Loomba and Martin Orkin (Eds.), *Post-Colonial Shakespeare*, London, Routledge, 1998, 43–63.

Burton, Jonathan H., 'English Anxiety and the Muslim Power of Conversion: Five Perspectives on "Turning Turk" in Early Modern Texts', Presented at the 'Conference at the University of Michigan', 25 January 2002.

Campbell, Mary B., 'Shakespeare's Use of the Voyagers in *The Tempest*', *PMLA*, 41: 3, 1926, 688–726.

Carnicelli, D. D., 'The Widow and the Phoenix: Dido, Carthage, and Tunis in *The Tempest*', *Harvard Library Bulletin*, 27, 1979, 389–433.

Clegg, Cyndia Susan, 'English Renaissance Books on Islam and Shakespeare's *Othello*', *Pacific Coast Philology*, 41, 2006, 1–12.

Collins, Kris, 'White-Washing the Black-a-Moor: Othello, Negro Minstrely and Parodies of Blackness', *Journal of American Culture*, 19:3, 1996, 87–101.

Corporaal, Marguérite, '"Moor, She was Chaste, She Loved Thee, Cruel Moor": *Othello* as a Starting Point for Alternative Dramatic Representations of the Female Voice', *Comitatus*, 33, 2002, 99–111.

Dabbagh Al-, Abdullah, 'Shakespeare's Orientalism: *Hamlet, King Lear* and Sufism', Presented at the Conference 'Between Empires: "Orientalism" Before 1600', Cambridge, 12–15 July 2001.

Dabbagh Al-, Abdullah, 'The Oriental Framework of *Romeo and Juliet*', *Comparatist*, 24, 2000, 64–82.

Dannenfeldt, K.H., 'The Renaissance Humanists and the Knowledge of Arabic', *Studies in the Renaissance*, 2, 1955, 142–64.

Danson, Lawrence, 'England, Islam, and the Mediterranean: *Othello* and Others', *Journal of Early Modern Cultural Studies*, 2002, 1–25.

DePanizza, Lorch Maristella, 'Honest Iago and the Lusty Moor: The Humanistic Drama of Honestas/

Voluptas in a Shakespearean Context', in J.R. Mulryne and M. Shewring (Eds.), *Theatre of the English and Renaissance*, Basingstoke, Macmillan, 1991, 204–20.

Dombrowsk, Rosemarie, 'Amalgamated Otherness: Caliban and the Colonialist Agenda of Elizabethan Travel Literature and Ethnography', Paper presented at the 'Rocky Mountain Medieval Renaissance Assocation Conference', 23–5 May 2002, University of Nevada, Las Vegas.

Draper, John W., 'Shakespeare and Barbary', in John W. Draper (Ed.), *Orientalia and Shakespeareana*, New York, Vantage Press, 129–38.

Draper, John W., 'Shakespeare and the Turk', *Journal of English and Germanic Philology*, October 1956, 55, 523–32.

Draper, John W., 'Shakespeare and Abbas the Great', *Philological Quarterly*, 30, 1951, 410–25.

Edelman, Charles, '*The Battle of Alcazar*, Muly Mollocco, and Shakespeare's *2 and 3 Henry VI*', *Notes and Queries*, 2002, 196–7.

Ekelbald, Inga-Stina, '*King Lear* and Selimus', *Notes and Queries*, May 1957, 193–4.

Enamul Karim, Md., 'The East in Shakespeare's Tragedies', in Syed Sajjad Hussain (Ed.), *Homage to Shakespeare*, Dacca, Bangladesh, Department of English, Dacca University, 1965, 60–70.

Euridge, Gareth M., 'Before Orientalism: The Allure of Islam in Renaissance England', Presented at Modern Language Association, Chicago, 27–9 December 1995.

Euridge, Gareth M., '"Turning Turk": Conversion to Islam in English Renaissance Thought', *Durham University Journal,* 86, 1994, 33–43.

Everett, Barbra, '"Spanish" Othello: The Making of Shakespeare's Moor', *Shakespeare Survey,* 35, 1982, 101–12.

Fleissner, Robert F., 'The Moor's Nomenclature', *Notes and Queries,* 25, 1978, 143.

Floyd-Wilson, Mary, 'Moors, Race, and the Study of English Renaissance Literature; A Brief Retrospective', *Literature Compass,* 3 July 2006, Online.

Gehl, Robert, 'Something is Stirring in the East: Racial Identity, Confronting the "Other" and Miscegenation in *Othello* and *The Lord of the Rings*', in Janet Brennan Croft (Ed.), *Tolkien and Shakespeare: Essays on Shared Themes and Language,* London, McFarland, 2007, 251–66.

Gérard, Albert, '"Egregiously an Ass": The Dark Side of the Moor. A View of Othello's Mind', *Shakespeare Survey,* 10, 1957, 98–106.

Ghazoul, Ferial, '*The Arabian Nights* in Shakespearean Comedy: 'The Sleeper Awakened' and *The Taming of the Shrew*', in Ferial Ghazoul, *Nocturnal Poetics: The Arabian Nights in Comparative Context,* Cairo, The American University in Cairo, 1996, 58–70.

Ghazoul, Ferial, 'The Arabization of Othello', *Comparative Literature,* 50:1, 1998, 1–31.

Habib, Imtiaz, 'Sir Peter Negro, Othello and the Lost Blacks of Elizabethan England: Colonial Inscription and Postcolonial Excavation', *Literature Interpretation Theory,* 9: 1, 1998, 15–30.

Hall, Kim F., 'Guess Who's Coming to Dinner? Colonization and Miscegenation in *The Merchant of Venice*', *Renaissance Drama,* 23, 1992, 87–111.

Harris, Bernard, 'A Portrait of a Moor', *Shakespeare Survey,* 11, 1958, 89–97.

Harris, Jonathan Gil, 'Rematerializing Shakespeare's Intertheatricality: The Occidental/Oriental Palimpsest', in Bryan Reynolds and William N. West (Eds.), *Rematerializing Shakespeare: Authority and Representation on the Early Modern English Stage,* Basingstoke, Palgrave Macmillan, 2005, 75–94.

Hawamdeh, Mufeed F., 'Shakespeare's Treatment of the Moor in *Othello*', *International Journal of Islamic and Arabic Studies,* 4:1, 1987, 93–114.

Hawamdeh, Mufeed F., 'Allusions to Muhammad in Shakespeare: A Lexico-Cultural Study', *Damascus University Journal,* 13, 1988, 53–72.

Hawamdeh, Mufeed F., 'The Treatment of Turks in Shakespeare', *International Journal of Islamic and Arabic Studies,* 1988.

Hoenselaars, A. J., 'The Elizabethans and Turks at Constantinople', *Cahiers Elisabethians,* 47, 1995, 29–42.

Hornback, Robert, 'Emblems of Folly in the First Othello: Renaissance Blackface, Moor's Coat, and "Muckender"', *Comparative Drama,* 35:1, 2001, 69–99.

Howard, Jean E., 'Shakespeare, Geography, and the Works of Genre on the Early Modern Stage', *Modern Language Quarterly,* 64: 3, 2003, 301–22.

Hunter, G.K., 'Elizabethan and Foreigners', *Shakespeare Survey,* 17, 1964, 37–52.

Hutchings, Mark, '"Turkish" or "Arabic" Emir? *The Merry Wives of Windsor,* II.i.176', *Notes and Queries,* 47: 4, 2000, 449–51.

Jackson, Ken, 'The Abrahamic in Shakespeare's *Titus Andronicus* and Other Plays', Paper Presented at the Conference '1453 to 1699: Cultural Encounters between East and West', Institute of English Studies, London, 5–7 December 2002.

Jafri, Naqi Hussain, 'Image of the Orient in Shakespeare', *The Aligarh Critical Miscellany,* 11: 1, 1998, 15–29.

Lim, Walter S. H., 'Jacobean Rule and Early Modern Orientalism in Shakespeare's *Antony and Cleopatra*', Presented at the Conference 'Colonial, Imperial, and Post-Colonial Shakespeare', Kent State University, 14–16 November, 2002.

Lim, Walter S. H., 'Representing the Other: *Othello,* Colonialism, Discourse', *The Upstart Crow: A Shakespeare Journal,* 13, 1993, 57–78.

Loomba, Ania, 'Shakespeare and Cultural Difference', in Terrence Hawkes (Ed.), *Alternative Shakespeare 2*, London, Routledge, 1996, 162–87.

Maclean, Gerald, 'Before Orientalism? Islam, Ottomans, and Moors in the English Renaissance', *Review*, Virginia, USA, 22, 2000, 229–48.

Mafe, Diana Adesola, 'From Ògún to Othello: (Re)acquainting Yoruba Myth and Shakespeare's Moor', *Research in African Literatures*, 35:3, 2004, 46–61.

Malieckal, Bindu, '"Bondslaves and Pagans Shall Our Statesmen Be": Moors, Turks, and Venetians in *Othello*', *Shakespeare Yearbook*, 10, 1999, 162–189.

Malieckal, Bindu, '"O Treason of the Blood": Moors and Miscegenation in Shakespeare', Presented at the 'South Atlantic Modern Language Association Conference', Savannah, Georgia, November 1996.

Matar, Nabil and Stoeckel, Rudolph, 'Europe's Mediterranean Frontier: The Moor', in Andrew Hadfield and Paul Hammond (Eds.), *Shakespeare and Renaissance Europe*, London, Arden Shakespeare, 2004, 220–52.

Matar, Nabil, 'Before Orientalism: The Allure of Islam in Renaissance England', Paper presented at Modern Language Association, Chicago, 1995.

Matinuddin, Abu Rushd, 'Shakespeare and the East', in Syed Sajjad Hussain (Ed.), *Homage to Shakespeare*, Dacca, Bangladesh, Department of English Dacca University, 1965, 29–39.

McJannet, Linda, 'Mapping the Ottomans on the Renaissance Stage', *Journal of Theatre and Drama*, 2, 1996, 9–34.

Neill, Michael, '"Mulattos', 'Blacks', and 'Indian Moors": Othello and Early Modern Constructions of Human Difference', *Shakespeare Quarterly*, 49:4, 1998, 361–74.

Parker, Patricia, 'Black Hamlet: Battening on the Moor', *Shakespeare Studies*, 31, 2003, 127–64.

Parker, Patricia, 'Fantasies of "Race" and "Gender": Africa, Othello and Bringing to Light', in Margo Hendricks and Patricia Parker (Eds.), *Women, Race, and Writing in the Early Modern Period*, New York, Routledge, 1994, 84–100.

Potter, Lois, 'Pirates and Turning Turk in Renaissance Drama', in Jean-Pierre Maquerlot and Michele Willems (Eds.), *Travel and Drama in Shakespeare's Time*, New York, Cambridge University Press, 1996, 14–31.

Rice, Warner G., 'To Turn Turk' *Modern Language Notes*, 46, 1931, 153–4.

Rosen, Alan, 'The Rhetoric of Exclusion: Jew, Moor and the Boundaries of Discourse in *The Merchant of Venice*' in Joyce Green MacDonald (Ed.), *Race, Ethnicity, and Power in the Renaissance*, Madison, NJ, Farleigh Dickinson University Press, 1997, 67–79.

Ross, Lawrence J., '"Marble", "Crocodile", and "Turban'd Turk" in "Othello"', *Philological Quarterly*, 40, October 1961, 476–84.

Schmuck, Stephan, 'From Sermon to Play: Literary Representations of "Turks" in Renaissance England 1550–1625', *Literature Compass*, 2, 156, 2006, 1–29.

Schwoebel, Robert, 'Coexistence, Conversion, and the Crusade Against the Turks', *Studies in the Renaissance*, 12, 1965, 164–87.

Shetawi al-, Mahmoud F., 'The Oriental in Shakespeare', *Arab Journal for the Humanities*, 17:68, 1999, 310–30.

Skura, Meredith Anne, 'Discourse and the Individual: The Case of Colonialism in *The Tempest*', *Shakespeare Quarterly*, 40, 1989, 42–69.

Spencer, T., 'Turks and Trojans in the Renaissance', *Modern Language Review*, 47, 1952, 330–3.

Srigley, Michael, '"Heavy-Headed Revel East and West": Hamlet and Christian IV of Denmark', in Gunnar Sorelius (Ed.), *Shakespeare and Scandinavia: A Collection of Nordic Studies*, London, Associated University Presses, 2002, 168–92.

Takaki, Ronald, '*The Tempest* in the Wilderness: The Racialization of Savagery', *Journal of American History*, 79, 1992, 892–912.

Vitkus, Daniel, 'Turning Turk in *Othello*: The Conversion and Damnation of the Moor', *Shakespeare Quarterly*, 48, 1997, 145–76.

Vitkus, Daniel, 'Trafficking with the Turk: English Travelers in the Ottoman Empire During the Early Seventeenth Century', in Jyotsna G. Singh and Ivo Kamps. (Eds.), *Travel Knowledge: European Discoveries in the Early Modern Period*, New York: St. Martin's Press, 2000, 35–52.

Wann, Louis, 'The Oriental in Elizabethan Drama', *Modern Philology*, 12 January 1915, 163–87.

Whitney, Lois, 'Did Shakespeare Know "Leo Africanus"?', *Publication of Modern Language Association,* 37, 1922, 470–83.

Wilson, Diana de Armas, 'Turning Turk: Cervantes, Shakespeare and Ottomite Islam', 50th Anniversary Cervantes Lecture, Fordham University, 11 April 2002.

Wilson, Richard, 'Voyage to Tunis: New History and the Old World of *The Tempest*', *English Literary History,* 64, 1997, 333–57.

Wunder, Amanda, 'Western Travelers, Eastern Antiquities, and the Image of the Turk in Early Modern Europe', *Journal of Early Modern History,* 7:1–2, 2003, 89–119.

Doctoral Dissertation/s

Artemel, S.S., 'The Idea of Turkey in the Elizabethan Period and in the Early Seventeenth Century, with Special Reference to Drama', University of Durham, 1965–6.

Barthelemy, Anthony Gerard, 'The Representation of Moors in English Drama: 1589–1695', Yale University, 1984.

Beshti el-, Bashir Mahmud, 'The Displacement Towards the East: The Oriental in English Renaissance Literature and Culture', University of California, Berkeley, 1989.

Burton, Jonathan, '"Turn'd Turk": Islam and English Drama, 1579–1624', City University of New York, 1999.

Fattouh, Essam, 'Ca...Ca.. Caliban: Cultural Constructions of Otherness in English Renaissance Drama', State University of New York at Stony Brook, 1993.

Kadi Al-, Thaer T., '"Here is my Space" : Shakespeare's Treatment of the Orient in *Othello, Antony and Cleopatra* and the *Tempest*', Indiana University of Pennsylvania, 2000.

Kanaan, F., 'Shakespeare on the Arab Page and Stage', University of Manchester, 1998.

Kang, Nae Heui, 'The Renaissance Representation of the Other: Travel Literature, Spenser, Shakespeare, and Milton', Marquette University, 1986.

Mayo Lopez, Jose, 'The Tragedy of Being a Moor, or Racialism in Shakespeare's *Othello*', Salamanca University, 1972.

Mugawar, Fahd M.T.S., 'The Oriental Element in the Elizabethan Drama with Special Reference to Marlowe, Shakespeare and Ben Jonson', Aligarh Muslim University, Aligarh, India, 2004.

Obaid, Thoraya Ahmed, 'The Moor Figure in English Renaissance Drama', Wayne State University, 1974.

Qazi, Munir Ahmad, 'Three Eastern Folktales and Shakespeare's *'Romeo and Juliet'*: A Comparison in Themes, Motifs, and Modes of Transference', University of Toledo, 1982.

Rais, Mahmoud, 'The Representation of the Turk in English Renaissance Drama, Cornell University', 1973.

Rice, Warner G., 'Turk, Moor, and Persian in English Literature from 1550 to 1660, with Particular Reference to the Drama', University of Harvard, 1931.

Robinson, Benedict, 'The Romance of the East: Islam and English Literature after the Reformation (Edmund Spenser, William Shakespeare, John Milton)', Columbia University, 2002.

Tounsi, Mohamed Mohamed, 'Shakespeare in Arabic: A Study of the Translation, Reception, and Influence of Shakespeare's Drama in the Arab World', University of Northern Colorado, 1989.

Twaij, Mohammed Baqir, 'Shakespeare in the Arab World', Northwestern University, 1973.

P.B. Shelley

(1792–1822)

- *From the Arabic: An Imitation*
- *The Indian Serenade*
- *The Revolt of Islam*
- *"Zeinab and Kathema' in the Witch of Atlas*
- *Queen Mab*
- *Alastor*

Article/s

Cameron, Kenneth N., 'A Major Source of *The Revolt of Islam*', *PMLA*, 56, 1941, 175–206.

Draper, John W., 'Shelley and Arabic-Persian Lyric Style', in John W. Draper (Ed.), *Orientalia and Shakespeareana*, New York, Vantage Press, 184–8.

Griffith, Ben W. Jr., '*The Revolt of Islam* and Byron's *The Corsair*', *Notes and Queries*, 201, June 1956, 265.

Grimes, Kyle, 'Censorship, Violence, and Political Rhetoric: *The Revolt of Islam* in its time', *Keats-Shelley Journal*, 43, 1994, 98–116.

Gutschera, Deborah A., 'The Drama of Reenactment in Shelley's *The Revolt of Islam*', *Keats-Shelley Journal*, 35, 1986, 115–25.

Haddad, Emily A., 'To Instruct Without Displeasing: Percy Shelley's *The Revolt of Islam* and Robert

Southey's *Thalaba the Destroyer*', in Emily A. Haddad, *Oriental Poetics*, Aldershort, UK, Ashgate, 2002, 11–53.

Hai, Abedl M., 'Shelley and the Arabs: An Essay in Comparative Literature', *Journal of Arabic Literature*, 3, 1972, 72–89.

Haswell, Richard H., 'Shelley's *The Revolt of Islam*: "The Connexion of Its Parts"', *Keats-Shelley Journal*, 256, 1976, 81–102.

Issawi, Charles, '"We Are all Greeks..." Shelley and the Near East', *Encounter*, 72:5, May 1989, 54–7.

Kabitoglou, E. Douka, 'Shelley's (Feminist) Discourse on the Female: *The Revolt of Islam*', *Arabeiten aus anglistik und Amerikanistik*, 15:2, 1990, 139–50.

Kitzberger, Ingrid Rosa, 'Archetypal Images of Transformation and the Self in Percy Bysshe Shelley's *The Revolt of Islam*', in Sabine Coelsch-Foisner, Wolfgang Görtschacher, and Holger M. Klein (Eds.), *Trends in English and American Studies: Literature and the Imagination: Essays in Honour of James Lester Hogg*, Lewiston, NY, Mellen Press, 1996, 171–87.

Makdisi, Saree, 'Versions of the East: Byron, Shelley, and the Orient', in Alan Richardson and Sonia Hofkosh (Eds.), in *Romanticism, Race, and Imperial Culture, 1780–1834*, Bloomington, Indiana University Press, 1996, 203–36.

Murray, E.B., '"Elective Affinity" in *The Revolt of Islam*', *Journal of English and Germanic Philology*, 678, 1968, 570–85.

Orel, Harold, 'Shelley's *The Revolt of Islam:* The Last Great Poem of the English Enlightenment?', *Studies on Voltaire and the Eighteenth Century*, 89, 1972, 187–207.

Rossington, Michael, 'Shelley and the Orient', *The Keats-Shelley Review*, 6, Autumn 1995, 18–36.

Sperry, Stuart, 'The Sexual Theme in Shelley's *The Revolt of Islam*', *Journal of English and Germanic Philology*, 82:1, 1983, 32–49.

Wu, Ya-Feng, '*The Assassins*: Shelley's Appropriation of History', *The Keats-Shelley Review*, 9, Spring 1995, 51–62.

Doctoral Dissertation/s

Ackerman, Jan Condra Bryant, 'The Education of a Poet: A Study of Shelley's *The Revolt of Islam*', University of Arizona, 1976.

Asfour, Mohammad Hassan, 'The Crescent and the Cross: Islam and the Muslims in English Literature from Johnson to Byron', Indiana University, 1973.

Bazei al-, Saad Abdulrahman, 'Literary Orientalism in Nineteenth-Century Anglo-American Literature: Its Formation and Continuity', Purdue University, 1983.

Broking, M. Elisabeth, "Common Sympathies": Shelley's "*Revolt of Islam*"', Rice University, 1985.

Harley, Robert Arnold, 'Images of Change in "*The Revolt of Islam*"', Columbia University, 1971.

Hejazi al-, Ali Ahmad Ali, 'Arabo-Islamic Mythology in English Poetry, 1755–1825, University of Wisconsin-Milwaukee, 1979.

Husain, I., 'The Oriental Elements in English Poetry (1784–1859)', University of Edinburgh, 1934.

Martinez, Alicia, 'The Hero and Heroine of Shelley's *The Revolt of Islam*', Columbia University, 1974.

Neal, Shirley Winifred Zwoyer, 'Family Relationships in '*The Revolt of Islam*', University of Illinois at Urbana-Champaign, 1973.

Rishmawi, George Khalil, 'Oriental Elements in English Romantic Poetry: Shelley and Byron', State University of New York at Buffalo, 1983.

Ruff, James Lynn, 'Image, theme and Structure in "*The Revolt of Islam*"', Northwestern University, 1968.

Sahaj Pal, T. R., 'Oriental Influence in the Poetry of P. B. Shelley', MA, University of Belfast, 1964–5.

Stavrou, Stavros, 'Seeking the Exotic Romantic Orientalism in Keats, Shelley, and Byron', Dalhousie University, 1991.

Sultana, Fehmida, 'Romantic Orientalism and Islam: Southey, Shelley, Moore, and Byron', Tufts University, 1989.

White, Deborah Elise, 'Action, Suffering, and Allegory: Shelley's *Revolt of Islam*', Yale University, 1993.

Robert Southey

(1774–1843)

- *Chronicle of the Cid*
- *Curse of Kehama*
- *Imitated from the Persian*
- *Ode on the Battle of Algiers*
- *Thalaba the Destroyer*
- *Don Roderick*
- *Mohammed*
- *The Kalendar*

Book/s

Curry, Kenneth, *Southey*, London, 1975.

Pratt, Lynda (Ed.), *Robert Southey and the Contexts of English Romanticism*, Aldershort, UK, Ashgate, 2006.

Article/s

Ahmad, Munir, 'From China to Peru: The Origin and Development of Southey's Mythological Poems', *Aligarh Journal of English Studies*, 12:2, 1987, 179–202.

Beyer, W.W., 'Southey, Orientalism and *Thalaba*', in Warner W. Beyer, *The Enchanted Forest*, Oxford, 1963, 234–45.

Brown, Wallace C., 'Robert Southey and the English Interest in the Near East', *Journal of English Literary History*, 5 September 1938, 218–24.

Butler, Marilyn, 'Plotting the Revolution: The Political Narratives of Romantic Poetry and Criticism', in Kenneth R. Johnston (et al.) (Eds.), *Romantic Revolutions: Criticism and Theory*, Bloomington, 1990, 133–57.

Butler, Marilyn, 'The Orientalism of Byron's *Giaour*', in Bernard Beatty and Vincent Newey (Eds.), *Byron and the Limits of Fiction*, Liverpool, 1988, 78–96.

Carnall, Goeffrey, 'A Note on Southey's Later Religious Opinions', *Philological Quarterly*, 31, 1952, 399–406.

Chandler, David, 'Robert Southey and *The Prelude's* "Arab Dream"', *Review of English Studies*, 54:214, 2003, 203–19.

Dowden, W.S., 'The Source of the Metermpsychosis in Southey's *Thalaba*', *Modern Language Notes*, 66, 1951, 555–6.

Fulford, T., 'Heroic Voyagers and Superstitious Natives: Southey's Imperialist Ideology', *Studies in Travel Writing*, 2, 1998, 46–64.

Fulford, T., 'Plants, Pagodas and Penises: Southey's Oriental Imports', in Lynda Pratt (Ed.), *Robert Southey and the Contexts of English Romanticism*, Aldershort, UK, Ashgate, 2006, 187–201.

Haddad, Emily A., 'To Instruct Without Displeasing: Percy B. Shelley's *The Revolt of Islam* and Robert Southey's *Thalaba the Destroyer*', in Emily A. Haddad, *Oriental Poetics*, Aldershort, UK, Ashgate, 2002, 11–53.

Haddad, Emily A., 'Truth in Illustrating Robert Southey and Thomas Moore', in Emily A. Haddad, *Oriental Poetics*, Aldershort, UK, Ashgate, 2002, 113–7.

Hoffpauir, Richard, 'The Thematic Structure of Southey's Epic Poetry', *The Wordsworth Circle*, 6, 1975, 240–8.

Kidwai, A.R., 'A Bibliography of Southey's Oriental Reading' in A.R. Kidwai, *Orientalism in Lord Byron's Turkish Tales*, Lewiston, Mellen University Press, 1995, 266–74.

Kidwai, A.R. and Newey, Vincent, 'The Outline of Coleridge's and Southey's 'Muhammad', *Notes and Queries*, 238, March 1993, 38–9.

Meachen, Edward, 'History and Transcendence in Robert Southey's Epic Poems', *Studies in English Literature*, 19, 1979, 589–608.

Ober, W.U., 'Muhammad': The Outline of a Proposed Poem by Coleridge and Southey', *Notes and Queries*, New Series, 5, 1958, 448.

Saglia, Diego, 'Words and Things: Southey's East and the Materiality of Oriental Discourse', in Lynda Pratt (Ed.), *Robert Southey and the Contexts of English Romanticism*, Aldershort, UK, Ashgate, 2006, 167–86.

Simmons, Clare A., '"Useful and Wasteful Both": Southey's Thalaba the Destroyer and the Function of Annotation in the Romantic Oriental Poem', *Genre*, 27:1/2, 1994, 83–104.

Doctoral Dissertation/s

Ahmad, M., 'Oriental Influence in English Poetry of the Romantic Period', University of Birmingham, 1959–60.

Asfour, Mohammad Hassan, 'The Crescent and the Cross: Islam and the Muslims in English Literature from Johnson to Byron', Indiana University, 1973.

Bazei al-, Saad Abdulrahman, 'Literary Orientalism in Nineteenth-Century Anglo-American Literature: Its Formation and Continuity', Purdue University, 1983.

Hejazi al-, Ali Ahmad Ali, 'Arabo-Islamic Mythology in English Poetry, 1755–1825', University of Wisconsin-Milwaukee, 1979.

Husain, I., 'The Oriental Elements in English Poetry (1784–1859)', University of Edinburgh, 1934.

Sharafuddin, M. A., 'Islam and Romanticism: A Study of Orientalism in English Verse Narrative, 1798–1817', University of York, 1988.

Sultana, Fehmida, 'Romantic Orientalism and Islam: Southey, Shelley, Moore, and Byron', Tufts University, 1989.

Edmund Spenser

(1552–99)

- *Faerie Queene I, ii*
- *Faerie Queene I, iv*
- *Faerie Queene I, x*
- *Faerie Queene II, viii*
- *Faerie Queene IV, xi*
- *Faerie Queene VI, vii*

Article/s and Conference Presentation/s

Feinstein, Blossom, 'The *Faerie Queene* and Cosmogonies of the Near East', *Journal of the History of Ideas,* 29: 4, 1968, 531–50.

Fuchs, Barbara, 'Spanish Lessons: Spenser and the Irish Moriscos', *Studies in English Literature, 1500–1900,* 42:1, 2002, 43–62.

Heberle, Mark, 'Pagans and Saracens in Spenser's *The Faerie Queene'* in Cornelia N. Moore and Raymond A. Moddy (Eds.), *Comparative Literature East and West: Traditions and Trends,* Honolulu, University of Hawaii, 1989, 81–7.

Hollings, Marion, 'Gender, Gardens, and Orientalism in Spenser's Bower of Bliss', Presented at the 'Rocky Mountain Medieval and Renaissance Association Conference', Tempe, Arizona, May 1999.

Hollings, Marion, 'Temperaunce, Turkish Baths, and the Threat of Islam: Bathing in Spenser's Paradise', Presented at the 'Conference on Virile Women, Consuming Men: Gender and Monstrous Appetites in the Middle Ages and the Renaissance', University of Wales, Aberswyth, April 2000.

Hollings, Marion, 'Sarazin, Paynim, and Other Strangers: Spenser's Discourses of Orientalism in *The Faerie Queene*', Presented at 'The Place of Spenser: Words, Worlds, Works', Pembroke College, Cambridge University, Cambridge, England, July 2001.

Lim, Walter S. H., 'Figuring Justice: Imperial Ideology and the Discourse of Colonialism in Book V of *The Faerie Queene* and *A View of the Present State of Ireland*', *Renaissance and Reformation,* 19, 1995, 45–70.

Robinson, Benedict Scott, *Islam and Early Modern English Literature: The Politics of Romance from Spenser to Milton,* New York , Palgrave Macmillan, 2007.

Doctoral Dissertation/s

Dhesi, Nirmal Singh, 'The Paynims and Saracens of Spenser's '*The Faerie Queene*', Michigan State University, 1968.

Kang, Nae Heui, 'The Renaissance Representation of the Other: Travel Literature, Spenser, Shakespeare, and Milton', Marquette University, 1986.

Peernajmodin, H., 'Orientalist Representations of Persia in the Works of Spenser, Marlowe, Milton, Moore and Morier', University of Birmingham, 2002.

Robinson, Benedict, 'The Romance of the East: Islam and English Literature after the Reformation (Edmund Spenser, William Shakespeare, John Milton)', Columbia University, 2002.

Alfred Tennyson

(1809–92)

- *Locksley Hall*
- *Fatima*
- *Persia*
- *The Expedition of Nadir Shah into Hindostan*
- *The Fall of Jerusalem*
- *Akbar's Dream*
- *Written by an Exile of Bassorah*
- *Recollections of the Arabian Nights*

Book/s

McBratney, John, *Rebuilding Akbar's Fane; Tennyson's Reclamations of the East*, West Virginia University Press, 1993.

Paden, W.D., *Tennyson in Egypt: A Study of the Imagery in His Earlier Work*, Lawrence, KS, University of Kansas Publications, 1942.

Article/s

Haddad, Emily A., 'Alfred Tennyson's Basra: Natural Phenomena and Urban Construction', in Emily A. Haddad, *Oriental Poetics*, Aldershort, UK, Ashgate, 2002, 147–51.

Haddad, Emily A., 'Grounding a Poetics in the *1001 Nights*: Tennyson', in Emily A. Haddad, *Oriental Poetics*, Aldershort, UK, Ashgate, 2002, 183–6.

Haddad, Emily A., 'The Oriental and Tennyson's P(a)lace of Art', in Emily A. Haddad, *Oriental Poetics*, Aldershort, UK, Ashgate, 2002, 187–91.

John, Brian, 'Tennyson's "Recollections of the *Arabian Nights*" and the Individuation Process', *Victorian Poetry*, 4, 1966, 275–9.

McBratney, John, 'Rebuilding Akbar's "Fane": Tenneyson's Reclamation of the East', *Victorian Poetry*, 32.4, 1993, 411–7.

Shatto, Susan, 'The Strange Charm of 'Far, Far Away': Tennyson, the Continent, and the Empire', in Michael Cotsell (Ed.), *Creditable Warriors, 1830–1876*, London, Ashfield, 1990, 119–29.

Shaw, Marion, 'Tennyson's Dark Continent', *Victorian Poetry* 32:2, 1994, 157–69.

Stevens, Paul and Sapra, Rahul, 'Akbar's Dream: Moghul Toleration and English/British Orientalism', *Modern Philology*, 104:3, 2007, 379–411.

Ziolkowski, E. J., 'Waking up from Akbar's Dream: The Literary Prefiguration of Chicago's 1893 World's Parliament of Religions', *Journal of Religion*, 73:i, 1993, 42–60.

Doctoral Dissertation/s

Hawari, R., 'The Arabian Background of Tennyson, Thomson and Meredith', B.Litt., University of Oxford, 1962–3.

Hawari, R., 'A Study of the 'Exotic' East in the Works of Thackeray, with Reference to the Cult of the

Oriental in Eighteenth and Nineteenth Century', London, Birckbeck College, 1966–7.

Khatib al-, Issam, 'The Orientalism of Alfred Lord Tennyson', Case Western Reserve University, 1967.

Zaidi, Syed Faiz, 'Image of the Orient in Victorian Poetry with Special Reference to Tennyson, Browning and Arnold', Aligarh Muslim University, Aligarh, India, 2003.

William M. Thackeray
(1811-63)

- *Tremendous Adventures of Major Gahagan*
- *Story of the Sultan Stork*
- *Journey from Cornhill to Grand Cairo*
- *Legend of Jawbrahim Heraudee,* **Punch**, *vol. I*
- *Turkish Letters,* **Punch**, *vol. IV*
- *Punch in the East,* **Punch**, *vol. VIII*
- *The Visit of Mehemet Ali,* **Punch**, *vol. XI*
- *The Ghazoul or Oriental,* **Punch**, *vol. XII*
- *Love Song,* **Punch**, *vol. XIX*
- *Fragments from the History of Cashmere,* **Punch**, *vol. XIX*
- *Panorama of the Ingleez,* **Punch**, *vol. XXI*
- *Important from the East,* **Punch**, *vol. XXVI*
- *Letters from the East,* **Punch**, *vol. XXVIII*

Article/s

Brantlinger, Patrick, 'Thackeray's India', in Patrick Brantlinger (Ed.), *Rule of Darkness*, Ithaca, Cornell University Press, 73–107.

Oscar Wilde

(1854–1900)

- *The Decay of Lying*
- *Athanasia*

Article/s

Haddad, Emily A., 'Orientalist Poetics, Oscar Wilde: Culmination', in Emily A. Haddad, *Oriental Poetics*, Aldershort, UK, Ashgate, 2002, 199–201.

Haddad, Emily A., 'Orientalist Poetics, Oscar Wilde', in Emily A. Haddad, *Oriental Poetics*, Aldershort, UK, Ashgate, 2002, 152–4.

Marez, Curts, 'The Other Addict: Reflections on Colonialism and Oscar Wilde's Opium Smoke Screen', *ELH*, 64:1, 1997, 257–87.

Nunokawa, Jeff, 'Oscar Wilde in Japan: Aestheticism, Orientalism and the Derealization of the Homosexual', in Jonathan Freedman (Ed.), *Oscar Wilde: A Collection of Critical Essays*, New Jersey, Prentice Hall, 153–7.

Zhou, Xiaoyi, 'Oscar Wilde's Orientalism and Late Nineteenth-Century European Consumer Culture', *Ariel*, 28:4, 1997, 49–71.

Doctoral Dissertation/s

Kaufman, Ester, 'The Use of Oriental Material by James Thomson, Oscar Wilde, and Rudyard Kipling', Cornell University, 1947.

William Wordsworth

(1770–1850)

- *Ecclesiastical Sonnet No. XXXIV*
- *The Armenian Lady's Love*
- *The Nightingale (The Prelude)*
- *Richard I*
- *The Haunted Tree*

Article/s

Bahti, Timothy, 'Figures of Interpretation, the Interpretation of Figures: A Reading of Wordsworth's Dream of the Arab', *Studies in Romanticism*, 18, 1979, 601–27.

Chandler, David, 'Robert Southey and *The Prelude's* "Arab Dream"', *Review of English Studies*, 54:214, 2003, 203–19.

Haddad, Emily A., 'A Confederation of the Middle East and Art: Wordsworth', in Emily A. Haddad, *Oriental Poetics*, Aldershort, UK, Ashgate, 2002, 155–6.

Haddad, Emily A., 'William Wordsworth and the Nature of the Middle East', in Emily A. Haddad, *Oriental Poetics*, Aldershort, UK, Ashgate, 2002, 103–8.

Kelley, Theresa M., 'Deluge and Buried Treasure in Wordsworth's Arab Dream', *Notes and Queries*, 27, 1980, 70–1.

Kelley, Theresa M., 'Spirit and Geometric Form: The Stone and the Shell in Wordsworth's Arab Dream', *Studies in English Literature 1500–1900*, 22, 1982, 563–82.

Most, Glenn W., 'Wordsworth's 'Dream of the Arab' and Cervantes', *English Language Notes*, 22:3, 1985, 52–8.

Ragussis, Michael, 'Language and Metamorphosis in Wordsworth's Arab Dream', *Modern Language Quarterly*, 36, 1975, 148–65.

Tarawreh, Yousef, 'Islamic Reflection: Revisionist Portrayals of Arab Civilization with Particular Reference to Wordsworth, Pope, Cervantes, and Dante', *International Journal of Islamic and Arabic Studies*, 4, 1987, 55–74.

Doctoral Dissertation/s

Barker, C., 'The Stone and the Shell: The Image of the Arab and the Romantic Sublime in the Poetry of Wordsworth and Coleridge', University of Exeter, 2006.

Khan, H.A., 'A Study of the Relationship Between the Sensuous and the Mystical in Wordsworth, with Some Oriental Parallels'.

W.B. Yeats
(1865–1939)

- *The Gift of Harun Alrashid*
- *Mosada*
- *Ego Dominus Tuus*
- *Street Dances*
- *Solomon to Sheba*
- *Solomon and the Witch*
- *Calvary*
- *The Cat and the Moon*

Book/s

Jeffares, A., Norman and Cross, K.G.W., *In Excited Reverie: A Centenary Tribute to William Butler Yeats 1865–1939*, New York, St. Martin's Press, 1965.

Article/s

Ali, Salah Salim, 'Ishraqi Themes in the Poetry and Prose of William Blake and William B.Yeats', *Hamdard Islamicus*, 16:iii, 1993, 37–61.

Bushrui, Suhiel Badi, 'Yeats's Arabic Interests' in A. Norman Jeffares and K.G.W. Cross (Eds.), *In Excited Reverie: A Centenary Tribute to W.B. Yeats*, London, Macmillan, 1965, 280–314.

Islam, Shamsul, 'The Influence of Eastern Philosophy on Yeats's Later Poetry', *Twentieth Century Literature*, 19, 1973, 283–90.

Yamazaki, Hiroyuki, 'Yeats and Orientalism', in Toshi Furomoto, (et al.) (Eds.)., *International Aspects of Irish Literature*, Gerrards Cross, Smythe, 1996, 82–92.

Doctoral Dissertation/s

Chamrawi El-, A.A.W., 'Some Eastern and Esoteric Aspects in the Work of W.B. Yeats', University of Exeter, 1977.

Chang, Ming-Chu, 'William Butler Yeats and the Orient', University of Colorado, 1949.

Farag, F.F., 'Oriental Mysticism in W. B. Yeats', University of Edinburgh, 1959–60.

2

Critical Books on Literary Orientalism

Abu-Lughod, Ibrahim, *Arab Rediscovery of Europe: A Study in Cultural Encounters*, Princeton, Princeton University Press, 1963.

Adams, Percy G., *Travelers and Travel Liars, 1600–1800*, Berkeley, University of California Press, 1962.

Addison, James T., *The Christian Approach to the Moslem*, New York, 1942.

Agius, D., *Arab Influence in Medieval Europe*, Reading, Ithaca Press, 1994.

Ahmed, Leila, *Edward W. Lane: A Study of His Life and Works and of British Ideas of the Middle East in the Nineteenth Century*, London, Longman/Librairie du Liban, 1978.

Akalin, Esin, *Discovering Self and Other, Representations of Ottoman Turks in English Drama (1656–1792)*, National Library of Canada, 2001.

Akbari, Suzanne Conklin, *Idols in the East: European Representations of Islam and the Orient, 1100–1450*, Cornell University Press, 2009.

Allen, M.D., *The Medievalism of Lawrence of Arabia*, Philadelphia, Pennsylvania State University Press, 1991.

Alloula, Malek, *The Colonial Harem*, 1981, Tr. Myrna Godzich and Wlad Godzich, Minneapolis, University of Minnesota Press, 1986.

Almond, Ian, *The New Orientalists: Postmodern Representations of Islam from Foucault to Baudrillard*, London, I. B. Tauris, 2007.

Andrea, Bernadette Diane, *Women and Islam in Early Modern English Literature*, Cambridge, Cambridge University Press, 2007.

Anidjar, Gil, *Semites: Race, Religion, Literature*, Stanford Clif., Stanford University Press, 2008.

Arac, Jonathan and Ritvo, Harriet (Eds.), *Macropolitics of Nineteenth-Century Literature: Nationalism, Exoticism, Imperialism*, Philadelphia, University of Pennsylvania Press, 1991.

Arberry, A.J., *Asiatic Jones*, London, 1946.

Archer, John Michael, *Old Worlds: Egypt, Southwest Asia, India, and Russia in Early Modern English Writings*, Stanford, Stanford University Press, 2001.

Arnold, T. and Guillaume, A. (Eds.), *The Legacy of Islam*, Oxford, University of Oxford, 1931.

Aydin, Kamil, *Images of Turkey in Western Literature*. Huntingdon, Eothen Press, 1999.

Bacchilega, Cristina and Moore, Cornelia N. (Eds.), *Constructions and Confrontations: Changing*

Representations of Women and Feminisms, East and West: Selected Essays, Honolulu, College of Languages, Linguistics and Literature, University of Hawaii and the East-West Center, 1996.

Ballaster, Ros (Ed.), *Fables of the East: Selected Tales*, London, Oxford University Press, 2005.

Ballaster, Ros, *Fabulous Orients: Fictions of the East in England, 1662–1785*, London, Oxford University Press, 2005.

Bangura, Ahmed S., *Islam and the West African Novel: the Politics of Representation*, Boulder, CO, Rienner, 2000.

Barbour, Richmond, *Before Orientalism: London's Theatre of the East, 1576–1626*, Cambridge, Cambridge University Press, 2003.

Barfoot, C. C. (Ed.), *Aldous Huxley between East and West*, Amsterdam, Rodopi, 2001.

Barfoot, C. C. and D'haen, Theo (Eds.), *Oriental Prospects: Western literature and the Lure of the East*, Amsterdam, Rodopi, 1998.

Barker, F., Hulme, P., Iversen, D. and Loxley, L. (Eds.), *Europe and Its Others*, Colchester, University of Essex, 1985.

Barker, Francis (et al.) (Eds.), *Literature, Politics and Theory*, London, Methuen, 1986.

Bartels, Emily C., *Spectacles of Strangeness: Imperialism, Alienation and Marlowe*, Philadelphia, University of Pennsylvania Press, 1993.

Barthelemy, A.G., *Black Face, Maligned Race: the Representation of Blacks in English Drama*, London, Louisiana State University Press, 1987.

Baudet, Henri, *Paradise on Earth: Some Thoughts on European Images of Non-European Man*, Tr. Elizabeth Wentholt, New Haven, CT, Yale University Press, 1965.

Beaulieu, Jill and Roberts, Mary (Eds.), *Orientalism's Interlocutors: Rewriting the Colonial Encounter*, Durham, NC, Duke University Press, 2002.

Beck, Brandon H., *From the Rising of the Sun: English Images of the Ottoman Empire to 1715*, New York, Peter Lang, 1987.

Beckett, Katherine Scarfe, *Anglo-Saxon Perceptions of the Islamic World*, Cambridge, Cambridge University Press, 2003.

Beckingham, C.F., *Between Islam and Christendom: Travellers, Facts and Legends in the Middle Ages and the Renaissance*, London, Varorium Reprints, 1983.

Behdad, Ali, *Belated Travelers: Orientalism in the Age of Colonial Dissolution*, Durham, NC, Duke University Press, 1994.

Bennett, Clinton, *Victorian Images of Islam*, London, Grey Seal, 1992.

Bernadette Andrea (Ed.), *English Women Staging Islam, 1696–1707*. Forthcoming from Center for Reformation and Renaissance Studies/ University of Toronto Press.

Bernstein, M. and Studlar, G., *Vision of the East: Orientalism in Film*, London, I.B. Tauris, 1997.

Birchwood, Matthew, *Staging Islam in England: Drama and Culture, 1640–1685*, Cambridge, D.S. Brewer, 2007.

Bisaha, Nancy, *Creating East and West: Renaissance Humanists and the Ottoman Turks.* Philadelphia, University of Pennsylvania Press, 2004.

Bitterli, Urs, *Cultures in Conflict: Encounters Between European and Non-European Cultures, 1492–1800*, Tr. Ritchie Robertson, Stanford, Stanford University Press, 1986.

Blanks, David, *Images of Other: Muslims and Europe before 1700*, Cairo, American University in Cairo Press, 1997.

Blanks, David R. and Frassetto, Michael (Eds.), *Western Views of Islam in Medieval and Early Modern Europe: Perception of Others*, New York, St. Martin's Press, 1999.

Bose, S., *Attitudes to Imperialism: Kipling, Forster and Paul Scott*, Delhi, Amar Prakashan, 1990.

Boukelmoun, Jamaa, *Misrepresenting the Arabs in T.E. Lawrence's Seven Pillars of Wisdom, Leon Uris' The Haj, and Michael Ondaatje's The English Patient*, Cleveland, Cleveland State University, 2007.

Brantlinger, Patrick, *Rule of Darkness: British Literature and Imperialism, 1830–1914*, Ithaca, Cornell University Press, 1988.

Bryan, W.F. and Dempster, G. (Eds.), *Sources and Analogues of Chaucer's Canterbury Tales*, Chicago, University of Chicago Press, 1941.

Burton, Jonathan, *Traffic and Turning: Islam and English Drama, 1579–1624*, London, Association University Press, 2005.

Caesar, Judith, *Crossing Borders: An American Woman in the Middle East*, Syracuse, Syracuse University Press, 1997.

Calkin, Siobhain Bly, *Saracens and the Making of English Identity: The Auchinleck Manuscript*, New York, Routledge, 2005.

Campbell, Mary B., *The Witness and the Other World: Exotic European Travel Writing, 400–1600*, Ithaca and London, Cornell University Press, 1988.

Cannon, Garland Hampton, *Sir William Jones, Orientalist, and Annotated Bibliography of His Works*, Honolulu, University of Hawaii Press, 1952.

Cannon, Garland Hampton, *The Life and Mind of Oriental Jones: Sir William Jones, the Father of Modern Linguistics*, Cambridge, Cambridge University Press, 1990.

Cannon, Garland Hampton and Brine, Kevin R. (Eds.), *Objects of Enquiry: The Life, Contribution, and Influences of Sir William Jones, 1746–1794*, New York, New York University Press, 1995.

Caracciolo, Peter L., *The Arabian Nights in English Literature: Studies in the Reception of the The Thousand and One Nights into British Culture*, London, St. Martin's Press, 1968.

Cawley, Robert Ralston, *The Voyagers and Elizabethan Drama,* New York, Kraus Reprint Corporation, 1966.

Cawley, Robert Ralston, *Unpathed Waters: Studies in the Influence of the Voyagers on English Literature,* London, Frank Cass, 1967.

Cawley, Robert Ralston, *Milton and the Literature of Travel,* Princeton, Princeton University Press, 1951.

Chakravorty, D.K., *A Passage to the Orient,* Delhi, Amar Prakashan, 1988.

Chesterton, G. K., *Turkey and the Turk,* Sussex, St Dominic's Press, 1930.

Chew, Samuel C., *The Crescent and the Rose: Islam and England during the Renaissance,* New York, Oxford University Press, 1937.

Christy, Arthur, *The Orient in American Transcendentalism: A Study of Emerson, Thoreau, and Alcott,* New York, Columbia University Press, 1932.

Cirakman, Asli, *From the 'Terror of the World' to the 'Sick Man of Europe': European Images of Ottoman Empire and Society from the Seventeenth Century to the Nineteenth,* Oxford, Peter Lang, 2001.

Clark, Steve and Suzuki, Masashi, *Reception of Blake in the Orient,* London, Continuum Int. Publishing Group, 2006.

Clerk, Blame, *Oriental England: A Study of Oriental Influences in Eighteenth-Century England,* Shanghai, Kelley & Walsh, 1939.

Cochran, Peter (Ed.), *Byron and Orientalism*, Cambridge, Cambridge Scholars, 2006.

Codwell, J.F. and Macleod, D.S. (Eds.), *Orientalism Transposed: The Impact of the Colonies on British Culture*, Aldershot, UK, Ashgate, 1998.

Coles, Paul, *The Ottoman Impact on Europe*, London, Thames and Hudson, 1968.

Conant, M.P., *The Oriental Tale in England in the Eighteenth Century*, New York, 1908.

Cooper, Helen, *The Structure of Canterbury Tales*, Athens, University of Georgia Press, 1983.

Creelman, David, *Setting in the East: Maritime Realist Fiction*, Montreal, McGill-Queen's University Press, 2003.

Curry, Kenneth, *Southey*, London, 1975.

D'Amico, Jack, *The Moor in English Renaissance Drama*, Tampa, FL, University of South Florida Press, 1991.

Da'mi-Al, Muhammed A., *Arabian Mirrors and Western Soothsayers: Nineteenth-Century Literary Approaches to Arab-Islamic History*, New York, Peter Lang, 2002.

Dahiyat, Eid Abdallah, *John Milton and the Arab-Islamic Culture*, Amman, Shukayr & Akasheh, 1987.

Dallmayr, F., *Beyond Orientalism: Essays on Cross-Cultural Encounter*, New York, State University of New York Press, 1996.

Damiani, Anita, *Enlightened Observers: British Travellers to the Near East 1715–1850*, Beirut, American University of Beirut, 1979.

Daniel, Norman, *Heroes and Saracens: A Reinterpretation of the 'Chanson de Geste'*, Edinburgh, University of Edinburgh, 1984.

Daniel, Norman, *Islam and the West: The Making of an Image*, Edinburgh, Edinburgh University Press, 1962.

Daniel, Norman, *The Arabs and Medieval Europe*, London, Longman, 1975.

Danish, Ishtiaq, *The English and the Arab: The Making of an Image*, Delhi, Karakush Publishers, 1992.

Das, G.K., *E.M. Forster's India*, London, Macmillan, 1977.

De Guary, G. & Winstone, H.V.E. (Eds.), *The Spirit of the East: An Anthology of Prose and Verse, Inspired by the People, Places and Legends of the East*, London, 1979.

Deneau, Daniel P., *Byron's Narrative Poems of 1813: Two Essays*, Salzburg, 1975.

Dimmock, Matthew, *'New Turkes': Dramatizing Islam and the Ottomans in Early Modern England*, Aldershot, Ashgate, 2005.

Disuqi-al, Rasha, *The Muslim Images in the Twentieth Century Anglo-American Literature*, Islamabad, Islamic Research Institute, 1996.

Doherty, Gerald, *Oriental Lawrence*, New York, Lang, 2001.

Draper, John, *Orientalia and Shakespeareana*, New York, Vantage Press, 1977.

Drew, John, *India and the Romantic Imagination*, Delhi, Oxford University Press, 1987.

Earle, Peter, *Corsairs of Malta and Barbary*, London, Sidgwick & Jackson, 1970.

Erickson, John, *Islam and Postcolonial Narrative*, Cambridge, Cambridge University Press, 1998.

Fausett, D., *The Strange Surprizing Sources of Robinson Crusoe*, Amsterdam, Rodopi, 1994.

Fedden, Robin, *English Travellers in the Near East*, London, 1958.

Fleissner, Robert F., *T. S. Eliot and the Heritage of Africa: the Magus and the Moor as Metaphor*, New York, Paris, Lang, 1992.

Folz, Robert, *The Concept of Empire in Western Europe from the Fifth to the Fourteenth Centuries*, London, Edward Arnold, 1969.

Franklin, Caroline, *Byron's Heroines*, Oxford University Press, 1992.

Franklin, Michael J. (Ed.), *Representing India: Indian Culture and Imperial Control in Eighteenth-Century British Orientalist Discourse, Sources and Perspectives of the Eighteenth Century*, London, Routledge, 2000.

Franklin, Michael J. (Ed.), *Romantic Representations of British India*, London, Routledge, 2006.

Franklin, Michael J., *Sir William Jones: A Critical Biography*, Cardiff, University of Wales Press, 1995.

Franklin, Michael J., *Sir William Jones: Selected Poetical and Prose Works,* Cardiff, University of Wales Press, 1995.

Freeth, Zehra and Winstone, H .V. F., *Explorers of Arabia: From the Renaissance to the End of the Victorian Era,* London, George Allen & Unwin, 1978.

Friedman, John Block, *The Monstrous Races in Medieval Art and Thought,* Cambridge, MA, Harvard University Press, 1981.

Fuchs, Barbara, *Mimesis and Empire: The New World, Islam, and European Identities,* Cambridge, Cambridge University Press, 2003.

Fujita, Minoru and Pronko, Leonard (Eds.), *Shakespeare East and West,* New York, St. Martin's Press, 1996.

Fulford, Tim and Kitson, Peter J. (Eds.), *Romanticism and Colonialism: Writing and Empire, 1780–1830,* Cambridge, Cambridge University Press, 1998.

Galin, Muge, *Between East and West: Sufism in the Novels of Doris Lessing,* Albany, New York State University Press, 1997.

Ganim, John M., *Medievalism and Orientalism: Three Essays on Literature, Architecture, and Cultural Identity,* Basingstoke, Palgrave Macmillan, 2005.

Germaner, Semra, and Inankur, Zeynep, *Orientalism and Turkey,* Tr. Nigar Alemdar and Jeremy Salt, Istanbul, Turkish Cultural Service Foundation, 1989.

Gillies, John, *Shakespeare and the Geography of Difference*, Cambridge, Cambridge University Press, 1994.

Goffman, Daniel, *Britons in the Ottoman Empire 1642–1660*, Seattle and London, University of Washington Press, 1998.

Goffman, Daniel, *The Ottoman Empire and Early Modern Europe*, Cambridge, Cambridge University Press, 2002.

Goytisolo, Juan, *Saracen Chronicles: A Selection of Literary Essays*, Tr. H. Lane, London, Quartet Books, 1992.

Graham, Kenneth W. (Ed.), *Vathek and the Escape from Time: Bicentenary Revaluations*, New York, AMS, 1990.

Greenberger, Allen, *The British Image of India: A Study in the Literature of Imperialism 1880–1960*, New York, Oxford University Press, 1969.

Greene, Molly, *A Shared World: Christians and Muslims in the Early Modern Mediterranean*, Princeton, Princeton University Press, 2000.

Grosrichard, Alain, *The Sultan's Court: European Fantasies of the East*, Tr. Liz Heron, Verso, London, 1998.

Grundy, Isobel, *Lady Mary Wortley Montagu*, Oxford, Oxford University Press, 1999.

Gunny, A., *Images of Islam in Eighteenth-Century Writings*, London, Grey Seal, 1996.

Gwynn, Stephen, *Thomas Moore*, London, 1905.

Habib, Imtiaz, *Shakespeare and Race: Postcolonial Praxis in the Early Modern Period*, Lanham, MD, University Press of America, 2000.

Haddad, Emily A., *Orientalist Poetics: the Islamic Middle East in Nineteenth-century English and French Poetry*, Aldershot, Ashgate, 2002.

Hadfield, Andrew, *Literature, Travel and Colonial Writing in the English Renaissance, 1545–1625*, Oxford, Clarendon, 1998.

Hage el-, George Nicolas, *William Blake and Kahlil Gibran: Poets of Prophetic Vision*, State University of New York at Binghamton, 1981.

Hammat, Abdelhalim, *Orientalism in Edward FitzGerald Seen Through His Adaptation of Omar Khayyam's Quatrains*, Algiers, University of Algiers, Institute of Foreign Languages, 1978.

Hampson, Robert, *Cross-Cultural Encounters in Joseph Conrad's Malay Fiction*, Basingstoke, Palgrave, 2000.

Hasan, Masoodul, *Sufism and English Literature – Chaucer to the Present Age: Echoes and Image*, New Delhi, Adam Publishers, 2007.

Heffernan, Carol F., *The Orient in Chaucer and Medieval Romance*, Woodbridge, Suffolk, Brewer, 2003.

Higgins, Iain Macleod, *Writing East: The 'Travels' of Sir John Mandeville*, Philadelphia, Pennsylvania University Press, 1997.

Hoenselaars, A.J., *Images of Englishmen and Foreigners in the Drama of Shakespeare and His Contemporaries; A Study of Stage, Characters and National Identity in English Renaissance Drama, 1558–1642*, London, Associated University Presses, 1992.

Hoeveler, Diane Long and Cass, Jeffrey (Eds.), *Interrogating Orientalism: Contextual Approaches and Pedagogical Perspectives*, Columbus, Ohio State University Press, 2006.

Hollings, Marion, *International Conference on Cultural Diversity*, Nashville, TN, 2003.

Hopkirk, Peter, *Quest for Kim: In Search of Kipling's Great Game*, Oxford, Oxford University Press, 2001.

Hosein, Imran N. (Ed.), *George Bernard Shaw and the Islamic Scholar: Text and Commentary of their Historic Conversation in 1935*, Bayshore, NY, USA, Masjid Dar Al-Quran, 2001.

Hourani, Albert, *Islam in European Thought*, Cambridge, Cambridge University Press, 1991.

Howard, Clare, *English Travellers of the Renaissance*, London, Burt Franklin, 1914.

Inden, Ronald, *Imagining India*, Oxford, Blackwell, 1990.

Issawi, C., *Cross-Cultural Encounters and Conflicts*. New York, Oxford University Press, 1998.

Jeffares, A. Norman and Cross, K.G.W., *In Excited Reverie: A Centenary Tribute to William Butler Yeats 1865–1939*, New York, St. Martin's Press, 1965.

Jeffreys, Peter, *Eastern Questions: Hellenism and Orientalism in the Writings of E. M. Forster and C. P. Cavafy*, Greensboro, NC, ELT Press, 2005.

Jones, Eldered, *Othello's Countrymen: Africans in English Renaissance Drama,* Oxford, Oxford University Press, 1965.

Jubb, Margaret, *Legend of Saladin in Western Literature and Historiography*, Queenston, Ontario, E. Mellen Press, 2000.

Jutzi, Alan H. (Ed.), *In Search of Sir Richard Burton: Papers from a Huntington Library Symposium,* San Mariono, CA, Huntington Library, 1993.

Kabbani, Rana, *Europe's Myths of Orient,* Bloomington, 1986.

Kahf, Mohja, *Western Representations of the Muslim Woman: From Termagant to Odalisque,* Austin, University of Texas Press, 1999.

Kamps, Ivo and Singh, Jyotsna (Eds.), *Travel Knowledge: European Discoveries in the Early Modern Period,* New York, Palgrave Macmillan, 2001.

Kaul, R.K., *Studies in William Jones: An Interpreter of Oriental Literature,* Shimla, India, Indian Institute of Advanced Study, 1995.

Kedar, Benjamin, *Crusade and Mission: European Approaches towards the Muslims,* Princeton, Princeton University Press, 1984.

Keirnan, V.G., *The Lords of Human Kind: European Attitudes Towards the Outside World in the Imperial Age,* London, 1969.

Kern, Robert, *Orientalism, Modernism, and the American Poem,* Cambridge, Cambridge University Press, 1996.

Khan, Jalal Uddin and Hare, Adrian E. (Eds.), *English and Islam: Creative Encounters 96*, Kuala Lumpur, International Islamic University, 1996.

Kidwai, A.R., *Stranger than Fiction: Images of Islam and Muslims in English Fiction*, New Delhi, A.P.H. Publishing Corporation, 2000.

Kidwai, A.R., *Orientalism in Lord Byron's 'Turkish Tales'*, Lewiston, Mellen University Press, 1995.

Kidwai, A.R., *The Crescent and the Cross: Image of the Orient in English Literature upto 1832*, Aligarh, Aligarh Muslim University, 1997.

King, Richard, *Orientalism and Religion: Post-Colonial Theory, India and the Mystic East*, London, Routledge, 1999.

Kishi, Tetsuo and Pringle, Roger and Wells, Stanley (Eds.), *Shakespeare and Cultural Traditions: The Selected Proceedings of the International Shakespeare Association World Congress, Tokyo, 1991*, Newark, Delaware University Press, 1994.

Klein, Christina, *Cold War Orientalism: Asia in the Middlebrow Imagination, 1945–1961*, Berkeley, California University Press, 2003.

Kobor, Kelli Michele, *Orientalism, the Construction of Race, and the Politics of Identity in British India,1800–1930*, Duke University, 1998.

Kopf, David, *British Orientalism and the Bengal Renaissance*, Berkeley, University of California, 1969.

Labib, Tahar (Ed.), *Imagining the Arab Other: How Arabs and non-Arabs view each other*, Library of

Modern Middle East Studies, 69, London, I.B. Tauris, 2008.

Lacey, R. Kevin and Poole, Francis (Eds.), *Mirrors on the Maghrib: Critical Reflections on Paul Bowles and Other American Writers in Morocco*, Delmar, New York, Caravan Books, 1996.

Leask, Nigel, *British Romantic Writers and the East; Anxieties of Empire*, Cambridge, Cambridge University Press, 1992.

Lennon, Joseph, *Irish Orientalism: A Literary and Intellectual History*, Syracuse, NY, Syracuse University Press, 2004.

Lewis, Bernard (etal.) (Eds.), *As Others See Us: Mutual Perceptions, East and West*, New York, International Society for the Comparative Study of Civilizations, 1985.

Lewis, Bernard (et al.) (Eds.), *Cultures in Conflict: Christians, Muslims and Jews in the Age of Discovery*, Oxford, Oxford University Press, 1995.

Lewis, Reina, *Rethinking Orientalism: Women, Travel, and the Ottoman Harem*, New Brunswick, NJ, Rutgers University Press, 2004.

Lewis, Reina, *Gendering Orientalism*, London, Routledge, 1995.

Lim, Walter S. H. *The Arts of Empire: The Poetics of Colonialism from Raleigh to Milton*, Newark, University of Delaware Press, 1998.

Lockman, J.N., *Parallel Captures: 'Lord Jim' and Lawrence of Arabia*, Huddersfield, UK, Falcon Books, 1998.

Loomba, Ania, *Shakespeare, Race and Colonialism*, Oxford, Oxford University Press, 2002.

Low, Gail Ching-Liang, *White Skins/Black Masks: Representation and Colonialism*, London, Routledge, 1996.

Lowe, Lisa, *Critical Terrains: French and British Orientalisms*, New York, Cornell University Press, 1991.

Luedtke, Luther S., *Nathaniel Hawthorne and the Romance of the Orient*, Bloomington, Indiana University Press, 1989.

Ma, Sheng-Mei, *'The Deathly Embrace': Orientalism and Asian American Identity*, Minneapolis, Minnesota University Press, 2000.

Mabro, Judy, *Veiled Half-Truths: Western Travellers' Perceptions of Middle Eastern Women*, London, I.B. Tauris, 1991.

Macfie, A.L. (Ed.), *Orientalism: A Reader*, Edinburgh, Edinburgh University Press, 2000.

MacKenzie, J.M., *Orientalism: History, Theory and the Arts*, Manchester, Manchester University Press, 1995.

MacLean, Gerald M., *Looking East: English Writing and the Ottoman Empire Before 1800*, Basingstoke, Palgrave Macmillan, 2007.

MacLean, Gerald M., *The Rise of Oriental Travel: English Visitors to the Ottoman Empire, 1580–1720*, Basingstoke, Palgrave Macmillan, 2004.

MacLean, Gerald M., *Re-Orienting the Renaissance: Cultural Exchanges with the East*, New York, Palgrave Macmillan, 2005.

Maier, John R., *Desert Songs: Western Images of Morocco and Moroccan Images of the West*, Albany, NY, State University of New York Press, 1996.

Makdisi, Saree, *Romantic Imperialism: Universal Empire and the Culture of Modernity*, New York, Cambridge University Press, 1998.

Malak, Amin, *Muslim Narratives and the Discourse of English*, Albany, State University of New York Press, 2005.

Mansoor, M., *The Story of Irish Orientalism*, London, Longmans, Green and Co., Ltd., 1944.

Manton, Richard (Ed.), *The Victorians in the Harem*, New York, Grove Press, 1986.

Marshall, P.J. and Williams, S.G., *The Great Map of Mankind: British Perceptions of the World in the Age of Enlightenment*, London, Dent, 1982.

Massoud, Mary (Ed.), *Literary Inter-Relations: Ireland, Egypt, and the Far East*, Gerrards Cross, Smythe, 1996.

Matar, Nabil, *Turks, Moors, and Englishmen in the Age of Discovery*, New York, Columbia University Press, 1999.

Matar, Nabil, *Islam in Britain, 1558–1685*, Cambridge, Cambridge University Press, 1998.

Matar, Nabil and MacLean, Gerald, *Britain and the Muslim World, 1558–1714*, Oxford, Oxford University Press, 2008.

Mazzeo, Tilar J. (Ed.), *Travels, Explorations and Empires: Writings from the Era of Imperial Expansion, 1770–1835*, London, Pickering & Chatto, 2001.

McBratney, John, *Rebuilding Akbar's Fane; Tennyson's Reclamations of the East*, West Virginia University Press, 1993.

McJannet, Linda, *The Sultan Speaks: Dialogue in English Plays and Histories About the Ottoman Turks*, London, Palgrave Macmillan, 2006.

Meester, Marie de, *Oriental Influences in the English Literature of the Nineteenth Century*, Amsterdam, 1914.

Melikian, Anahid, *Byron and the East*, Beirut, American University, 1977.

Melman, Billie, *Women's Orients: English Women and the Middle East, 1718–1918: Sexuality, Religion and Work*, Ann Arbor, MI, University of Michigan Press, 1992.

Menocal, Maria Rosa, *The Arabic Role in Medieval Literary History: A Forgotten Heritage*, Philadelphia, University of Pennsylvania Press, 1987.

Metlitzki, Dorothee, *The Matter of Araby in Medieval England*, New Haven, Yale University Press, 1977.

Michie, Helena and Thomas, Ronald (Eds.), *Nineteenth-Century Geographies: The Transformation of Space from the Victorian Age to the American*

Century, New Brunswick, NJ, Rutgers University Press, 2003.

Milligan, Barry, *Pleasures and Pains: Opium and the Orient in Nineteenth-Century British Culture*, Charlottesville, Virginia University Press, 1995.

Mishima, Toshiko, *Shakespeare and the Orient*, Tokyo, 1959.

Moore-Gilbert, B. J., *Kipling and Orientalism*, London, Croom Helm, 1986.

Moran, Berna, *The Bibliography of the English Publications about the Turks from the 15th Century to the 18th Century*, Istanbul, Istanbul University Press, 1964.

Morgan, Alllison, *Dante and the Medieval Other World*. Cambridge, Cambridge University Press, 1990.

Mousa, Suleiman, *T. E. Lawrence: An Arab View*, Tr. Albert Butros, London, Oxford University Press, 1966.

Moussa, Mahmoud F. (Ed.), *William Beckford of Fonthill, 1760–1844: Bicentenary Essays*, Cairo, Dar-al Marifah, 1960.

Mukherjee, S.N., *Sir William Jones: A Study in 19th-Century British Attitudes to India*, London, Sangam Books, 1987.

Mukherjee, Sujit, *Forster and Further: The Tradition of Anglo-Indian Fiction*, Hyderabad, Orient Longman, 1993.

Muldoon, James, *Popes, Lawyers and Infidels: The Church and the non-Christian World, 1250–1550*, Philadelphia, University of Pennsylvania Press, 1979.

Munster, Robert and Gross, Clyde, *Englishmen Abroad: Being an Account of their Travel in Seventeenth Century*, Lewiston, NY, Edwin Mellen Press, 1986.

Murray, Alexander (Ed.), *Sir William Jones, 1746–1794: A Commemoration*, Oxford, Oxford University Press, 1998.

Mutman, Mahmut and Meyda, Yegenoglu (Eds.), *Orientalism and Cultural Differences*, Santa Cruz, University of California at Santa Cruz, 1992.

Myers, Eugene A., *Arabic Thought and the Western World in the Golden Age of Islam*, New York, Ungar, 1964.

Nash, Geoffrey P., *From Empire to Orient: Travellers to the Middle East 1830–1926*, London, Tauris, 2005.

Nasir, S.J., *The Arabs and the English*, London, 1976.

Nielson, J., and Khasawnih, S.A., *Arabs and the West: Mutual Images*, Amman, Jordan University Press, 1998.

Nittel, Jana, *Wondrous Magic: Images of the Orient in 18th and 19th Centuries' British Women Travel Writing*, Cambridge, MA, Galda & Wilch, 2001.

Obeidat, Marwan M., *American Literature and Orientalism*, Berlin, K. Schwarz, 1998.

Orr, Bridget Erica, *Empire on the English Stage 1660–1714*, Cambridge, Cambridge University Press, 2001.

Osborne, Edna, *Oriental Diction and Theme in English Verse, 1740–1840*, Lawrence, KS, University of Kansas Press, 1916.

Oueijan, Naji B., *A Compendium of Eastern Elements in Byron's Oriental Tales*, New York, Lang, 1996.

Oueijan, Naji. *The Progress of an Image: East in English Literature*, New York, Peter Lang, 1996.

Pachori, Satya S. (Ed.), *Sir William Jones – A Reader*, New Delhi, Oxford University Press, 1993.

Paden, W.D., *Tennyson in Egypt: A Study of the Imagery in His Earlier Work*, Lawrence, KS, University of Kansas Press, 1942.

Pagden, Anthony, *European Encounters with the New World*, New Haven, Yale University Press, 1993.

Pagden, Anthony, *Lords of all the World: Ideologies of Empire in Spain, Britain and France, c. 1500–c. 1800.* New Haven, Yale University Press, 1995.

Palacios, Miguel Asin, *Islam and the Divine Comedy*, Tr. Harold Sunderland, London, Frank Cass, 1960.

Parker, Kenneth (Ed.), *Early Modern Tales of the Orient*, London, Routledge, 1999.

Parr, Anthony (Ed.), *Three Renaissance Travel Plays*, Manchester, Manchester University Press, 1999.

Parry, Benita, *Delusions and Discoveries: Studies on India in the British Imagination*, Berkeley, University of California Press, 1972.

Peltre, Christine, *Orientalism in Art*, U.S., Abbeville Press, 1998.

Penrose, Boies, *Travel and Discovery in the Renaissance*. Cambridge, MA, Harvard University Press, 1952.

Porter, Dennis, *Haunted Journeys: Desire and Transgression in European Travel Writing*, Princeton, NJ, Princeton University Press, 1991.

Prasad, Ram Chandra, *Early English Travellers in India: A Study in the Travel Literature of the Elizabethan and the Jacobean Periods with Particular Reference to India*, Delhi, Motilal Banarsi Dass, 1965.

Prochazka, Martin (Ed.), *Byron: East and West*, Prague, Univerzita Karjova, 2000.

Raizis, M.B. (Ed.), *Byron and the Mediterranean World*, Athens, Hellenic Byron Society, 1995.

Richard, J., *Relations Between East and West in the Middle Ages*, Edinburgh, Edinburgh University Press, 1977.

Robinson, Benedict Scott, *Islam and Early Modern English Literature : The Politics of Romance from Spenser to Milton*, New York , Palgrave Macmillan, 2007.

Robinson, Jeremy, *Lawrence Durrell: Between Love and Death, Between East and West*, Kidderminster, Crescent Moon, 1995.

Rodinson, Maxime, *Europe and the Mystique of Islam*, Tr. Roger Veinus, Seattle, University of Washington Press, 1987.

Rubies, Joan Pau, *Travel and Ethnology in the Renaissance: South India through European Eyes 1250–1625*, Cambridge, Cambridge University Press, 2000.

Sahni, Chaman L., *Forster's A Passage to India: The Religious Dimension*, New Jersy, Humanities Press, 1981.

Said, Edward, *Orientalism*, New York, Pantheon Books, 1978.

Sardar, Ziauddin, *Orientalism*, Philadelphia, Open University Press, 1999.

Schacht, Joseph (Ed.), *The Legacy of Islam*, Oxford, Clarendon Press, 1974.

Schiffer, Reinhold, *Oriental Panorama: British Travellers in 19th-Century Turkey*, Amsterdam, Rodopi, 1999.

Schildgen, Brenda Deen, *Dante and the Orient*, Champaign, IL, University of Illinois Press, 2002.

Schildgen, Brenda Deen, *Pagans, Tartars, Moslems and Jews in Chaucer's Canterbury Tales*, Gainesville, University Press of Florida, 2001.

Schneider, Elisabeth, *Coleridge, Opium and 'Kubla Khan'*, Chicago, 1953.

Schwab, Raymond, *The Oriental Renaissance: Europe's Rediscovery of India and the East, 1680–1880*,

Tr. G. Patterson-Black and Victor Reinking, New York, Columbia University Press, 1984.

Schwartz, Stuart (Ed.), *Implicit Understandings: Observing, Reporting, and Reflecting on the Encounters Between Europeans and Other Peoples in the Early Modern Era*, Cambridge, Cambridge University Press, 1994.

Schwoebel, Robert, *The Shadow of the Crescent: The Renaissance Image of the Turk (1453–1517)*, New York, St. Martin's Press, 1967.

Searight, Sarah, *The British in the Middle East*, New York, Atheneum, 1970.

Semaan, Khalil I, *Islam and the Medieval West: Aspects of International Relations*, Albany, State University of New York, 1980.

Setton, Kenneth M., *Venice, Austria and the Turks in the Seventeenth Century*, Philadelphia, American Philosophical Society, 1991.

Setton, Kenneth M., *Western Hostility to Islam and Prophecies of Turkish Doom*, Philadelphia, American Philosophical Society, 1992.

Shaban, Faud, *Islam and Arabs in Early American Thought: The Roots of American Orientalism in America*, Durham, NC, Acorn Press, 1991.

Shahane, V.A., *Perspectives on E.M. Forster's A Passage to India: A Collection of Critical Essays*, New York, Barnes and Noble, 1968.

Sharafuddin, Mohammed, *Islam and Romantic Orientalism: Literary Encounters with the Orient*, New York, Tauris, 1994.

Sharpe, J., *Allegories of Empire: The Figure of Woman in the Colonial Text*, Minneapolis, University of Minnesota Press, 1993.

Shaw, Ezel Kural and Heywood, C. J., *English and Continental Views of the Ottoman Empire, 1500–1800*, Los Angeles, University of California Press, 1972.

Singleton, Brian, *Oscar Asche, Orientalism, and British Musical Comedy*, London, Praeger, 2004.

Smith, B.P., *Islam in English Literature*, New York, Caravan Books, 1977.

Southern, R.W., *Western Views of Islam in the Middle Ages*, Cambridge, MA, Harvard University Press, 1962.

Stanivukovic, Goran V., *Remapping the Mediterranean World in Early Modern English Writings*, New York, Palgrave Macmillan, 2007.

Starkey, Paul (Ed.), *Unfolding the Orient: Travellers in Egypt and the Near East*, Reading, UK, Ithaca Press, 2000.

Stetkevych, Jaroslav, *Arabic Poetry and Orientalism*, Oxford, St. Johns College Research Centre, 2004.

Stevens, M.A. (Ed.), *The Orientalists: Delacroix to Matisse: The Allure of North Africa and the Near East*, London, Weidenfeld and Nicolson, 1984.

Steward, Lawrence D., *Paul Bowles: The Illumination of North Africa*, Carbondale, IL, Southern Illinios University Press, 1974.

Sweetman, John, *The Oriental Obsession*, Cambridge, Cambridge University Press, 1988.

Tabachnick, Stephen Ely (Ed.), *Explorations in Doughty's Arabia Deserta*, Athens, University of Georgia Press, 1987.

Teltscher, Kate, *India Inscribed: European and British Writing on India, 1600–1800*, Delhi, Oxford University Press, 1995.

Thornton, Lynne, *The Orientalists: Painters and Travellers: 1828–1908*, Paris, ACR, 1983.

Tokson, Elliot H., *The Popular Image of the Black Man in English Drama, 1550–1688*, Boston, MA, G.K. Hall and Co., 1982.

Tolan, John Victor (Ed.), *Medieval Christian Perceptions of Islam*, New York, Garland, 1995.

Tolan, John Victor (Ed.), *Saracens: Islam in the Medieval European Imagination*, New York, Columbia University Press, 2002.

Trivedi, Harish, *Colonial Transactions: English Literature and India*, Manchester, Manchester University Press, 1993.

Turner, Bryan S. (Ed.), *Orientalism: Early Sources*, London, Routledge, 1999.

Turner, Bryan S., *Orientalism, Postmodernism and Globalism*, London, Routledge, 1994.

Vitkus, Daniel J., *Turning Turk: English Theatre and the Multicultural Mediterranean*, New York, Palgrave Macmillan, 2003.

Vitto, Cindy, *The Virtuous Pagan in Middle English Literature*, Philadelphia, The American Philosophical Society, 1989.

Wann, Louis, *The Oriental in Restoration Drama*, Madison, University of Wisconsin Press, 1918.

Watkins, Daniel P., *Social Relations in Byron's Eastern Tales*, London, Associated University Presses, 1987.

Watt, W. Montgomery, *The Influence of Islam on Medieval Europe*, Edinburgh, Edinburgh University Press, 1972.

Watt, W. Montgomery, *Muslim-Christian Encounters: Perceptions and Misperceptions*, London, Routledge, 1991.

Wazzan, A.M., *Essays in Comparative Literature: An Islamic Perspective*, London, 1985.

Weir, David, *Brahma in the West: William Blake and the Oriental Renaissance*, Albany, New York State University Press, 2003.

Winks, Robin W. and Rush, James R. (Eds.), *Asia in Western Fiction*, Manchester, Manchester University Press, 1990.

Wurgaft, Lewis D., *The Imperial Imagination: Magic and Myth in Kipling's India*, Middletown, CT, Wesleyan University Press, 1983.

Yamanaka, Yuriko and Nishio, Tetsuo, *The Arabian Nights and Orientalism: Perspectives from East and West*, London, Tauris, 2006.

Yegenoglu, Meyda, *Colonial Fantasies: Towards a Feminist Reading of Orientalism*, Cambridge, Cambridge University Press, 1998.

Yohannan, John D., *Persian Poetry in England and America: A 200–Year History*, New York, Caravan Books, 1977.

Yokota-Murakami, Takayuki, *Don Juan East/West: On the Problematics of Comparative Literature*, Albany, New York State University Press, 1998.

Yosef, Eitan Bar-, *The Holy Land in English Culture 1799–1917: Palestine and the Question of Orientalism*, Oxford, Oxford University Press, 2005.

Yoshihara, Mari, *Embracing the East: White Women and American Orientalism*, Oxford, Oxford University Press, 2003.

Ziter, Edward, *The Orient on the Victorian Stage*, Cambridge, Cambridge University Press, 2003.

3

Articles and Conference Presentations on Literary Orientalism

Abdel-Hamid, M.S., 'Literature of Eastern Travel and the Romantic Movement', *Bulletin of the Faculty of Arts, University of Cairo*, 19 May 1957, 25–32.

Abdelwahed, Said T., 'Samuel Johnson's *Rasselas* and the Culture of the East', *Annals of the Faculty of Arts* (Ain Shams University), 24:ii, 1996–7, 69–78.

Abdul Muttaleb, Fuad, 'Sean O'Casey in the Arab World', *Research Journal of Aleppo University (Humanities)*, 21, 1991, 41–65.

Abu-Baker, Mohamed Hassan, 'The Representation of Islam in Medieval Western Narratives', *International Journal of Arabic English Studies*, 5, 2004, 45–58.

Ackland, Michael, 'Writing the East: Homosexuality and the Epic Endeavor of Harold Stewart', *Antipodes*, 15:1/2, 2001, 18–21.

Adolf, H., 'Christendom and Islam in the Middle Ages: New Light on "Grail Stone" and "Hidden Host"', *Speculum*, 32, 1957, 103–15.

Adolf, H., 'New Light on Oriental Sources for Wolfram's *Parzival* and Other Grail Romances', *PMLA,* 62: 2, 1947, 306–24.

Ahmad, Munir, 'From China to Peru: The Origin and Development of Southey's Mythological Poems', *Aligarh Journal of English Studies,* 12:2, 1987, 179–202.

Ahmed, Leila, 'Western Ethnocentrism and Perceptions of the Harem', *Feminist Studies,* 8:3, 1982, 524–5.

Akbari, Suzanne Conklin, 'Imagining Islam: The Role of Images in Medieval Depictions of Muslims', *Scripta Mediteterranea,* 19–20, 1998–9, 9–27.

Akbari, Suzanne Conklin, 'Dissimilarity or Assimi-lation: The Representation of the East in Middle English Romances', Presentation to the Annual Meeting of the Medieval Academy, 1996.

Akbari, Suzanne Conklin. 'Women as Mediator in Medieval Depictions of Muslims: The Case of Floripas', Paper presented at 'Marco Polo and the Encounter of East and West Conference', University of Toronto, 24 May 2002.

Albet-Mas, Abel, and Nogue-Font, Joan, 'Voices from the Margins: Gendered Images of "Otherness" in Colonial Morocco', *Gender, Place and Culture,* 5, 1998, 229–311.

Alexander, B., 'The Decay of Beckford's Genius' in Fatma Moussa Mahmoud (Ed), *William Beckford of Fonthill, 1760–1844,* Cairo, Dar al-Marifah, 1961.

Alfrey, Shawn H., '"Oriental Peaceful Penetration": Gertrude Stein and the End of Europe', *Massachusetts Review*, 38:3, 1997, 405–16.

Ali, Muhsin Jassim, '*The Arabian Nights* in Eighteenth-Century English Criticism', *Muslim World*, 67, 1977, 12–32.

Ali, Muhsin Jassim, '*Rasselas* as a Colonial Discourse', *Central Institute of English & Foreign Languages Bulletin*, 8:1, 1996, 47–60.

Ali, Muhsin Jassim, 'The Growth of Scholarly Interests in the *Arabian Nights*', *Muslim World*, 70, 3–4, 1980, 196–212.

Ali, Salah Salim, 'Ishraqi Themes in the Poetry and Prose of William Blake and William B. Yeats', *Hamdard Islamicus*, Karachi, Pakistan 16:iii, 1993, 37–61.

Allen, M.D., 'The New Path: English Women Travelers in the Middle East', *West Virginia University Philological Papers*, 40, 1994, 1–5.

Almond, Philip. 'Western Images of Islam, 1700–1900', *Australian Journal of Politics and History*, 49: 3, 2003, 412–24.

Alshetawi, Mahmoud F., 'Shakespeare's Journey into the Arab World: An Initial Bibliography', *Shakespeare Yearbook*, 13, 2002, 442–99.

Andrea, Bernadette, '"She that Spake to the Great Turk": Early Modern Englishwomen in the Ottoman Empire', Presented at the 'Comparative Literature Colloquia', Green College, University of British Columbia, 2 November 1995.

Andrea, Bernadette, 'English Women and Islam, 1610–1690', in Mihoko Suzuki (Ed.), *History of British Women's Writings, 1610–1690*, Forthcoming from Palgrave Macmillan.

Andrea, Bernadette, 'Lady Sherley: The "First" Persian in England?', in Nabil Matar and Bindu Malieckal (Eds.), *Muslim and Non-Muslim Women in the Empires of Islam, 1453–1798*, Special issue of *The Muslim World*, 95.2, 2005, 279–95.

Andrea, Bernadette, 'Renaissance Orientalist/Renaissance Orientalism? Edward Pococke, Chair of Arabic Studies, Oxford, 1636', Presented at 'Cornell University Graduate Student Conference', 7 April 1995.

Andrea, Bernadette, 'Travels Through Islam in Early Modern English Studies', *CLIO*, 35:2, 2006, 225–43.

Andrea, Bernadette, 'Women and their Rights: Fethullah Gulen's Gloss on Lady Montagu's *Embassy* to the Ottoman Empire', in Robert A. Hunt and Yuksel A. Aslandogan (Eds.), *Muslim Citizens of the Globalized World: Contributions of the Gulen Movement*, Somerset, NJ, The Light and IID Press, 2006, 137–54.

Andrea, Bernadette, 'The "Matter of Araby" in Seventeenth-Century England', Presented at the 'Fifth International Conference on the Seventeenth Century', Durham, England, 12–15 July 1993.

Anis, Mohammed, 'British Travellers' Impressions of Egypt in the Late Eighteenth Century', *Bulletin of the*

Faculty of Arts, University of Cairo, 13 December 1951, 9-37.

Anon, 'William Beckford and Islam', *Connoisseur*, 191, 1976, 250–3.

ApRoberts, Ruth, 'Mahomet, or Turning to the East' in Ruth ApRoberts, *The Ancient Dialect: Thomas Carlyle and Comparative Religion*, Berkeley, University of California Press, 1988, 87–101.

Arab, Si Abderrahmane, 'A Yankee Candide on the Barbary Shore: Royall Tyler's *The Algerine Captive, published in 1797'*, *Journal of Algerian Studies*, 2, 1997, 81–9.

Araci, Emre, '"Turkish" Imagery in Elizabethan Drama', *RNL*, 4, 1973, 82–98.

Araci, Emre, 'Turkish Women and the Amazons in English Renaissance Drama', *Bogazici University Journal, Humanities*, 7, 1979, 133–8.

Aravamudan, Srinivas, 'In the Wake of the Novel: The Oriental Tale as National Allegory', *Novel*, 33:1, 1999, 5–31.

Aravamudan, Srinivas, 'Lady Mary Worley Montagu in the *Hammam:* Masquerade, Womanliness, and Levantinization', *English Literature History*, 62, 1995, 69–104.

Arberry, Arthur John, 'Persian Jones', *Asiatic Review*, 40, 1944, 186–196.

Arberry, Arthur John, 'Oriental Pearls at Random Strung', *Bulletin of the School of Oriental and African Studies*, 11, 1946, 699–712.

Armistead, Samuel G., 'Science and Literature in the Middle Ages: England, Spain and the Arabs', *Hispanic Review,* 46: 2, 1978, 235–40.

Artemel, S., 'Where the Turk's Horse Once Treads...' *Notes and Queries,* 18, 1971, 216–23.

Ascari, Maurizio, 'The Role of Addison's Dream Visions and Oriental Tales in the Nascent Poetics of Short Fiction', *Textus,* 18:1, 2005, 11–23.

Asfour, Mohammad, 'Thomas Moore and the Pitfalls of Orientalism', *International Journal of Islamic and Arabic Studies,* Indiana, 4, 1, 1987, 1–12.

Athamneh, Naser and Brandabur, Clare, 'George Eliot's *Daniel Deronda*: Apartheid Utopia', *Abhath al-Yarmouk', Literature and Linguistics Series,* 20:i, 2002, 37–76.

Atherton, J.S., 'Islam and the Koran in *Finnegans Wake*', *Comparative Literature,* 1954, 240–55.

Attar, Samar, 'Serving God or Mammon? Echoes from Hayy Ibn Yaqzan and Sindbad the Sailor in *Robinson Crusoe*', in Brian Stimpson, (Ed.), *Robinson Crusoe: Myths and Metamorphoses,* London, Macmillan, 1996, 78–97.

Austin, Greta, 'Marvelous Peoples or Marvelous Races? Race and the Anglo-Saxon Wonders of the East', in Timothy S. Jones and David A. Sprunger (Eds.), *Marvels, Monsters, and Miracles: Studies in the Medieval and Early Modern Imaginations,* Kalamazoo, MI: Medieval Inst. Pubs, 2002, 25–51.

Avcioglu, Nebahat, 'The Ottomans and the Allegories of Tyranny in the Frontispiece to George Sandys' *A Relation of a Journey (1615)*', Presented at the Conference 'Between Empires: "Orientalism" Before 1600', Cambridge, 12–15 July 2001.

Aybet, Gülgûn Üçel, 'The Influence of Turkish Culture in the Literature, Music and Drama of Baroque England', in Hasan Celâl Güzel (et al.) (Ed.), *The Turks, 3: Ottomans,* Yeni Türkiye, 2002, 985–95.

Aycock, Roy E., 'Lord Byron and Bayle's *Dictionary*', *Year Book of English Studies,* 1975, 142–52.

Aydin, Kamil, 'Travel Writers and their Oriental Women', *The Fountain,* London, 1:2, 1993, 29–31.

Aydin, Kamil, 'Western Images of Muslim Turks Prior to the 20th Century: A Short Outline', *Hamdard Islamicus,* Karachi, Pakistan, 16:4, 1993, 103–25.

Aydin, Kamil, 'Western Presentation of the Ottoman Turks', *The Fountain,* London, 1:1, 1993, 7–10.

Azinfar, Fatemeh, 'The Saracens, *La Chanson de Roland,* and the Birth of Medieval Epic', *South Asian Review,* 19: 16, 1995, 25–31.

Azm El-, S.J., 'Orientalism and Orientalism in Reverse', *Khamsin,* 8, 5–26.

Babbit, Irving, 'Romanticism and the Orient', *Bookman,* 74, December 1931, 349–57.

Bach, E., 'Sheikh Fantasies: Orientalism and Desire in the Desert Romance', *Hecate*, St. Lucia, Queensland, Australia, 22:1, 1997, 9–40.

Bahti, Timothy, 'Figures of Interpretation, the Interpretation of Figures: A Reading of Wordsworth's Dream of the Arab', *Studies in Romanticism*, 18, 1979, 601–27.

Baird, James, 'Critical Problems in the Orientalism of Western Poetry', *Asia and the Humanities*, II, 38–65.

Bakay, Gönül, '21st Century Reflections on Images of the Turk in the Renaissance Literature of England', Presented at the Conference 1453 to 1699: Cultural Encounters between East and West', Institute of English Studies, London, 5–7 December 2002.

Baker, Ernest, 'The Oriental Tale from *Rasselas* to *Vathek*', in Ernest Baker (Ed.), *History of English Novel*, 5, 55–76.

Bakshi, Parminder Kaur, 'Homosexuality and Orientalism: Edward Carpenter's Journey to the East', *Prose Studies*, 13:1, 1990, 151–77.

Baldwin, Marshall W., 'Western Attitudes towards Islam', *Catholic Historical Review*, 27, 1942, 403–11.

Ballard, Roger, 'Islam and the Construction of Europe', in W.A.R. Shadid and P. S. Van Koningsveld (Eds.), *Muslims in the Margin: Political Response to the Presence of Islam in Western Europe*, Kampen, Kok Pharos, 1996, 15–51.

Ballaster, Ros, 'Orienting the English Novel: The Shaping Genius of the Eastern Tale in Eighteenth-Century Britain' in (Ed.), Jenny Mander, *Remapping the Rise of the European Novel*, Oxford, Voltaire Foundation, 2007, 237–48.

Ballaster, Ros, 'Performing Roxane: The Oriental Woman as the Sign of Luxury in Eighteenth-Century Fictions', in Maxine Berg and Elizabeth Eger (Eds.), *Luxury in the Eighteenth Century: Debates, Desires and Delectable Goods*, Basingstoke, Palgrave Macmillan, 2003, 165–77.

Banerjee, Pompa, 'The White Othello: Turkey and Virginia in John Smith's *True Travels*', in Robert Appelbaum and John Wood Sweet (Eds.), *Envisioning an English Empire: Jamestown and the Emergence of a North Atlantic World*, Philadelphia, University of Pennsylvania Press, 2005, 135–51.

Banerjee, Pompa, 'Milton's India and *Paradise Lost*', *Milton Studies*, 37, 1999, 142–65.

Baneth, Émilienne, '"Ship Me Somewhere East of Suez": Rudyard Kipling's Strange Exile from Himself', *Jouvert*, 6:1–2, 2001.

Barber, Malcolm, 'Confronting The Crusade: How the West Saw Medieval Islam', *History Today*, 47, 1997, 44–50.

Barber, Malcolm, 'Lepers, Jews and Moslems: The Plot to Overthrow Christendom in 1321', *History Today*, 66, 1981, 1–17.

Barbour, John D., 'The Ethics of Intercultural Travel: Thomas Merton's Asian Pilgrimage and Orientalism', *Biography*, 28:1, 2005, 15–26.

Barbour, John D., 'Thomas Merton's Pilgrimage and Orientalism', in Eric Ziolkowski(Ed.), *Literature, Religion, and East/West Comparison*, London, Assoc. University Presses, 2005, 243–59.

Barbour, Richmond, '"There is Our Commission": Writing and Authority in *Measure for Measure* and the London East India Company', *Journal of English and Germanic Philology*, 99:2, 2000, 193–214.

Barfield, Steven, '"Jewelinthecrown.co.uk": Orientalism's Strange Persistence in British South Asian Writing', in Silvia Nagy-Zekmi (Ed.), *Paradoxical Citizenship: Edward Said*, Lanham, MD, Lexington, 2006, 111–20.

Barnes, Rebecca, 'Steinbeck's East of Eden', *Explicator*, 55:3, 1997, 159–60.

Bartels, Emily C. 'The Double Vision of the East: Imperialist Self-Construction in Marlowe's *Tamburlaine*', *Renaissance Drama*, 23, 1992, 3–24.

Bartels, Emily C., 'Making More of the Moor: Aaron, Othello and Renaissance Refashioning of Race', *Shakespeare Quarterly*, 41, 1990, 433–54.

Bartels, Emily C., 'Malta, the Jew, and the Fictions of Difference: Colonialist Discourse in Marlowe's *The Jew of Malta*', *English Literary Renaissance*, 20, 1990, 1–16.

Bartels, Emily C., 'Othello and the Moor', in Garrett A. Sullivan, (et al.) (Eds.), *Early Modern English Drama: A Critical Companion*, Oxford, Oxford University Press, 2006, 140–51.

Bartholomeusz, Dennis, 'Shakespeare Imagines the Orient: The Orient Imagines Shakespeare', in Tetsuo Kishi (et al.) (Ed.), *Shakespeare and Cultural Traditions: The Selected Proceedings of the International Shakespeare Association World Congress*, Tokyo, 1991, London, Associated University Presses, 1994, 188–204.

Basker, James G., 'Multicultural Perspectives: Johnson, Race and Gender', in Philip Smallwood (Ed.), *Johnson Re-Visioned: Looking Before and After*, Lewisburg, Bucknell University Press, 2001, 64–79.

Bate, Jonathan, '*Othello* and the Other; or, Turning Turk: The Subtleties of Shakespeare's Treatment of Islam', *Times Literary Supplement*, 19 October 2001, 14–15.

Battenhouse, Roy W., '*Tamburlaine*'s Passions', in Clifford Leech (Ed.), *Marlowe: A Collection of Critical Essays*, New Jersey, Prentice-Hall Inc., 1964, 57–68.

Baumer, Franklin L., 'England, the Turk, and the Common Corps of Christendom', *American Historical Review*, 50: 1, 1944, 26–48.

Bausani, Alessandro, 'The Western European Image and the Response to Arab Civilization: A Historical Overview and an Interpretation', in Derek Hopwood (Ed.), *Euro-Arab Dialogue: The Relations Between the Two Cultures*,

London, Routledge Kegan & Paul, 1985, 45–59.

Bazi'i, Sa'd al-, 'The Revulsion Against Islam: Romanticist Critics and the East', *Abhath al-Yarmouk: Literature and Linguistics Series*, 15:i, 1997, 75–96.

Beatty, Bernard, 'Calvin in Islam: A Reading of *Lara* and *The Giaour*', *Romanticism*, 5:1, 1999, 70–86.

Beckingham, C.F., 'Misconceptions of Islam: Medieval and Modern', *Journal of the Royal Society of Arts*, 124, 1976, 606–11.

Behdad, Ali, 'Orientalism after *Orientalism*', *L'Esprit-Createur*, 34:2, 1994, 3–44.

Behdad, Ali, 'Colonial Narrative and its Discontents', *Victorian Literature and Culture*, 22, 1994, 233–48.

Behler, Ernst, 'Ideas of the "State of Nature" and "Natural Man" in the Arabic Tradition of the Middle Ages and Their Entrance into Western Thought', *Arcadia*, 3: 1, 1968, 1–26.

Bell, Elizabeth S., 'Dashing Off to Baghdad, A Sense of Place in a Piece of Time', *South Atlantic Review*, 61:4, 1996, 39–52.

Bell, Millicent, 'Shakespeare's Moor', *Raritan*, 21:4, 2002, 1–14.

Bellamy, James A., 'Arabic Names in *Chanson De Roland*: Saracen Gods, Frankish Swords, Roland's Horse, and the Olifant', *Journal of the American Oriental Society*, 107: 2, 1987, 267–77.

Ben Rejeb, Lotfi, 'Barbary's 'Character' in European Letters, 1514–1830: An Ideological Prelude to Colonization', *Dialectical Anthropology*, 6, 1982, 345–55.

Bennett, Matthew, 'First Crusaders' Images of Muslims: The Influence of Vernacular Poetry', *Forum for Modern Language Studies,* 22: 2, 1986, 101–22.

Berg, Maxine, 'Manufacturing the Orient: Asian Commodities and European Industry 1500–1800', in *Prodotti e tecniche d'oltremare neele economie europee secc. xiii-xvii,* Le Monnier, 1998, 185–419.

Berkaoui, Khalid, 'Colonial Irony: The Andalusian Moor in Congreve's *The Mourning Bride*', in Mohamed Dahbi, Mohamed Ezroura and Lahcen Haddad Rabat (Eds.), *Cultural Studies, Interdisciplinarity, and the University*, Morocco, Faculty of Letters and Human Sciences, 1996, 167–73.

Berland, Kevin, 'The Paradise Garden and the Imaginary East: Alterity and Reflexivity in British Oriental Romances', *Eighteenth Century Novel,* 2, 2002, 137–59.

Bernadette Andrea, 'Persia, Tartaria, and Pamphilia: Ideas of Asia in Mary Wroth's *Urania*', Forthcoming in Walter S. H. Lim and Debra Johanyak (Eds.), *The English Renaissance, Orientalism, and the Idea of Asia,* Palgrave MacMillan.

Bernadette Andrea, 'Islam, Women, and Western Responses: The Contemporary Relevance of Early Modern Investigations.' Forthcoming in *Women's Studies: An Interdisciplinary Journal.*

Bernard, Camille, 'Some Aspects of Delacroix's Orientalism', *Bulletin of the Cleveland Museum of Arts*, 58, April 1971, 123–7.

Beyer, W.W., 'Southey, Orientalism and *Thalaba*', in Warner W. Beyer, *The Enchanted Forest*, Oxford, 1963, 234–45.

Bhabha, Homi K., 'The Other Question ... The Stereotype and Colonial Discourse', *Screen*, 24:3, November/December 1993, 18–36.

Bhattacharya, N., 'Ethnopolitical Dynamics and the Language of Gendering in Dryden's *Aureng-Zebe*', *Cultural Critique*, 25, 1993, 152–76.

Birchwood, Matthew, 'Reforming the Turk and Reclaiming the Stage in William Devenant's *The Siege of Rhodes*', Presented at the 'Early Modern/ Renaissance Postgraduate Conference', University of Newcastle upon Tyne, 5–6 April 2001.

Birns, Nicholas, 'Christian-Islamic Relations in Dante and Chaucer: Reflections on Recent Criticism', in Joan E. Hallisey and Mary-Ann Vetterling (Eds.), *Proceedings: Northeast Regional Meeting of the Conference on Christianity and Literature*, Weston, MA, Regis College, 1996.

Blackstone, Bernard, 'Byron and Islam: The Triple Eros', *Journal of European Studies*, 4, 1974, 325–63.

Blanks, David R., 'Western Views of Islam in the Premodern Period; A Brief History of Past Approaches', in David R. Blanks and Michael Frassetto (Eds.), *Western Views of Islam in Medieval and Early Modern Europe: Perception of Other*, New York, St. Martin's Press, 1999, 11–53.

Bleeth, Kenneth A., 'Orientalism and the Critical History of Chaucer's *Squire's Tale*', in Kathryn L. Lynch (Ed.), *Chaucer's Cultural Geography*. London, Routledge, 2002, 21–31.

Boerth, Robert, 'The Mediterranean and the Mediterranean World on the Stage of Marlowe and Shakespeare', *Journal of Theatre and Drama*, 2, 1996, 35–58.

Bohls, Elizabeth A., 'Aesthetics and Orientalism in Lady Mary Wortley Montagu's *Letters*', *Studies in Eighteenth-Century Culture*, 23, 1994, 179–205.

Bohrer, Frederick N., 'The Sweet Waters of Asia: Representing Difference/ Differencing Representation in the Nineteenth Century', in Hackforth-Jones and Roberts (Eds.), *Edges of Empire: Orientalism and Visual Culture*, Oxford, Blackwell, 2004, 121–38.

Boone, Joseph A., 'Vacation Cruises; or, The Homoerotics of Orientalism', *Publications of the Modern Language Association of America*, 110:1, 1995, 89–107.

Bosworth, C.E., 'James Elroy Flecker: Poet, Diplomat, Orientalist', *Bulletin of the John Rylands University Library of Manchester*, 69, 1987, 359–78.

Bosworth, C. E., 'Arabic Influences in the Literature of Nineteenth and Early Twentieth Century Britain: Tradition and Modernity', in J.R. Smart (Ed.), *Arabic Language and Literature*, Richmond, Surrey, Curzon Press, 1996, 155–85.

Bowen, Roger, 'Closing the "Toybox": Orientalism and Empire in the *Alexandria Quartet*', *Studies in the Literary Imagination*, 24:1, 1991, 9–18.

Bowen, Roger, 'Investing in Conrad, Investing in the Orient: Margaret Drabble's *The Gates of Ivory*', *Twentieth Century Literature*, 45:3, 1999, 278–98.

Bowen, Roger, 'The Artist at His Papers': Durrell, Egypt, and the Poetry of Exile', *Twentieth Century Literature*, 33, 1987, 465–84.

Bowers, Terence, 'Robert Curzon, Orientalism, and the Ars Peregrinationis', *Victorian Institute Journal*, 33, 2005, 117–47.

Bradham, JoAllen, 'An Ass Charged with Books: Pope's *Dunciad* and the *Koran*', *South Atlantic Review*, 60:1, 1995, 1–15.

Brantlinger, Patrick, 'Nations and Novels: Disraeli, George Eliot, and Orientalism', *Victorian Studies*, 35:3, 1992, 255–75.

Brantlinger, Patrick, 'Thackeray's India', in Patrick Brantlinger (Ed.), *Rule of Darkness*, Ithaca, Cornell University Press, 73–107.

Brantlinger, Patrick, 'Victorians and Africans: The Genealogy of the Myth of the Dark Continent', in Henry Louis Gates Jr. (Ed.), *Race, Writing and Cultural Difference*, Chicago and London, Chicago University Press, 1985, 185–222.

Breckenridge, Carol A. and Veer, Peter van der, 'Orientalism and the Postcolonial Predicament Perspectives on South Asia', in Carol

A. Breckenridge and Peter van der Veer (Eds.), *Orientalism and the Postcolonial Predicament: Perspectives on South Asia,* Philadelphia, PA, USA, University of Pennsylvania Press, 1993, 1–19.

Breckwoldt, Inge C., 'The Effect of the Other: Saracens in Malory's *Morte DArthur*', Presented at 'Studientag zum Englischen Mittelalter, 5 March 2004, Friedrich-Schiller-Universitat, Jena.

Brennan, Timothy, 'The Illusion of a Future: Orientalism as Travelling Theory', *Critical Inquiry,* 26:3, 2000, 558–83.

Bringhurst, Robert, 'The Koran, the *Wake*, and Atherton', *Wake Newsletter,* December 1973, 92–3.

Brooks, Christopher, 'Goldsmith's *Citizen of the World*: Knowledge and The Imposture of "Orientalism"', *Texas Studies in Literature and Language*, 35:1, 1993, 124–44.

Brotton, Jerry, '"This Tunis, Sir, was Carthage": Contesting Colonialism in *The Tempest*', in Ania Loomba and Martin Orkin (Eds.), *Post-Colonial Shakespeare,* London, Routledge, 1998, 23–42.

Brotton, Jerry, 'Carthage and Tunis: *The Tempest* and Tapestries', in Peter Hulme and William H. Sherman. (Eds.), *'The Tempest' and Its Travels,* Philadelphia, University of Pennsylvania Press, 2000, 132–7.

Brown, Wallace C., 'Byron and English Interest in the Near East', *Studies in Philology,* 34, 1937, 55–64.

Brown, Wallace C., 'English Travel Books and Minor Poetry about the Near East, 1775–1825', *Philological Quarterly*, 16, 1937, 249–71.

Brown, Wallace C., 'Prose Fiction and English Interest in the Near East, 1775–1825', *PMLA*, 53, 1938, 827–36.

Brown, Wallace C., 'Robert Southey and the English Interest in the Near East', *Journal of English Literary History*, 5 September 1938, 218–24.

Brown, Wallace C., 'The Popularity of English Travel Books about the Near East, 1775–1825', *Philological Quarterly*, 15, 1936, 70–80.

Brown, Wallace C., 'Thomas Moore and English Interest in the East', *Studies in Philology*, 34, 1937, 578–88.

Brown, William J., 'Marlowe's Debasement of Bajazet: Foxe's *Actes and Monuments* and *Tamberlaine, Part I*', *Renaissance Quarterly*, 24, 1971, 38–48.

Buchan, James, 'Romancers Entwined: How T.E. Lawrence and John Buchan Invented One Another', *The Times Literary Supplement*, London, No. 4652, May 1992, 13–4.

Bullough, G., 'Beckford's Early Travels and His "Dream of Delusion"' in Fatma Mahmoud Moussa (Ed.), *William Beckford of Fonthill, 1760–1844*, Cairo, Dar al-Marifah, 1960.

Burian, Orhan, 'Interest of the English in Turkey as Reflected in English Literature of the Renaissance', *Oriens*, 5, 1952, 209–29.

Burley, Stephanie, 'The Death of Zofloya; or, The Moor as Epistemological Limit', in Ruth Bienstock Anolik and Douglas L. Howard (Eds.), *The Gothic Other: Racial and Social Constructions in the Literary Imagination,* London: McFarland, 2004, 197–211.

Burrow, J. A., '"Alterity" and Middle English Literature', *The Review of English Studies,* 50: 200, 1999, 483–93.

Burshatin, Israel, 'The Docile Image: The Moor as a Figure of Force, Subservience, and Nobility in the *Poema de mio Cid*', *Kentucky Romance Quarterly,* 31, 1984, 269–80.

Burshatin, Israel, 'The Moor in the Text: Metaphor, Emblem, and Silence', *Critical Inquiry,* 12, 1985, 98–118.

Burton, Jonathan H., 'A Most Wily Bird, Leo Africanus, *Othello* and the Trafficking in Difference', in Ania Loomba and Martin Orkin (Eds.), *Post-Colonial Shakespeare,* London, Routledge, 1998, 43–63.

Burton, Jonathan H., 'Anglo-Ottoman Relations and the Image of the Turk in *Tamburlaine*', *Journal of Medieval and Early Modern Studies,* 30: 1, 2000, 125–56.

Burton, Jonathan H., 'English Anxiety and the Muslim Power of Conversion: Five Perspectives on "Turning Turk" in Early Modern Texts', Presented at the 'Conference at the University of Michigan', 25 January 2002.

Bushrui, Suhiel Badi, 'Yeats's Arabic Interests' in A. Norman Jeffares and K.G.W. Cross (Eds.), *In*

Excited Reverie: A Centenary Tribute to W.B. Yeats, London, Macmillan, 1965, 280–314.

Bushrui, Suhiel Badi, 'Yeats, India, Arabia, and Japan: The Search for a Spiritual Philosophy', in W. Zach and H. Kosok (Eds.), *Literary Interrelations: Ireland, England and the World, 2: Comparison and Impact*. Tübingen, Narr, 1987, 221–34.

Butler, Beverley, 'Egypt: Constructed Exiles of the Imagination' in B. Bender and M. Winer *(Ed.)*, *Contested Landscapes: Movement, Exile and Place*, Oxford, Berg, 2001, 303–17.

Butler, Marilyn, 'Byron and the Empire in the East', in Andrew Rutherford (Ed.), *Byron: Augustan and Romantic*, London, 1990, 63–81.

Butler, Marilyn, 'Orientalism' in David B. Pirie (Ed.) *The Penguin History of Literature: Romantic Period*, London, Penguin, 1994, 394–447.

Butler, Marilyn, 'Plotting the Revolution: The Political Narratives of Romantic Poetry and Criticism', in Kenneth R. Johnston (et al.) (Eds.), *Romantic Revolutions: Criticism and Theory*, Bloomington, 1990, 133–57.

Butler, Marilyn, 'The Orientalism of Byron's *Giaour*', in Bernard Beatty and Vincent Newey (Eds.), *Byron and the Limits of Fiction*, Liverpool, 1988, 78–96.

Caesar, Judith, 'Arabs in Contemporary American Literature: Cultural Violence and Brand-Name Bigotry', *North Dakota Quarterly*, 61:3, 1993, 79–90.

Calbi, Maurizio, '"Unshap't Bodies": Masculinity Travels East', Paper Presented at the Conference '1453 to 1699: Cultural Encounters between East and West', Institute of English Studies, London, 5–7 December 2002.

Calkin, Siobhain Bly, 'Defining Christian Knighthood in a Saracen World: Changing Depictions of the Protagonist in *Sir Bevis of Hampton*" in Jennifer Fellows and Ivana Djordjevic (Eds.), *A Companion to Bevis of Hampton*, Cambridge, Boydell and Brewer, 2008, 127–42.

Calkin, Siobhain Bly, 'Marking Religion on the Body: Saracens, Categorization, and *The King of Tars*', *Journal of English and Germanic Philology*, 104: 2, 2005, 219–39.

Calkin, Siobhain Bly, 'Muslim, Christian, and Christian: Saracens, 'Gregeys' and Guy's 'meyne' *Guy of Warwick*', 42nd International Congress on Medieval Studies, Kalamazoo, Michigan, 10–13 May 2007.

Calkin, Siobhain Bly, 'Saracens, Saints, and Lumps of Flesh: Thinking the Issues of English Identity in Eastern Contexts in the Auchinleck Manuscript', Invited Lecture at the University of Texas at Arlington, 11 April 2005.

Calkin, Siobhain Bly, 'The Anxieties of Encounter and Exchange: Saracens and Christian Heroism in *Sir Beves of Hamtoun*', *Florilegium*, 21, 2004, 135–58.

Calkin, Siobhain Bly, 'Violence, Saracens, and English Identity in *Of Arthur and of Merlin*', *Arthuriana*, 14: 2, 2004, 17–36.

Cameron, Kenneth N. 'A Major Source of *The Revolt of Islam*', *PMLA*, 56, 1941, 175–206.

Campbell, Charles, 'Johnson's Arab: Anti-Orientalism in *Rasselas*', *Abhath al-Yarmouk Literature and Linguistics*, 12:1, 1994, 51–66.

Campbell, Mary B., 'On Renaissance Voyage Literature and Ethnographic Pleasure', *Studies in Travel Writing*, I, 1997, 216–38.

Campbell, Mary B., 'Shakespeare's Use of the Voyagers in *The Tempest*', *PMLA*, 41: 3, 1926, 688–726.

Cannon, Garland, 'Jones's Founding and Directing of the Asiatic Society', *British Library India Office Library and Records Report for 1984–85*, 11–28.

Cannon, Garland, 'Orientalism and Sir William Jones', *Michigan Alumnus Quarterly Review*, 62:10, 1955, 70–8.

Cannon, Garland, 'Sir William Jones and Literary Orientalism', in C.C. Barfoot and Theo D'haen (Eds.), *Oriental Perspectives: Western Literature and the Lure of the East*, Amsterdam, Rodopi, 1998, 27–41.

Cannon, Garland, 'Sir William Jones's Persian Linguistics', *Journal of the American Oriental Society*, 78, 1958, 262–73.

Cannon, Garland, 'The Construction of the European Image of the Orient: A Bicentenary Reappraisal of Sir William Jones as Poet and Translator', *Comparative Criticism*, 8, 1986, 167–88.

Cantarino, V., 'Dante and Islam: History and Analyses of a Controversy', in William De and Gino Rizzu (Eds.), *A Dante Symposium in Commemoration of 700th Anniversary of the Poet's Birth (1265–1965)*, Chapel Hill, University of North Carolina Press, 1965, 175–98.

Caraher, Brian G., 'A "Ruin of all Space, Shattered Glass and Toppling Masonry": Joyce's Orientalism in the Context of 11 September 2001 and 1922', *Textual Practice*, 18:4, 2004, 497–520.

Cardwell, Richard A., 'Byron and the Orient: Appropriation or Speculation', in Peter Cochran (Ed.), *Byron and Orientalism*, Cambridge, Cambridge Scholars, 2006, 152–74.

Carnall, Goeffrey, 'A Note on Southey's Later Religious Opinions', *Philological Quarterly*, 31, 1952, 399–406.

Carnicelli, D. D., 'The Widow and the Phoenix: Dido, Carthage, and Tunis in *The Tempest*', *Harvard Library Bulletin*, 27, 1979, 389–433.

Carver, James E., 'The Northern Homily Cycle, and Missionaries to the Saracens', *Modern Language Notes*, 53: 4, 1938, 258–61.

Cass, Jeffrey, ''The Scraps, Patches, and Rags of Daily Life': Gaskell's Oriental Other and the Conservation of Cranford', *Papers on Language and Literature*, 35:4, 1999, 417–33.

Cass, Jeffrey, 'Homoerotics and Orientalism in William Beckford's *Vathek*: Liberalism and the Problem of Pederasty', in Diane Long Hoeveler and

Jeffrey Cass (Eds.), *Interrogating Orientalism: Contextual Approaches and Pedagogical Perspectives*, Columbus, Ohio State University Press, 2006, 107–20.

Cass, Jeffrey, 'Interrogating Orientalism: Theories and Practices', in Diane Long Hoeveler and Jeffrey Cass (Eds.), *Interrogating Orientalism: Contextual Approaches and Pedagogical Perspectives*, Columbus, Ohio State University Press, 2006, 25–45.

Cass, Jeffrey, 'Miltonic Orientalism: Jane Eyre and the two Dalilas', *Dickens Studies Annual*, 33, 2003, 191–213.

Chandler, David, 'Robert Southey and *The Prelude's* "Arab Dream"', *Review of English Studies*, 54:214, 2003, 203–19.

Chang, Juliana, '"I Cannot Find Her": The Oriental Feminine, Racial Melancholia, and Kimiko Hahn's *The Unbearable Heart*', *Meridians*, 4:2, 2004, 239–60.

Charry, Brinda, 'Saint, Knight, Pilgrim: Christian Masculinity in the Islamic World', Presented at the 'Group for Early Modern Cultural Studies Conference', 2002.

Chejne, Anwar, 'The Role of al-Andalus in the Movement of Ideas Between Islam and the West', in Khalil I. Semaan (Ed.), *Islam and the Medieval West: Aspects of Inter-Cultural Relations*, Albany, New York, State University of New York, 1980, 114–20.

Chitty, C. W., 'Aliens in England in the Sixteenth Century', *Race,* 8, 1996, 129–45.

Christensen, Jerome, 'Perversion, Parody and Cultural Hegemony: Lord Byron's Oriental Tales', *South Atlantic Quarterly,* 88, Summer 1989, 570–603.

Christison, Katheline, 'The Arab in Recent Popular Fiction', *Middle East Journal,* 41, 1987, 397–411.

Chubbuck, Katharine, '"Ah! That the Desert Were My Dwelling Place": The Romance of Persia in the Early Writings of Gertrude Bell', in Paul and Janet Starkey (Eds.), *Interpreting the Orient: Travellers in Egypt and the Near East,* Reading, Ithaca, 2001, 199–207.

Cirakman, Asli, 'From Tyranny to Despotism; the Enlightenment's Unenlightened Image of the Turks', *International Journal of Middle East Studies,* Cambridge, UK, 33:1, 2001, 49–68.

Clark, G.N., 'Barbary Corsairs in the Seventeenth Century', *Cambridge Historical Journal,* 8, 1945–6, 22–35.

Clark, Robert L.A., 'Queering Orientalism: The East as Closet in Said, Ackerley, and the Medieval Christian West', *Medieval Encounters,* 5:3, 1999, 336–49.

Clarke, Blake, 'The Orient in England as Reflected in Eighteenth Century Drama', *Bulletin of Vanderbilt University,* 37, 1937, 7–8.

Cleary, Thomas R., 'Fielding's First Assault on George Whitefield and Parson Adams' 'Good Turk'', *New Rambler,* 1974, 40–6.

Clegg, Cyndia Susan, 'English Renaissance Books on Islam and Shakespeare's *Othello*', *Pacific Coast Philology*, 41, 2006, 1–12.

Cochran, Peter, 'Byron's and "Tully's Tripoli"', *Byron Journal*, 20, 1992, 77–88.

Cochran, Peter, 'Byron's Orientalism', in Peter Cochran (Ed.), *Byron and Orientalism*, Cambridge, Cambridge Scholars, 2006, 1–33.

Cochran, Peter, 'Harold Goes to Hell: The Orientalism of *Childe Harold's Pilgrimage*', in Peter Cochran (Ed.), *Byron and Orientalism*, Cambridge, Cambridge Scholars, 2006, 34–66.

Cochran, Peter, 'Studies of Byron's Orientalism', in Peter Cochran (Ed.), *Byron and Orientalism*, Cambridge, Cambridge Scholars, 2006, 67–151.

Cohen, Jeffrey Jerome, 'On Saracen Enjoyment: Some Fantasies of Race in Late Medieval France and England', *Journal of Medieval and Early Modern Studies*, 31: 1, 2001, 113–46.

Cole, R., 'Sixteenth-century Travel Books as a Source of European Attitudes toward Non-White and Non-Western Culture', *Proceedings of the American Philosophical Society*, 116, 1972, 59–67.

Coleman, Daniel, 'Masculinity's Severed Self: Gender and Orientalism in Out of Egypt and Running in the Family', *Studies in Canadian Literature/ Études en Littérature Canadienne*, 18:2, 1993, 62–80.

Colish, Marcia L., 'The Virtuous Pagan: Dante and the Christian Tradition', in Jaroslav Jan Pelikan, Duncan Fisher and William Caffero (Eds.), *The Unbounded Community, Papers in Christian Ecumenism in Honour of Jaroslav Pelikan,* New York, Garland, 1996, 43–92.

Collins, Kris, 'White-Washing the Black-a-Moor: Othello, Negro Minstrely and Parodies of Blackness', *Journal of American Culture,* 19:3, 1996, 87–101.

Comfort, William Wistar, 'The Literary Role of the Saracens in the French Epic', *Publications of the Modern Language Association,* 55, 1940, 621–59.

Conger, S. M., 'Maternal Negotiations with the Underworld: Origins and Ends in William Beckford's *Vathek* and Mary Shelley's *Proserpine*', in Werner Schneiders, Jane Godden (et al.) (Eds.), *Transactions of the Ninth International Congress on the Enlightenment Münster ... 1995,* vol. I, Oxford: Voltaire Foundation, 1996, 448–51.

Cook, G., 'The Poetry of High Imperialism:. Sir Alfred Lyall and the British Raj in India', The Islamic Monologues, *International Journal of Indian Studies,* 3:i, 1993, 69–83.

Cordery, Leona F., 'The Saracens in Middle English Literature: A Definition of Otherness', *Al-Masâq: Islam and the Medieval Mediterranean,* 14:ii, 2002, 87–99.

Corporaal, Marguérite, '"Moor, She Was Chaste, She Loved Thee, Cruel Moor": *Othello* as a Starting Point for Alternative Dramatic Representations of the Female Voice', *Comitatus*, 33, 2002, 99–111.

Cruz, Jo Ann Hoeppner Moran, 'Popular Attitudes Towards Islam in Medieval Europe', in David R. Blanks and Michael Frassetto (Eds.), *Western Views of Islam in Medieval and Early Modern Europe: Perception of Other*, New York, St. Martin's Press, 1999, 55–81.

Cunninghan, J.S. and Warren, Roger, '*Tamburlaine the Great* Rediscovered', in John Russell Brown (Ed.), *Marlowe: Tamburlaine the Great, Edward the Second and the Jew of Malta*, London, Macmillan, 1982, 139.

Da'mi Al-, Muhammed A., 'Mistaking the *Arabian Nights* for Socio-Historical Document', *al-Ma'thurat al-Sha'biyyah*, Doha, Qatar, 49, January 1998, 7–19.

Da'mi Al-, Muhammed A., 'On Carlyle's Concept of the Arab-Islamic Orient: A Study in *The Hero as Prophet*', in Muhsin Al-Musawi (Ed.), *Orientalism*, 2, Baghdad, Cultural Affairs, 1987, 62–86.

Da'mi Al-, Muhammed A., 'Orientalism and Arab-Islamic History: An Inquiry into Orientalists' Motives and Compulsions', *Arab Studies Quarterly*, 20:4, 1998, 1–10.

Da'mi Al-, Muhammed A., 'Some Aspects of the *Arabian Nights'* Impact on Nineteenth-Century American Culture', *Al-Ma'thurat al-Sha'biyyah*, 31, 1993, 7–16.

Da'mi al-Muhammed A., 'Arab Heroism for Victorian Britain: Carlyle's Contrasts of Faith and Doubt', in Muhammed al-Da'mi, *Arabian Mirrors and Western Soothsayers*, New York, Lang, 2002, 65–98.

Dabbagh Al-, Abdallah, 'Orientalism and Literary Translation', *Dirasat*, Amman, Jordan, 22:2, 1995, 21–32.

Dabbagh Al-, Abdullah, 'Orientalism and Literary Orientalism', in Muhsin Al-Musawi (Ed.), *Orientalism*, vol. IV, Baghdad, Cultural Affairs, 1990, 14–24.

Dabbagh Al-, Abdullah, 'Shakespeare's Orientalism: *Hamlet, King Lear* and Sufism', Presented at the Conference 'Between Empires: "Orientalism" Before 1600', Cambridge, 12–15 July 2001.

Dabbagh Al-, Abdullah, 'The Oriental framework of *Romeo and Juliet*', *Comparatist*, 24, 2000, 64–82.

Dabbagh Al-, Abdullah, 'The Oriental Sources of Courtly Love', *International Journal of Arabic English Studies*, 3, 2002, 21–32.

Daffron, Eric, 'Disorienting the Self: The Figure of the White European Man in Byron's Oriental Tales and Travels', in Jay Losey and William D. Brewer (Eds.), *Mapping Male Sexuality: Nineteenth-Century England*, Madison, NJ, Fairleigh Dickinson University Press, 2001, 69–90.

Dahab, F. Elizabeth, 'Beginning, Orientalism, and After: On Edward Said (1935–2003)', *Canadian Review of Comparative Literature/Revue*

Canadienne de Littérature Comparée, 29:4, 2002, 552–67.

Dale, Leigh and Gilbert, Helen, 'Looking the Same? A Preliminary (Post-Colonial) Discussion of Orientalism and Occidentalism in Australia and Japan', *Yearbook of Comparative and General Literature*, 41, 1993, 35–50.

Daniel, Norman, 'The Development of the Christian Attitude to Islam', *Dublin Review*, Winter, 1957/8.

Dannenfeldt, K.H., 'The Renaissance Humanists and the Knowledge of Arabic', *Studies in the Renaissance*, 2, 1955, 142–64.

Danson, Lawrence, 'England, Islam, and the Mediterranean: *Othello* and Others', *Journal of Early Modern Cultural Studies*, 2002, 1–25.

Davis, Kathleen, 'Time Behind the Veil: The Media, the Middle Ages and Orientalism', in Jeffery Jerome Cohen (Ed.), *The Postcolonial Middle Ages*, New York, St. Martin's Press, 2000, 105–22.

Degenhardt, Jane, 'From Body to Symbol, (or Castration to Re-virgination): The Limits of Faith in Massinger's "*The Renegado*"', Paper presented at the Conference '1453 to 1699: Cultural Encounters between East and West', Institute of English Studies, London, 5–7 December 2002.

Degenhardt, Jane, 'Catholic Martyrdom in Dekker and Massinger's *The Virgin Martir* and the Early

Modern Threat of "Turning Turk"', *ELH*, 73:1, 2006, 83–117.

Delany, Sheila, 'Chaucer's Orientalism in the Legend', Presented at the 'New York Medieval Club Conference', 1995.

Delany, Sheila, 'Chaucer's Prioress, the Jews and the Muslims', *Medieval Encounters,* 5: 2, 1999, 198–213.

Delany, Sheila, 'Geographies of Desire: Orientalism in the *Legend of Good Women*', *Chaucer Yearbook: A Journal of Late Medieval Studies,* 1, 1992, 1–32.

Deledalle-Rhodes, Janice, 'The True Nature of Doughty's Relationship with the Arabs' in Stephen E. Tabachnic (Ed.), *Explorations in Doughty's Arabia Deserta,* Athens, University of Georgia Press, 1987, 111–29.

Dellal, Mohamed, 'Tangier: An Exotic Haven, or Achilles' Heel', in R. Kevin Lacey (Ed.), *Mirrors on the Maghrib,* State University of New York at Binghamton, 1996, 17–27.

DelPlato, Joan, 'A English "Feminist" in the Turkish Harem: A Portrait of Lady Mary Wortley Montagu', in Frederick M. Keener and Susan E. Lorsch (Eds.), *Eighteenth-Century Women and the Arts,* Greenwood, IL, 1988, 163–78.

Demata, Massimiliano, 'A Bibliography of Byron's Oriental Reading: Addenda and Corrections', *Notes and Queries,* 46:1, 1999, 39–41.

DeMott, Robert, 'Steinbeck's Other Family: New Light on East of Eden' *Steinbeck Newsletter*, 7:1, 1994, 1–4.

Dent, Robert W., 'The Love-sick King: Turk Turned Dane', *Modern Language Review*, 56, October 1961, 555–7.

Denuccio, Jerome D., 'Fact, Fiction, Fatality: Poe's "The Thousand-and-Second Tale of Scheherazade"', *Studies in Short Fiction*, 27, 1990, 365–70.

DePanizza, Lorch Maristella, 'Honest Iago and the Lusty Moor: The Humanistic Drama of Honestas/ Voluptas in a Shakespearean Context', in J.R. Mulryne and M. Shewring (Eds.), *Theatre of the English and Renaissance*, Basingstoke, Macmillan, 1991, 204–20.

DeWind, John S., 'The Empire as Metaphor: England and the East in The Mystery of Edwin Drood', *Victorian Literature and Culture*, 21, 1993, 169–89.

Dickey, Jerry R., '"Myths of the East, Myths of the West": Shattering Racial and Gender Stereotypes in the Plays of David Henry Hwang', in Barbara Howard Meldrum (Ed.), *Old West - New West: Centennial Essays*, Moscow, Idaho University Press, 1993, 272–80.

Dimmock, Matthew, 'Machomet Dyd before as Luther Doth Nowe': Islam, the Ottomans and the English Reformation', *Reformation* vol. IX, 2004, 99–130.

Dimmock, Matthew, 'Swapping the "Geneua Bible" for the "Turkish Alcoran": *The Battle of Alcazar* and Early English Representations of the Ottoman Turk', Presented at the 'Early Modern/ Renaissance Postgraduate Conference',

University of Newcastle upon Tyne, 5–6 April 2001.

Dine, Philip, 'Anglo-Saxon Literary and Filmic Representations of the French Army in Algeria', in Martin S. Alexander, Martin Evans and J.F.V. Keiger (Eds.), *The Algerian War and the French Army, 1954–62: Experiences, Images, Testimonies*, Basingstoke, Palgrave Macmillan, 2002, 137–51.

Disuqi, Rasha al-, 'Orientalism in *Moby Dick*', *The American Journal of Islamic Social Sciences*, 4:1, 1987, 117–25.

Dombrowsk, Rosemarie, 'Amalgamated Otherness: Caliban and the Colonialist Agenda of Elizabethan Travel Literature and Ethnography', Presented at the 'Rocky Mountain Medieval Renaissance Association Conference', 23–5 May 2002, University of Nevada, Las Vegas.

Douglas, Christopher, 'Tracking "The Wild Man of the Green Swamp": Orientalism, Clichés, and The Preoccupation of Language', *English Studies in Canada*, 23:3, 1997, 331–55.

Dowden, W.S., 'The Source of the Metermpsychosis in Southey's *Thalaba*', *Modern Language Notes*, 66, 1951, 555–6.

Draper, John W., 'Milton's Ormus', *Modern Language Review*, 20, 1925, 323–7.

Draper, John W., 'Shakespeare and Barbary', in John W. Draper (Ed.), *Orientalia and Shakespeareana*, New York, Vantage Press, 129–38.

Draper, John W., 'Shakespeare and the Turk', *Journal of English and Germanic Philology*, October 1956, 55, 523–32.

Draper, John W., 'Shelley and Arabic-Persian Lyric Style', in John W. Draper (Ed.), *Orientalia and Shakespeareana*, New York, Vantage Press, 184–8.

Draper, John W., 'Shakespeare and Abbas the Great', *Philological Quarterly*, 30, 1951, 410–25.

Drogin, David J., 'Inhabiting Representation: Ottoman Manipulation of European Images of the Turk', Presented at the Conference 'Between Empires: "Orientalism" Before 1600', Cambridge, 12–15 July 2001.

Drukker, Tamar, 'The East in Late-Medieval English Historiography', Presented at the Conference 'Between Empires: "Orientalism" Before 1600', Cambridge, 12–15 July 2001.

Dubino, Jeanne, 'Turkish Tales: Mary Wortley Montagu's *Turkish Embassy Letters* and Virginia Woolf's *Orlando*', *Selected Papers from the Annual Conference on Virginia Woolf*, 12, 2003.

Dutton, M., and Williams, Peter, 'Translating Theories: Edward Said on Orientalism, Imperialism and Alterity', *Southern Review*, Australia, 26:3, 1993, 314–57.

Dyer, Gary R., 'The "Vanity Fair" of Nineteenth-Century England: Commerce, Women, and the East in the Ladies' Bazaar', *Nineteenth-Century Literature*, 46:2, September 1991, 197–222.

Eade, John, 'Muslims in a "Green and Pleasant Land"; or, Who Belongs Where?' *Critical Survey*, 7:2, 1995, 172–82.

Edelman, Charles, '*The Battle of Alcazar*, Muly Mollocco, and Shakespeare's *2 and 3 Henry VI*', *Notes and Queries*, 2002, 196–7.

Edwards, Brian T., 'Yankee Pashas and Buried Women: Containing Abundance in 1950s Hollywood Orientalism', *Film and History*, 31:2, 2001, 13–24.

Ehrlich, Heyward, 'Araby in Context: The "Splendid Bazaar" Irish Orientalism, and James Clarence Mangan', *James Joyce Quarterly*, 35:2/3, 1998, 309–31.

Ekelbald, Inga-Stina, '*King Lear* and Selimus', *Notes and Queries*, May 1957, 193–4.

Ekhtiar, Shelly, 'Hayy ibn Yaqzan: the Eighteenth Century Reception of an Oriental Self-Taught Philospher', *Studies on Voltaire and the Eighteenth Century*, 302, 1992, 217–45.

Elsie, R., Benjamin Disraeli and Scanderbeg, 'The Novel "*The Rise of Iskander*" (1833) as a Contribution to Britain's Literary Discovery of Albania', *Südost-Forschungen*, 52, 1993, 25–52.

Enamul Karim, Md., 'The East in Shakespeare's Tragedies', in Syed Sajjad Hussain (Ed.) *Homage to Shakespeare*, Dacca, Bangladesh, Department of English, Dacca University, 1965, 60–70.

Escott, Angela, 'The Imperial Project: Resistance and Revolution in Hannah Cowley's Oriental

Musical Comedy', *Restoration and 18th Century Theatre Research,* 20:1/2, 2005, 80–96.

Euridge, Gareth M., 'Before Orientalism: The Allure of Islam in Renaissance England', Presented at Modern Language Association, Chicago, 27–9 December 1995.

Euridge, Gareth M., 'Conversion to Islam in English Renaissance Thought', Presented at National Social Science Association, Memphis, Tennessee, 14–16 November 1991.

Euridge, Gareth M., 'Islam in Interregnum and Restoration England', *The Seventeenth Century,* 6, 1991, 57–71.

Euridge, Gareth M., 'Muslims in Seventeenth-Century England', *Journal of Islamic Studies,* 8, 1997, 63–82.

Euridge, Gareth M., 'Renaissance England and Images of Sexuality among the Turks', Presented at the 'Carolinas Symposium on British Studies', Norfolk, Virginia, 15–16 October 1994.

Euridge, Gareth M., 'The East is a Foreign Country; They Do Things Similarly There: Internationalizing the Tudor Myth on the Elizabethan Stage', Presented at the Conference 'Between Empires: "Orientalism" Before 1600', Cambridge, 12–15 July 2001.

Euridge, Gareth M., 'The Renegade in English Seventeenth-Century Imagination', *Studies in English Literature,* 33, 1993, 489–505.

Euridge, Gareth M., 'The Representation of Muslim Women in the English Renaissance', *The Muslim World,* 86, 1996, 50–61.

Euridge, Gareth M., 'The Status of Muslims in Renaissance England', Presented at the 'Sixth International Conference on the Seventeenth Century', University of Durham, England, 24–7 July 1995.

Euridge, Gareth M., 'The Taming of the Turk', Presented at National Social Science Association, San Antonio, Texas, 10–12 November 1993.

Euridge, Gareth M., 'The Traveller as Captive: The Allure of Islam in Renaissance England', *Literature, Interpretation, Theory,* 7, 1996, 187–96.

Euridge, Gareth M., '"Turning Turk": Conversion to Islam in English Renaissance Thought', *Durham University Journal,* 86, 1994, 33–43.

Euridge, Gareth M., 'England and Islam in the Seventeenth Century', Presented at the American University in Cairo, 5 May 1996.

Euridge, Gareth M., 'Muslims in Early Modern England', Presented at the University of Delaware, 27 February 1996.

Euridge, Gareth M., 'The Comenian Legacy in England: The Case for the Conversion of the Muslims', Presented at Johann Amos Comenius: Educator, Philosopher, Theologian, Clark Library, U.C.L.A., 6–7 November 1992.

Evenson, Jennie M., 'Abundance, Trade, and Divine Will in The Travels of Sir John Mandeville',

Presented at the Conference 'Between Empires: "Orientalism" Before 1600', Cambridge, 12–15 July 2001.

Everett, Barbra, '"Spanish" Othello: The Making of Shakespeare's Moor', *Shakespeare Survey,* 35, 1982, 101–12.

Eversole, Richard, 'Imlac and the Poets of Persia and Arabia', *Philological Quarterly,* 58, 1979, 155–70.

Fallon, David, '"That Angel Who Rides on the Whirlwind": William Blake's Oriental Apotheosis of William Pitt', *Eighteenth-Century Life,* 31:2, 2007, 1–28.

Feinstein, Blossom, 'The *Faerie Queene* and Cosmogonies of the Near East', *Journal of the History of Ideas,* 29: 4, 1968, 531–50.

Fernea, Elizabeth Warnock, 'An Early Ethnographer of Middle Eastern Women: Lady Mary Wortley Montagu (1689–1762)', *Journal of Near Eastern Studies,* 40, 1981, 329–38.

Finkelstein, Dorothee, '"The Code of Chaucer's Secree of Secrees": Arabic Alchemical Terminology in the Canon's *Yeoman's Tale', Archiv fur das Studium der Neueren Sprachen und Literaturn,* 207, 1970, 260–76.

Flanagan, Kathleen, 'The Orient as Pretext for Aesthetic and Cultural Revolution in Modern American Poetry', in Carol Colatrella (Ed.), *Cohesion and Dissent in America,* Albany, State University of New York Press, 1994, 114–29.

Fleck, Richard F., 'Samuel Johson's *Rasselas*: A Perspective on Islam', *Weber Studies,* 10:1, Winter 1993, 50–7.

Fleissner, Robert F., 'The Moor's Nomenclature', *Notes and Queries*, 25, 1978, 143.

Fletcher, Robert P., '"Heir of all the Universe": Evolutionary Epistemology in Mathilde Blind's Birds of Passage: Songs of the Orient and Occident', *Victorian Poetry*, 43:4, 2005, 435–53.

Floyd-Wilson, Mary, 'Moors, Race, and the Study of English Renaissance Literature; A Brief Retrospective', *Literature Compass*, 3 July 2006, Online.

Folsom, James K., 'Beckford's *Vathek* and the Tradition of Oriental Satire', *Criticism*, 6, 1964, 53–69.

Foster, Shirley, 'Colonialism and Gender in the East: Representations of the Harem in the Writings of Women Travellers', *Yearbook of English Studies*, 34, 2004, 6–17.

Francaviglia, Richard, 'Crusaders and Saracens: the Persistence of Orientalism in Historically Themed Motion Pictures About the Middle East', in Richard Francaviglia and Jerry Rodnitzky (Eds.), *Lights, Camera, History: Portraying the Past in Film*, Texas, A&M University Press, 2007, 53–90.

Frank, Frederick, 'A Checklist of *Vathek* Criticism', in Kenneth W. Graham (Ed.), *Vathek and the Escape from Time: Bicentenary Revaluations*, New York, AMS, 247–68.

Franklin, Caroline, 'Juan's Sea Changes: Class, Race and Gender in Byron's *Don Juan*' in Nigel Wood (Ed.), *Don Juan, Theory in Practice Series,* London, Open University Press, 1993, 56–89.

Franklin, Caroline, 'Quiet Cruising o'er the Ocean Woman': Byron's *Don Juan* and the Woman Question, *Studies in Romanticism*, 29:4, Winter 1990, 603–31.

Franklin, Caroline, '"Some Samples of the Finest Orientalism": Byronic Philhellenism and Proto-Zionism at the time of the Congress of Vienna', in Tim Fulford (Ed.), *Romanticism and Colonialism: Writing and Empire, 1780–1830*, Cambridge, Cambridge University Press, 1998, 221–42.

Franklin, Michael J., 'Accessing India: Orientalism, anti-Indianism', and the Rhetoric of Jones and Burke', in Tim Fulford (Ed.), *Romanticism and Colonialism: Writing and Empire, 1780–1830*, Cambridge, Cambridge University Press, 1998, 48–66.

Franklin, Michael J., '"And the Celt knew the Indian": Sir William Jones, Oriental Renaissance and Celtic Revival', in Gerard Carruthers and Alan Rawes (Eds.), *English Romanticism and the Celtic World* , Cambridge, University of Cambridge Press, 2003, 20–37.

Franklin, Michael J., 'Cultural Possession, Imperial Control, and Comparative Religion: The Calcutta Perspectives of Sir William Jones and Nathaniel Brassey Halhed', *Yearbook of English Studies*, 32, 2002, 1–18.

Franklin, Michael J., '"I burn with a desire of seeing Shiraz": A New Letter from Sir William Jones to Harford Jones', *Review of English Studies,* N.S. 56:227, 2005, 748–56.

Franklin, Michael J., 'Orientalism: Literature and Scholarship' for the *Encyclopaedia of the Romantic Era* 1760–1850, (Ed.) Christopher Murray, New York and London, Fitzroy Dearborn, 2:832–5, 2004.

Franklin, Michael J., '"Passion's Empire": Sydney Owenson's "Indian Venture", Phoenicianism, Orientalism, and Binarism', *Studies in Romanticism,* 45:2, 2006, 181–97.

Franklin, Michael J., 'Sir William Jones and Asiatick Society of Bengal for *South Asian Literature in English: An Encyclopaedia',* Jaina C. Sanga, Westport, CT, and London, Greenwood, 2004, 18–19, 176–8.

Franklin, Michael J., 'Sir William Jones' in Meic Stephens (Ed.), *The Oxford Companion to the Literature of Wales,* Oxford, Oxford University Press, 1998.

Franklin, Michael J., 'The Building of Empire and the Building of Babel: Sir William Jones, Lord Byron, and their Productions of the Orient', in Martin Prochazka (Ed.), *Byron East and West,* Prague, Charles University, 2000, 63–78.

Frawley, Maria H., 'Desert Places/Gendered Spaces: Victorian Women in the Middle East', *Nineteenth Century Contexts,* 15:1, 1991, 49–64.

Frend, W. H. C., 'North Africa and Europe in the Early Middle Ages', *Transactions of the Royal Historical Society*, 5th series, 1955, 61–80.

Frye, Richard N., 'Persia in the Mind of the West', *Islam and Christian-Muslim Relations,* 14: 4, 2003, 403–6.

Fuchs, Barbara, 'Spanish Lessons: Spenser and the Irish Moriscos', *Studies in English Literature, 1500–1900,* 42: 1, 2002, 43–62.

Fulford, T., '"Getting and Sending": The Orientalization of Satire in Romantic London', in Jones, S.E. (Ed.) *The Satire Eye; Forms of Satire in the Romantic Period,* New York and Basingstoke, Palgrave, 2003, 11–31.

Fulford, T., 'Heroic Voyagers and Superstitious Natives: Southey's Imperialist Ideology', *Studies in Travel Writing*, 2, 1998, 46–64.

Fulford, T., 'Plants, Pagodas and Penises: Southey's Oriental Imports', in Lynda Pratt (Ed.), *Robert Southey and the Contexts of English Romanticism*, Aldershot, UK, Ashgate, 2006, 187–201.

Fulford, T., 'Seraglios and Raree Shows: Orientalism and Sexual Satires in Late Eighteenth-Century Britain', in S.E. Jones (Ed.), *The Satiric Eye: Forms of Satire in the Romantic Period,* Basingstoke, Palgrave, 2003.

Gairola, Rahul, 'Queering Orientalism: Sexual Otherness and Asian American Studies', *Amerasia Journal*, 31:1, 2005, 27–31.

Garber, Frederick, 'Beckford, Delacroix and Byronic Orientalism', *Comparative Literature Studies*, 18, 1981, 321–32.

Garber, Frederick, 'Byron's *Giaour* and the Mark of Cain', *Etudes Anglaises*, 26, April-June 1973, 150–9.

Gardiner, Anne Barbeau, 'Islam as Antichrist in the Writings of Abraham Woodhead: Spokesman for the Restoration Catholics', *Restoration*, 15:2, 1991, 89–98.

Gargano, Elizabeth, '"English Sheiks" and Arab Stereotypes: E. M. Hull, T. E. Lawrence, and the Imperial Masquerade', *Texas Studies in Literature and Language*, 48:2, 2006, 171–86.

Garland Cannon and Michael J. Franklin, 'A Cymmrodor Claims Kin in Calcutta : An Assessment of Sir William Jones as Philologer, Polymath, and Pluralist', THSC, N.S. 11, 2005, 50–69.

Garrett, J., 'Beckford's Amorality: Deconstructing the House of Faith', in Werner Schneiders and Jane Gooden (et al.) (Eds.), *Transactions of the Ninth International Congress on the Enlightenment Münster ... 1995*, vol. I, Oxford, Voltaire Foundation, 1996, 455–8.

Gehl, Robert, 'Something is Stirring in the East: Racial Identity, Confronting the "Other" and Miscegenation in *Othello* and *The Lord of the Rings*', in Janet Brennan Croft (Ed.), *Tolkien and Shakespeare: Essays on Shared Themes and Language*, London: McFarland, 2007, 251–66.

Gendron, Charisse, 'Images of Middle Eastern Women in Victorian Travel Books', *Victorian Newsletter*, 79, 1991, 18–23.

Gérard, Albert, '"Egregiously an Ass": The Dark Side of the Moor. A View of Othello's Mind', *Shakespeare Survey*, 10, 1957, 98–106.

Ghazoul, Ferial, 'Dialectics of the Self and the Other: Arabian Tales in American Literature', in Ferial Ghazoul, *Nocturnal Poetics: The Arabian Nights in Comparative Context*, Cairo, The American University in Cairo Press, 1996, 121–33.

Ghazoul, Ferial, '*The Arabian Nights* in Shakespearean Comedy: "The Sleeper Awakened" and *The Taming of the Shrew*', in Ferial Ghazoul, *Nocturnal Poetics: The Arabian Nights in Comparative Context*, Cairo, The American University in Cairo, 1996, 58–70.

Ghazoul, Ferial, 'The Arabization of Othello', *Comparative Literature*, 50:1, 1998, 1–31.

Gifford, James, 'Reading Orientalism and the Crisis of Epistemology in the Novels of Lawrence Durrell', *CLCWeb: Computers, Literature, and Culture*, 1:2, 1999.

Gill, R.B., 'The Enlightened Occultist: Beckford's Presence in *Vathek*', in Kenneth W. Graham (Ed.), *Vathek and the Escape from Time: Bicentenary Revaluations*, New York, AMS, 1990, 131–43.

Gindy, Nadia, 'While I was in Egypt, I Finished Dr. Thorne', in Paul and Janet Starkey (Eds.), *Interpreting the Orient: Travellers in Egypt and the Near East*, Reading, Ithaca, 2001, 139–51.

Gittes, Katherine Slater, '*The Canterbury Tales* and The Arabic Frame Tradition', *PMLA*, 98: 2, 1983, 238–51.

Giuliano, Cheryl Fallon, 'Gulnare/Kaled's 'Untold' Feminization of Byron's *Oriental Tales*', *Studies in English Literature,* 1500–1900, 33:4, 1993, 785–807.

Godsall, Jon R., 'Fact and Fiction in Richard Burton's *Personal Narrative of a Pilgrimage to Al-Madinah and Meccah*', 1855–6', *IRAS*, Series 3, 3, 1993, 331–51.

Goode, Greg, 'The Oriental in Crime Fiction: the Sinister Oriental', *Armchair Detective,* 15, 1982, 203–18.

Goodrich, Peter H., 'Beyond Palamedes: Malory's Other Saracens', Conference Paper presented at the 'Fortieth International Conference on Medieval Studies', 5–8 May 2005 at Western Michigan University.

Gourgouris, Stathis, 'Orientalism and the Open Horizon of Secular Criticism', *Social Text,* 87, 2006, 11–20.

Grady, Frank, '"Machomete" and Mandeville's Travels', in John Victor Tolan (Ed.), *Medieval Christian Perceptions of Islam: A Book of Essays*, New York, Garland, 1996, 271–88.

Graham, Kenneth W., 'Beckford's Adaptation of the Oriental Tale in *Vathek*', *Enlightenment Essays,* 5:1, 1974, 24–33.

Graham, Kenneth W., 'Perverse Interactions of the Gothic, Enlightened, and Oriental: William Beckford's *Vathek*; with, *The Episodes of Vathek*', in Kenneth W. Graham and Kevin Berland (Eds.), *William Beckford and the New*

Millennium, New York, AMS Press, 2004, 119–30.

Gregory, Allan, 'Thomas Moore's Orientalism', in Peter Cochran (Ed.), *Byron and Orientalism*, Cambridge, Cambridge Scholars, 2006, 173–82.

Grenby, M. O., 'Orientalism and Propaganda: The Oriental Tale and Popular Politics in Late Eighteenth-Century Britain', *Eighteenth Century Novel*, 2, 2002, 215–37.

Griffith, Ben W. Jr., '*The Revolt of Islam* and Byron's *The Corsair*', *Notes and Queries*, 201, June 1956, 265.

Grimes, Kyle, 'Censorship, Violence, and Political Rhetoric: *The Revolt of Islam* in its Time', *Keats-Shelley Journal*, 43, 1994, 98–116.

Grudin, Michaela Paasche, 'Credulity and the Rhetoric of Heterodoxy: From Averroes to Chaucer', *The Chaucer Review*, 35: 2, 2000, 204–22.

Gruesser, John C., '"*Ligeia*" and Orientalism', *Studies in Short Fiction*, 26:2, Spring 1989, 145–9.

Grundy, Isobel, '"The Barbarous Character We Give Them": White Women Travellers Report on Other Races', *Studies in Eighteenth-Century Culture*, 23, 1993, 73–86.

Gupta, J., 'The East in English Literature', *Calcutta Review*, 30, January 1929, 45–66.

Gutschera, Deborah A., 'The Drama of Reenactment in Shelley's *The Revolt of Islam*', *Keats-Shelley Journal*, 35, 1986, 115–25.

Habib, Imtiaz, 'Sir Peter Negro, Othello and the Lost Blacks of Elizabethan England: Colonial Inscription and Postcolonial Excavation', *Literature, Interpretation, Theory,* 9:1, 1998, 15–30.

Hachicho, Mohamad Ali, 'English Travel Books about the Arab Near East in the Eighteenth Century', *Welt des Islams,* 1964, 5–7.

Haddad, Emily A., '"Better than the Reality": The Egyptian Market in Nineteenth-Century British Travel Writing', in Diane Long Hoeveler and Jeffrey Cass (Eds.), *Interrogating Orientalism: Contextual Approaches and Pedagogical Perspectives,* Columbus, Ohio State University Press, 2006, 72–89.

Haddad, Emily A., 'A Confederation of the Middle East and Art: Wordsworth', in Emily A. Haddad, *Oriental Poetics,* Aldershot, UK, Ashgate, 2002, 155–6.

Haddad, Emily A., 'Alfred Tennyson's Basra: Natural Phenomena and Urban Construction', in Emily A. Haddad, *Oriental Poetics,* Aldershot, UK, Ashgate, 2002, 147–51.

Haddad, Emily A., 'Grounding a Poetics in the *1001 Nights*: Tennyson', in Emily A. Haddad, *Oriental Poetics,* Aldershot, UK, Ashgate, 2002, 183–6.

Haddad, Emily A., 'Matthew Arnold in Bukhara: Nature in the Middle Eastern City', in Emily A. Haddad, *Oriental Poetics,* Aldershot, UK, Ashgate, 2002, 141–6.

Haddad, Emily A., 'Nightingales and Roses I: Walter Savage Landor and Oriental Literature', in

Emily A. Haddad, *Oriental Poetics*, Aldershot, UK, Ashgate, 2002, 171–4.

Haddad, Emily A., 'Nightingales and Roses II: Moore and the Orient as an Ideal', in Emily A. Haddad, *Oriental Poetics*, Aldershot, UK, Ashgate, 2002, 175–7.

Haddad, Emily A., 'Orientalist Poetics, Oscar Wilde: Culmination', in Emily A. Haddad, *Oriental Poetics*, Aldershot, UK, Ashgate, 2002, 199–201.

Haddad, Emily A., 'Orientalist Poetics, Oscar Wilde', in Emily A. Haddad, *Oriental Poetics*, Aldershot, UK, Ashgate, 2002, 152–4.

Haddad, Emily A., 'Out of the Desert: Byron's *Turkish Tales*', in Emily A. Haddad, *Oriental Poetics*, Aldershot, UK, Ashgate, 2002, 136–40.

Haddad, Emily A., 'The Oriental and Tennyson's P(a)lace of Art', in Emily A. Haddad, *Oriental Poetics*, Aldershot, UK, Ashgate, 2002, 187–91.

Haddad, Emily A., 'To Instruct Without Displeasing: Percy B. Shelley's *The Revolt of Islam* and Robert Southey's *Thalaba the Destroyer*', in Emily A. Haddad, *Oriental Poetics*, Aldershot, UK, Ashgate, 2002, 11–53.

Haddad, Emily A., 'Truth in Illustrating Robert Southey and Thomas Moore', in Emily A. Haddad, *Oriental Poetics*, Aldershot, UK, Ashgate, 2002, 113–17.

Haddad, Emily A., 'William Wordsworth and the Nature of the Middle East', in Emily A. Haddad,

Oriental Poetics, Aldershot, UK, Ashgate, 2002, 103–8.

Haddawy, Husain, 'English Arabesque: Orientalism and the Oriental Mode in Eighteenth Century English Literature', *Ur*, 1983–4, 17–22.

Hadley, Elaine, 'Home as Abroad: Orientalism and Occidentalism in Early English Stage Melodrama', *Texas Studies in Literature and Language*, 41:4, 1999, 330–50.

Hage el-, George Nicolas, 'William Blake and Kahlil Gibran: Poets of Prophetic Vision', State University of New York at Binghamton, 1981.

Hahn, Friederike, 'One Osmond the Great Turk, Not Two', *Notes and Queries*, 54:1, 2007, 35–6.

Hai, Abedl M., 'Shelley and the Arabs: An Essay in Comparative Literature', *Journal of Arabic Literature*, 3, 1972, 72–89.

Haitham, Abdul Aziz Saab, 'Restoration Oriental Drama and Contemporary Ottoman History: Turkish Politics Rehearsed', Presented at '1453 to 1699: Cultural Encounters between East and West', Institute of English Studies, London, 5–7 December 2002.

Hall, Kim F., 'Guess Who's Coming to Dinner? Colonization and Miscegenation in *The Merchant of Venice*', *Renaissance Drama*, 23, 1992, 87–111.

Haltof, Marek, 'Australia and the 'Mysterious Orient' in C. J. Koch's *The Year of Living Dangerously*', *Analecta Husserliana*, 51, 1997, 43–54.

Hambly, Gavin R.G., 'Muslims in English-Language Fiction', in Robin W. Winks and James R. Rush (Eds.), *Asia in Western Fiction*, Manchester, Manchester University Press, 1990, 35–52.

Hamilton, M., 'The Image of Arabs in the Sources of American Culture: Bibliographic Essay', *Choice*, 28, 1991, 1271–81.

Hammani, Reza and Martina Rieker, 'Feminist Orientalism and Orientalist Marxism', *New Left Review*, 170, 1988, 93–106.

Hampson, Robert G., 'Conrad, Guthrie, and *"The Arabian Nights"*', *Conradiana: A Journal of Joseph Conrad Studies*, 18, 1986, 141–3.

Hampton, Timothy, '"Turkish Dogs": Rabelais, Erasmus, and the Rhetoric of Alterity', *Representations*, 41, 1993, 58–82.

Hanlon, David, 'Islam and Stereotypical Discourse in Medieval Castile and Leon', *Journal of Medieval and Early Modern Studies*, 30: 3, 2000, 479–504.

Harper, James, 'Turks as Trojans, Trojans as Turks: Visual Imagery of the Trojan War and the Politics of Cultural Identity in Fifteenth-Century Europe', in Ananya Jahanara Kabir and Deanne Williams (Eds.), *Postcolonial Approaches to the European Middle Ages: Translating Cultures*, Cambridge, Cambridge University Press, 2005, 151–79.

Harrington, Henry R., 'English Travellers and the Oriental Crowd: Kinglake, Curzon, and *The Miracle of the Holy Fire'*, *Harvard Library Bulletin*, 5:2, 1994, 73–86.

Harris, Bernard, 'A Portrait of a Moor', *Shakespeare Survey*, 11, 1958, 89–97.

Harris, Jonathan Gil, 'Rematerializing Shakespeare's Intertheatricality: The Occidental/ Oriental Palimpsest', in Bryan Reynolds and William N. West (Eds.), *Rematerializing Shakespeare: Authority and Representation on the Early Modern English Stage*, Basingstoke, Palgrave Macmillan, 2005, 75–94.

Hartman, Michelle, '"This Sweet/Sweet Music": Jazz, Sam Cooke, and Reading Arab American Literary Identities', *MELUS*, 31:4, 2006, 145–65.

Hasnat, A.B. Abul, 'Some Aspects of the Impact of Sir William Jones' Persian Studies on English Romantic Poetry', *Indo-Iranica*, 41, 1988, 72–90.

Haswell, Richard H., 'Shelley's *The Revolt of Islam*: The Connexion of Its Parts', *Keats-Shelley Journal*, 256, 1976, 81–102.

Hatem, Mervat, 'Through East Other's Eyes: The Impact on the Colonial Encounter on the Images of Egyptian, Levantine-Egyptian, and European Women, 1862–1920' in Nupur Chaudhuri and Margaret Strobel (Eds.), *Western Women and Imperialism: Complicity and Resistance*, Bloomington, Indiana University Press, 1992, 61–78.

Hawamdeh, Mufeed F., '"The Enchanted Island": A Thematic Study', *Arab Journal for the Humanities*, 6:24, 1986, 314–22.

Hawamdeh, Mufeed F., 'Marlovian Turkophobia: A Study of the Image and Role of Turks in *Tamburlaine the Great*, Parts 1 and 2', *Damascus University Journal for the Arts and Human and Educational Sciences*, 4:ii , 1998, 47–71.

Hawamdeh, Mufeed F., 'Shakespeare's Treatment of the Moor in *Othello*', *International Journal of Islamic and Arabic Studies*, 4:1, 1987, 93–114.

Hawamdeh, Mufeed F., 'Allusions to Muhammad in Shakespeare: A Lexico-Cultural Study', *Damascus University Journal*, 13, 1988, 53–72.

Hawamdeh, Mufeed F., 'The Treatment of Turks in Shakespeare', *International Journal of Islamic and Arabic Studies*, 1988.

Hawari, Rida, 'On Some Oriental Sources of English Literature in 18th and 19th Century England', *Bulletin of the Faculty of Arts, University of Riyadh*, 1, 1970, 7–19.

Heath, Michael J., 'Renaissance Scholars and the Origins of the Turks', *Bibliotheque d'Humanisme et Renaissance*, 41, 1979, 453–71.

Heberle, Mark, 'Pagans and Saracens in Spenser's *The Faerie Queene*' in Cornelia N. Moore and Raymond A. Moddy (Eds.), *Comparative Literature East and West: Traditions and Trends*, Honolulu, University of Hawaii, 1989, 81–7.

Heffernan, Teresa, 'Feminism Against the East/West Divide: Lady Mary's *Turkish Embassy Letters*', *Eighteenth-Century Studies*, 33:2, 2000, 201–15.

Heng, Geraldine, 'The Romance of England: Richard Coer de Lyon, Saracens, Jews, and the Politics of Race and Nation', in Jeffrey-Jerome Cohen, (Ed.), *The Postcolonial Middle Ages*, New York, St. Martin's, 2000, 135–72.

Herz, N., 'Byron's *Bride of Abydos*', *Notes and Queries*, 10th Series, 11 June 1909, 445.

Heseltine, J. E., 'The Royame of Perse', in A. J. Arberry (Ed.), *The Legacy of Persia*, Oxford, Clarendon Press, 1953, 359–87.

Heywood, C. J., 'Sir Paul Rycaut, A Seventeenth-Century Observer of the Ottoman State: Notes for a Study', in G. E. von Grunebaum (Ed.), *English and Continental Views of the Ottoman Empire, 1500–1800*, Los Angeles, University of California Press, 1972, 33–66.

Hilles, F.W., 'Self Portrait of the Great Orientalist', *Yale Review*, 60, 1971, 259–67.

Hockley, Luke, 'Detective Films and Images of the Orient: a Post-Jungian Reflection', in James S. Baumlin (et al.) (Ed.), *Post-Jungian Criticism: Theory and Practice*, Albany, New York State University Press, 2004, 75–91.

Hodges, Kenneth, 'Green Turks and English Knights: Sir Gawain, the Green Knight, and the Islamic al-Khidr', Presented at the 'Fortieth International Conference on Medieval

Studies', 5–8 May 2005 at Western Michigan University.

Hoenselaars, A. J., 'The Elizabethans and Turks at Constantinople', *Cahiers Elisabethians,* 47, 1995, 29–42.

Hoffpauir, Richard, 'The Thematic Structure of Southey's Epic Poetry', *The Wordsworth Circle,* 6, 1975, 240–8.

Hoeveler, Diane Long, 'The Female Captivity Narrative: Blood, Water, and Orientalism', in Diane Long Hoeveler and Jeffrey Cass (Eds.), *Interrogating Orientalism: Contextual Approaches and Pedagogical Perspectives,* Columbus, Ohio State University Press, 2006, 46–71.

Hollenbach, John W., 'The Image of the Arab in Nineteenth Century English and American Literature', *Muslim World,* 62, 1972, 159–208.

Hollings, Marion, 'Early Modern European Travel Narratives and Discourses of Barbarism', Presented at the Conference 'Between Empires: "Orientalism" Before 1600', Cambridge, 12–15 July 2001.

Hollings, Marion, 'Gender, Gardens, and Orientalism in Spenser's Bower of Bliss', Presented at the 'Rocky Mountain Medieval and Renaissance Association Conference', Tempe, Arizona, May 1999.

Hollings, Marion, 'Temperaunce, Turkish Baths, and the Threat of Islam: Bathing in Spenser's Paradise', Presented at the 'Conference on

Virile Women, Consuming Men: Gender and Monstrous Appetites in the Middle Ages and the Renaissance', University of Wales, Aberswyth, April 2000.

Hollings, Marion, 'Romancing the Turk: Trade, Race, Nation in Early Modern Romance and Travel', Presented at the GEMCS Conference, 2002.

Hollings, Marion, 'Sarazin, Paynim, and Other Strangers: Spenser's Discourses of Orientalism in *The Faerie Queene*', Presented at 'The Place of Spenser: Words, Worlds, Works', Pembroke College, Cambridge University, Cambridge, England, July 2001.

Holmberg, Rachel, 'Ravished: *The Renegado* and Anxieties of Conversion', Presented at the Group for Early Modern Cultural Studies Conference, 2002.

Holmes, Urban T., 'The Saracen Oath in the *Chansons de Geste*', *Modern Language Notes*, 43: 2, 1928, 84–7.

Hopwood, Derek, 'The Arabs and the West – The Cultural Divide: The British Image of the Arabs', *Arab Affairs*, 1, 1, Summer 1986, 30–6.

Hornback, Robert, 'Emblems of Folly in the First Othello: Renaissance Blackface, Moor's Coat, and "Muckender"', *Comparative Drama*, 35:1, 2001, 69–99.

Horwath, Peter, 'Why did the Turks Meet the Wortley Montagus at "Betsko" (1717)', *English Language Notes*, 29, 1992, 24–6.

Hossain, Mary, 'Women and Paradise', *Journal of European Studies*, 19, 1989, 293–310.

Howard, Jean E., 'An English Lass Amid the Moors: Gender, Race, Sexuality and National Identity in Heywood's *The Fair Maid of the West*', in Margo Hendricks and Patricia Parker, (Eds.), *Women, Race, and Writing in the Early Modern Period*, London, Routledge, 1994, 101–17.

Howard, Jean E., 'Shakespeare, Geography, and the Works of Genre on the Early Modern Stage', *Modern Language Quarterly*, 64: 3, 2003, 301–22.

Hudson, Nicholar, 'Open and Enclosed Readings of *Rasselas*', *The Eighteenth Century: Theory and Interpretation*, 31:1, 1990, 48–56.

Huggan, Graham, '(Not)Reading Orientalism', *Research in African Literatures*, 36:3, 2005, 124–36.

Hull, Gloria T., 'The Byronic Heroine and Byron's *The Corsair*', *Ariel*, 8, 1978, 71–83.

Humphreys, A.H., 'The Genius of the Place: Turkey in English Letters', *South Atlantic Quarterly*, 73, Summer 1974, 306–23.

Hunter, G.K., 'Elizabethan and Foreigners', *Shakespeare Survey*, 17, 1964, 37–52.

Hurley, Kelly, '"The Inner Chambers of All Nameless Sin": The Beetle, Gothic Female Sexuality, and Oriental Barbarism', in Lloyd Davis (Ed.), *Virginal Sexuality and Textuality in Victorian Literature*, Albany, New York State University Press, 1993, 193–213.

Hussain, Imdad, 'Beckford, Wainwright, De Quincey and Oriental Exoticism', *Venture*, 1, September 1960, 234–48.

Hussain, Imdad, 'Oriental Elements in English Poetry, 1784–1859', *Venture*, 1, June, 1960, 156–65.

Hussain, Imdad, 'Orientalism and Coleridge', *Venture*, 1 and 2, 1960, 33–46 and 1961, 44–55.

Hutchings, Mark, ''Turkish' or 'Arabic' Emir? *The Merry Wives of Windsor*, II.i.176', *Notes and Queries*, 47: 4, 2000, 449–51.

Hutchings, Mark, 'Anglo-Ottoman Relations and the English Stage, 1580–1600', Presented at the Conference 'Between Empires: 'Orientalism' Before 1600', Cambridge, 12–15 July 2001.

Hutchings, Mark, 'In Thrace; Brought up in Arabia: *The Jew of Malta*, II.iii.131', *Notes and Queries*, 47: 245, 2000, 428–30.

Hyland, Peter, 'Moors, Villainy and *The Battle of Alcazar*', *Parergon*, 16: 2, 1999, 85–99.

Idris, Farhad, 'The Native Returns: Conrad and Orientalism in V. S. Naipaul's *An Area of Darkness*', *South Carolina Review*, 32:2, 2000, 43–53.

Inden, R., 'Orientalist Constructions of India', *Modern Asian Studies*, 20:3, 1986, 401–48.

Irimia, Michaela, 'Defoe and Cantemir: Eighteenth-Century Explorers, West and East', in Kevin L. Cope and Laura Morrow (Eds.), *1650–1850: Ideas, Aesthetics, and Inquiries in the Early Modern Era*, New York, AMS Press, 1997, 239–49.

Irwin, Robert, 'Cucumbers in the Harem: Oriental Realities and the Deforming Western Gaze', *Times Literary Supplement*, London, 5012, April 1999, 3–4.

Irwin, Robert, 'Oriental Discourses in Orientalism', *Middle Eastern Lectures* (Tel Aviv), 3, 1999, 87–110.

Islam, Shamsul, 'The Influence of Eastern Philosophy on Yeats's Later Poetry', *Twentieth Century Literature*, 19, 1973, 283–90.

Islam, Shamsul, 'The Islamic Tradition in Kipling's Work', *Kipling Journal*, 37:174, 1970, 10–14.

Islam, Shamsul, 'Kipling's Use of Indo-Pakistani Languages', *Kipling Journal*, 37:171, 1969, 15–9.

Ismael, J.S., and Ismael, T.Y., 'Studying the Arabs: Myths and Metaphors', *Studies in Comparative International Development*, New Brunswick, N.J., 30:2, 1995, 45–57.

Issawi, Charles, ''We Are all Greeks…' Shelley and the Near East', *Encounter*, 72:5, May 1989, 54–7.

Jack, M., 'William Beckford: The Poor Arabian Story-Teller' in *Transactions of the Ninth International Congress on the Enlightenment, Münster ... 1995*, vol. I Oxford: Voltaire Foundation, 1996, 451–4.

Jackson, Ken, 'The Abrahamic in Shakespeare's *Titus Andronicus* and Other Plays', Paper Presented at the Conference '1453 to 1699: Cultural Encounters between East and West', Institute of English Studies, London, 5–7 December 2002.

Jafri, Naqi Hussain, 'Image of the Orient in Shakespeare', *The Aligarh Critical Miscellany,* 11: 1, 1998, 15–29.

Jahanpour, Farhang, 'Western Encounters with Persian Sufi Literature', *Sufi,* 35, 1997.

Jardine, Lisa, 'Medieval and Early Modern Interaction Between Europe and the Orient', Presented at the Conference 'Between Empires: "Orientalism" Before 1600', Cambridge, 12–15 July 2001.

Jarrett-Kerr and Martin, William R., 'Arnold Versus the Orient: Some Footnotes to a Disenchantment', *Comparative Literature Studies,* 12, 1975, 129–46.

John, Brian, 'Tennyson's 'Recollections of the *Arabian Nights*' and the Individuation Process', *Victorian Poetry,* 4, 1966, 275–9.

Johnson, Amy J., 'Orientalism and Gender: The Condition and Status of Women in Morocco', in Paul & Janet Starkey (Eds.), *Interpreting the Orient: Travellers in Egypt and the Near East,* Reading, Ithaca, 2001, 209–33.

Johnson, Galen, 'Muhammad and Ideology in Medieval Christian Literature', *Islam and Christian Muslim Relations,* 11: 3, 2000, 333–46.

Johnson, Lee, 'Delacroix and *the Bride of Abydos', Burlington Magazine,* 114, September 1972, 579–85.

Johnson, Rebecca Carol (et al.), '*The Arabian Nights,* Arab-European Literary Influence, and the Lineages of the Novel', *Modern Language Quarterly,* 68:2, 2007, 243–79.

Jones, C. M., 'The Conventional Saracen of the Songs of Geste', *Speculum*, 17, 1942, 201–25.

Jones, Norman, 'The Adaptation of Tradition: The Image of the Turk in Protestant England', *East European Quarterly*, 12, 1978, 161–75.

Jones, W.R., 'The Image of the Barbarian in Medieval Europe', *Comparative Studies in Society and History*, 13, 1971, 376–407.

Jones, Russell, 'Leigh Hunt's Oriental Motifs – 'Abou Ben Adhem', *Journal of the Royal Asiatic Society*, 7:iii, 1997, 389–97.

Jones-Wagner, Valentina, 'The Body of the Saracen Princess in *La Belle Helene de Constantinople*', *Bucknell Review*, 47: 2, 2004, 82–9.

Jowitt, Claire, 'Political Allegory in Late Elizabethan and Early Jacobean "Turk" Plays: *Lust's Dominion* and *The Turke*', *Comparative Drama*, 36: 3/4, 2002/03, 411–43.

Jubouri Al-, Dhai, 'Precursors of Orientalism: Early English Pilgrims in the Arab East', in Muhsin J. Al-Musawi (Eds.), *Orientalism*, Baghdad, Cultural Affairs, 3, 1989, 17–27.

Kabbani, Rana, 'Eastern Travelogues: The Cultural Foundation of Colonialism', *Arab Affairs*, 1:1, 1986, 37–45.

Kabitoglou, E. Douka, 'Shelley's (Feminist) Discourse on the Female: *The Revolt of Islam*', *Arabeiten aus anglistik und Amerikanistik*, 15:2, 1990, 139–50.

Kaczvinsky, Donald P., 'Memlik's House and Mountolive's Uniform: Orientalism, Ornamentalism, and

The Alexandria Quartet', *Contemporary Literature*, 48:1, 2007, 93–118.

Kappert, Petra, 'From Romanticization to Colonial Dominance: Historical Changes in the European Perception of the Middle East', in H. Hippler and A. Lueg (Eds.), *The Next Threat: Western Perceptions of Islam*, London, Pluto Press, 1995, 32–56.

Karim-Cooper, Farah, '"This Alters Not Thy Beauty": Face-Paint, Gender and Race in Richard Brome's *The English Moor*', *Early Theatre*, 10:2, 2007, 140–9.

Katz, Michael, 'Amy Lowell and the Orient', *Comparative Literature Studies*, 18, 1981, 124–40.

Kaul, R.K., 'Jones on Persian Poetry', in R.K. Kaul, *Studies in William Jones: An Interpreter of Oriental Literature*, Shimla, India, IIAS, 1995, 48–82.

Kaul, R.K., 'Orientalism and William Jones', in R.K. Kaul, *Studies in William Jones: An Interpreter of Oriental Literature*, Shimla, India, IIAS, 1995, 1–27.

Kaul, R.K., 'The Seven Odes: Jones on Arabic Poetry', in R.K. Kaul, *Studies in William Jones: An Interpreter of Oriental Literature*, Shimla, India, IIAS, 1995, 28–47.

Kazmi, Syed Nasir Raza, 'E.M. Foster and Anita Desai: Portraits of Indian Muslims in English Fiction', in Jalal Uddin Khan and Adrian E. Hare (Eds.) *English and Islam: Creative Encounters 96*, Kuala Lumpur, Malaysia, International Islamic University, 1996, 161–71.

Kelley, Theresa M., 'Deluge and Buried Treasure in Wordsworth's 'Arab Dream', *Notes and Queries*, 27, 1980, 70–1.

Kelley, Theresa M., 'Spirit and Geometric Form: The Stone and the Shell in Wordsworth's Arab Dream', *Studies in English Literature 1500–1900*, 22, 1982, 563–82.

Kelly, Gary, 'Social Conflict, Nation and Empire: From Gothicism to Romantic Orientalism', *Ariel*, 20:2, 1989, 3–18.

Kelly, Henry Ansgar, 'Jews and Saracens in Chaucer's England: A Review of the Evidence', *Studies in the Age of Chaucer*, 27, 2005, 129–69.

Kelly, Kathleen Coyne, '"Blue" Indians, Ethiopians and Saracens in Middle English Narrative Texts', *Parergon*, 11: 1, 1993, 35–52.

Kelly, Kathleen Coyne, 'The Bartering of the Blauncheflur in the Middle English *Floris and Blauncheflur*', *Studies in Philology*, 91: 2, 1994, 101–10.

Kelsall, Malcolm, '"Once Did She Hold the Gorgeous East in Fee ...": Byron's Venice and Oriental Empire', in Tim Fulford (Ed), *Romanticism and Colonialism: Writing and Empire, 1780–1830*, Cambridge, Cambridge University Press, 1998, 243–60.

Kelsall, Malcolm, 'Byron and the Women of the Harem', in Alice Levine and Robert N. Keane (Eds.), *Rereading Byron: Essays Selected from Hofstra University's Byron Bicentennial Conference*, New York, Garland, 1993, 165–73.

Kerr, Douglas, 'Not Knowing the Oriental', *New Zealand Journal of Asian Studies*, 5:2, 2003, 33–46.

Kerr, Douglas, 'Stories of the East: Leonard Woolf and the Genres of Colonial Discourse', *English Literature in Transition*, 41:3, 1998, 261–79.

Kershner, R. Brandon, 'Ulysses and the Orient', *James Joyce Quarterly*, 35:2/3, 1998, 273–96.

Kestner, Joseph, 'The Genre of Landor's *Gebir*', *The Wordsworth Circle*, 5:1, 1974, 41–9.

Khalaf, Elias Mustafa, 'Islam in Marlowe's *Tamburlaine the Great*', *Al-Balqa*, 4:i, 1996, 61–88.

Khan, Jalal Uddin, 'Reading the Muslim East in English Literature With*out* an Orientalist Perspective', in Jalal Uddin Khan and Adrian E. Hare (Eds.) *English and Islam: Creative Encounters 96*, Kuala Lumpur, Malaysia, International Islamic University, 1996, 277–87.

Khattab, Ezzat, 'Browning in Arabic', *Arab Studies Quarterly*, 5:2, 1983, 113–8.

Khattab, Ezzat, 'Muhammad in Marlowe's *Tamburlaine*', *Majallat Kulliyat al-Adab*, 1, 1970, 41–52.

Khoddam, Salwa, '"The Significance of the East in C. S. Lewis's *The Voyage of the Dawn Treader* and Other Narnia Stories: Topos or Cosmos?", *CSL: Bulletin of the New York, C. S. Lewis Society*, 29:5/6, 1998, 1–10.

Kidwai, A.R. and Newey, Vincent, 'Leigh Hunt's "Abraham and the Fire Worshipper" – A

Possible Source', *Notes and Queries*, 241, March, 1996, 44–5.

Kidwai, A.R. and Newey, Vincent, 'The Burning Heart in Poe's 'Al-Aaraf': Another Possible Source', *Notes and Queries*, 242, March 1997, 365–6.

Kidwai, A.R. and Newey, Vincent, 'The Outline of Coleridge's and Southey's 'Muhammad', *Notes and Queries*, 238, March 1993, 38–9.

Kidwai, A.R., 'A Bibliography of Byron's Oriental Reading', *Notes and Queries*, 237, June 1992, 167–8.

Kidwai A.R., 'Oriental Heroines in Lord Byron's *Turkish Tales*', *The Aligarh Journal of English Studies*, 20:1, 1998, 51–77.

Kidwai, A.R., '"A Vulgar Error": Byron on Women and Paradise', *Byron Journal*, 21, 1993, 87–8.

Kidwai, A.R., 'Byron's Allusion to Zuleika: A Note', *Byron Journal*, 19, 1999, 149.

Kidwai, A.R., 'Exotic East: Fiction and Fantasy in Western Literature', *Muslim World Book Review*, Leicester, UK, 17:2, 1997, 3–8.

Kidwai, A.R., 'Samples of the Finest Orientalism: Image of the Orient in Lord Byron's 'Turkish Tales', *Aligarh Critical Miscellany*, 9:1, 1996, 65–84.

Kidwai, A.R., 'The Tale of Calil' in A.R. Kidwai, *Orientalism in Lord Byron's Turkish Tales*, Lewiston, Mellen University Press, 1995, 259–65.

Kidwai, A.R., 'A Bibliography of Southey's Oriental Reading' in A.R. Kidwai, *Orientalism in Lord*

Byron's Turkish Tales, Lewiston, Mellen University Press, 1995, 266–74.

Kidwai, A.R., 'A Bibliography of Moore's Oriental Reading' in A.R. Kidwai, *Orientalism in Lord Byron's Turkish Tales*, Lewiston, Mellen University Press, 1995, 275–80.

Kidwai, A.R., 'Perceptions of Islam and Muslims in English Literature: A Survey', in Zafar Ishaq Ansari and John L. Esposito (Eds.), *Muslims and the West: Encounter and Dialogue*, Islamabad, Islamic Research Institute, International Islamic University; Washington, Center for Muslim-Christian Understanding, Georgetown University, 2001, 52–86.

Kidwai, A.R., 'Pulp Fiction or Hate Literature' in A.R. Kidwai (Ed.), *Stranger Than Fiction: Images of Islam and Muslims in English Fiction*', Delhi, A.P.H., 2000, 86–98.

Kinoshita, Sharon, 'Cairo Nights: *Floire et Blanchefleur* and the Crusader Imaginary', Presented at the Conference 'Between Empires: "Orientalism" Before 1600', Cambridge, 12–15 July 2001.

Kinoshita, Sharon, 'Fraternizing with the Enemy: Christian-Saracen Relations in *Raoul de Cambrai*', *L'épopée romane, Actes du XVe Congrès international Rencesvals*, Poitiers, Centre d'Etudes Supérieures de Civilisation Médiévale, 2, 2002, 695–703.

Kinoshita, Sharon, 'Pagans are Wrong and Christians are Right: Alterity, Gender and Nation in *The Chanson de Roland*', *Journal of Medieval and Early Modern Studies*, 31:1, 2001, 79–111.

Kirsch, Arthur C., 'The Significance of Dryden's *Aureng-Zebe*', *English Literary History*, 29: 2, 1962, 160–74.

Kitson, Peter J, 'Romanticism and Colonialism, Races, Places, Peoples, 1785–1800', in T.J. Fulford and P. Kitson (Eds.), *Romanticism and Colonialism: Writing and Empire, 1780–1830*, Cambridge, Cambridge University Press, 1998, 13–34.

Kitaeff, Lila, 'Three Kings: Neocolonial Arab Representation', *Jump Cut*, 46, 2003.

Kitzberger, Ingrid Rosa, 'Archetypal Images of Transformation and the Self in Percy B. Shelley's *The Revolt of Islam*', in Sabine Coelsch-Foisner, Wolfgang Görtschacher, and Holger M. Klein (Eds.), *Trends in English and American Studies: Literature and the Imagination: Essays in Honour of James Lester Hogg*, Lewiston, NY, Mellen Press, 1996, 171–87.

Klimova, Svetlana, 'Byron's *Turkish Tales* and Russian Byronism: Pushkin and the Early Nineteenth-Century Russian Reception of Byron', *Byron Journal*, 33:2, 2005, 117–25.

Klinger, H., 'The Tale of Calil', *Times Literary Supplement*, 2 August 1985, 851.

Knight, Sarah, '"So Rich a Prize as This": Persia in Marlowe's *Tamburlaine the Great*', Paper presented at the Conference '1453 to 1699: Cultural Encounters between East and West', Institute of English Studies, London, 5–7 December 2002.

Knobler, Adam, 'Timur the (Terrible/Tartar) Trope: A Case of Repositioning in Popular Literature and History', *Medieval Encounters*, 7:i, 2001, 101–12.

Knowlton, E.C., '"Indian Moors" and *Doctor Faustus*', *Cahiers Elisabethains*, 23, 1983, 93–7.

Knox-Shaw, Peter, '*Persuasion*, Byron, and the *Turkish Tale*', *Review of English Studies*, 44:173, 1993, 47–69.

Knox-Shaw, Peter, '*Vathek* and The Seven Fountains by Sir William Jones', *Notes and Queries*, 240, New Series 42:1, March 1995, 75–6.

Kolba, Gwin, J., 'The Paradise in Abyssinia and the Happy Valley in *Rasselas*', *Modern Philology*, 16, 1958, 10–16.

Konzett, Delia, 'War and Orientalism in Hollywood Combat Film', *Quarterly Review of Film and Video*, 21:4, 2004, 327–38.

Kopf, David, 'The Historiography of British Orientalism, 1772–1992', in Garland Cannon and Kevin R. Brine (Eds.), *Objects of Enquiry: The Life, Contributions, and Influences of Sir William Jones (1746–1794)*, New York, New York University Press, 1995, 141–60.

Koundoura, Maria, 'Between Orientalism and Philhellenism: Lady Mary Wortley Montagu's "Real" Greeks', *Eighteenth Century*, 45:3, 2004, 249–64.

Krotkoff, George, 'Hammer-Purgstall, Hajji Baba and the Moriers', *International Journal of Middle East Studies*, 19:1, February 1987, 203–8.

Lach, Donald F., 'Asia in the Eyes of the Europe: The Seventeenth Century', *Seventeenth Century,* 5: 1, 1990, 93–109.

Lach, Donald F. and Foss, T.N., 'Images of Asia and Asians in European Fiction, 1500–1800', in R.W. Winks and J.R. Rush (Eds.), *Asia in Western Fiction,* Manchester, Manchester University Press, 1990, 145–55.

Landry, Donna, 'Steal of a Turk: Restoration Horse-Trading and Eastern Bloodstock', *Prose Studies,* 29:1, 2007, 115–35.

Larrissy, Edward, 'Blake's Orient', *Romanticism,* 11:1, 2005, 1–13.

Larsen, Thorlief, 'The Historical and Legendary Background of Peele's *Battle of Alcazar*', *Transactions of the Royal Society of Canada,* 2, 1939, 185–97.

Le Gallienne, Richard, 'A Day with Dr Johnson at the Turk's Head', *Literary Digest International Book Review,* July 1923, 1:8, 25–7.

Leask, Nigel, 'Byron and the Eastern Mediterranean: Childe Harold II and the Polemic of Ottoman Greece', in Drummond Bone (Ed.), *The Cambridge Companion to Byron,* Cambridge University Press, 2005.

Leask, Nigel, 'Byron Turns Turk: Orientalism and the Eastern Tales', in Nigel Leask, *British Romantic Writers and the East: Anxieties of Empire,* Cambridge, Cambridge University Press, 1993, 13–67.

Leask, Nigel, 'Easts', in Nicholas Roe (Ed.), *Romantic Orientalism for Romanticism: An Oxford Guide*, Oxford University Press, 2005.

Leask, Nigel, 'Kubla Khan and Orientalism: The Road to Xanadu Revisited', *Romanticism*, 4:1, 1998, 1–21.

Leask, Nigel, 'Resolving the Corsair: Lara and The Island', in Jane Stabler (Ed.), *Byron: A Critical Reader*, London, Longman, 1998.

Leask, Nigel, 'Wandering Through Eblis: Absorption and Containment in Romantic Exoticism', in Tim Fulford and P.J. Kitson (Eds.), *Romanticism and Colonialism: Writing and Empire*, Cambridge, Cambridge University Press, 1998, 165–88.

Lennon, Joseph, 'James Stephens's Diminutive National Narratives: Imagining an Irish Nation Based on the "Orient"', *Comparatist*, 20, 1996, 62–81.

Lerner, Laurence, 'The Machiavel and the Moor', *Essays in Criticism*, 9, Oct. 1959, 339–60.

Lester, John, 'Conrad and Islam', *Conradiana*, 13:3, 1981, 163–79.

Lew, Joseph W., 'Lady Mary's Portable Seraglio', *Eighteenth-Century Studies*, 24:4, Summer 1991, 432–50.

Lew, Joseph W., 'The Deceptive Other: Mary Shelley's Critique of Orientalism in *Frankenstein*', *Studies in Romanticism*, 30:2, 1991, 255–83.

Lew, Joseph W., 'The Necessary Orientalist? *The Gioaur* and Nineteenth Century Imperialist Misogyny', in Alan Richardson and Sonia Hofkosh (Eds.), *Romanticism, Race, and Imperial Culture, 1780–1834*, Bloomington, IN, Indiana University Press, 1996, 173–202.

Lewis, Archibald R., 'The Islamic World and the Latin West, 1350–1500', *Speculum,* 65:4, 1990, 833–44.

Lewis, Bernard, 'Some English Travellers in the East', *Middle Eastern Studies,* 4, 1967–8, 296–315.

Lewis, Reina, 'Only Women Should Go to Turkey': Henriette Browne and Women's Orientalism', *Third Text,* 22, Spring 1993, 53–64.

Lewis, Reina, 'Oriental Femiminity as Cultural Commodity: Authorship, Authority and Authenticity' in Hackforth-Jones, Jocelyn and Roberts, Mary (Eds.), *Edges of Empire: Orientalism and Visual Culture,* Oxford, Blackwell, 2004, 70–94.

Lim, Walter S. H., 'Figuring Justice: Imperial Ideology and the Discourse of Colonialism in Book V of *The Faerie Queene* and *A View of the Present State of Ireland*', *Renaissance and Reformation,* 19, 1995, 45–70.

Lim, Walter S. H., 'Jacobean Rule and Early Modern Orientalism in Shakespeare's *Antony and Cleopatra*', Presented at the Conference 'Colonial, Imperial, and Post-Colonial Shakespeare', Kent State University, 14–16 November 2002.

Lim, Walter S. H., 'Representing the Other: *Othello*, Colonialism, Discourse', *The Upstart Crow: A Shakespeare Journal*, 13, 1993, 57–78.

Lim, Walter S. H., 'Epic, Colonialism, Empire: A Reading of Milton's *Paradise Lost* and *Paradise Regained*', in Robert Young, Ban Kah Choon and Robbie Goh (Eds.), *The Silent Word: Textual Meaning and the Unwritten*, Singapore, Singapore University Press and World Scientific Publishing, 1998, 45–57.

Ling, Jinqi, 'Before and After Orientalism', *Amerasia Journal*, 31:1, 2005, 42–7.

Little, Donald P., 'Three Arab Critiques of Orientalism', *Muslim World*, 69, 1979, 110–31.

Liu, Alan, 'Toward a Theory of Common Sense: Beckford's *Vathek* and Johnson's *Rasselas*', *Texas Studies in Literature and Language*, 26, 1984, 183–217.

Liu, Lidan, 'The Legacy and the Future of Orientalism', in Silvia Nagy-Zekmi (Ed.), *Paradoxical Citizenship: Edward Said*, Lanham, MD, Lexington, 2006, 129–43.

Lochon, Christian, 'Islamic Learning and the Medieval West', *Medieval World*, London, 4, 1992, 15–21.

Lockhart, L., 'Persia as Seen by the West', in A. J. Arberry (Ed.), *The Legacy of Persia*, Oxford, Clarendon Press, 1953, 318–58.

Logan, Deborah A., 'Harem Life, West and East', *Women's Studies*, 26:3/4, 1997, 449–74.

Loomba, Ania, 'Shakespeare and Cultural Difference', in Terrence Hawkes (Ed.), *Alternative Shakespeare 2*, London, Routledge, 1996, 162–87.

Loshitzky, Yosefa, 'Orientalist Representations: Palestinians and Arabs in Some Postcolonial Films and Literature', in E. Hallam and B.V. Street (Eds.), *Cultural Encounters: Representing Otherness*, London, Routledge, 2000, 51–71.

Lowe, Lisa, 'Orientalism as Literary Criticism: Reception of E.M. Forster's *A Passage to India*', in Lisa Lowe, *Critical Terrains: French and British Orientalisms*, Ithaca, Cornell University Press, 1991, 102–35.

Lowe, Lisa, 'Travel Narratives and Orientalism: Montagu and Montesquieu', in Lisa Lowe, *Critical Terrains: French and British Orientalisms*, Ithaca, Cornell University Press, 1991, 30–74.

Luchitskaya, Sveltana, 'Muslims in Christian Imagery of the Thirteenth Century: The Visual Code of Otherness', *Al-Masaq*, 12, 2000, 37–67.

Lulua, Abdul Wahid, 'Andalusian and English Lyrical Poetry: Probable Influence Through the Troubadours', in Jalal Uddin Khan and Adrian E. Hare (Eds.) *English and Islam: Creative Encounters 96*, Kuala Lumpur, Malaysia, International Islamic University, 1996, 1–21.

Lynch, Kathryn L., 'East Meets West in Chaucer's Squire's and Franklin's Tales', *Speculum*, 70:3, 1995, 530–51.

Lynch, K.L., 'Storytelling, Exchange and Constancy: East and West in Chaucer's *Man of Law's Tale*', *The Chaucer Review*, 33: 4, 1999, 409–22.

Macfie, Alexander Lyon, 'Kipling and Orientalism', *Kipling Journal*, 80:317, 2006, 46–53.

Macfie, Alexander Lyon, 'Representations of Lawrence of Arabia: From Said's Orientalism to David Lean's Film (1962)', *Journal of Postcolonial Writing*, 43:1, 2007, 77–87.

Maclean, Gerald M., 'Before Orientalism? Islam, Ottomans, and Moors in the English Renaissance', *Review*, Virginia, USA, 22, 2000, 229–48.

MacLean, Geralad M., 'Britons Abroad: Travellers and Traders in Maghrebian Ports, 1580–1720,' in Abdeljelil Temimi and Mohamed-Salah Omri, (Eds.), *The Movement of People and Ideas between Britain and the Maghreb*, Tunis, Fondation Temimi, 2003, 117–24.

MacLean, Gerald M., 'Learn of a Turk', *Prose Studies*, 29:1, 2007, 36–58.

MacLean, Geralad M., 'Milton, Islam and the Ottomans', in Sharon Achinstein and Elizabeth Sauer (Eds.), *Milton and Toleration*, Oxford, Oxford University Press, 2007.

MacLean, Geralad M., 'Of Pirates, Slaves and Diplomats: Anglo-American Writing about the Maghrib in the Age of Empire', in Claire Jowitt (Ed), *Pirates? The Politics of Plunder 1550–1650*, Palgrave Macmillan, 2006.

MacLean, Gerald M., 'On Turning Turk, but Failing: Daborne's Ward', Presented at the Conference 'Changing States: Travel and Conversion in the Early Modern Period', at University of Michigan, 25 January 2002.

MacLean, Gerald M., 'On Turning Turk, or Trying to: National Identity in Robert Daborne's *A Christian Turn'd Turk*', *Explorations in Renaissance Culture,* 29: 2, 2003, 225–52.

MacLean, Geralad M., 'Strolling in Seventeenth-Century Syria', in (Ed.), Marius Kociejowski, *Syria Through Travellers' Eyes,* London, Eland, 2006.

MacLean, Gerald M., 'The Sultan's Beasts: English Travellers Encounter Ottoman Fauna', Presented at the Conference '1453 to 1699: Cultural Encounters between East and West', Institute of English Studies, London, 5–7 December 2002.

Mafe, Diana Adesola, 'From Ògún to Othello: (Re)acquainting Yoruba Myth and Shakespeare's Moor', *Research in African Literatures,* 35:3, 2004, 46–61.

Mahood, M.M., 'Marlowe's Heroes', in R.J. Kaufmann (Ed.), *Elizabethan Drama: Modern Essays in Criticism* New York, Oxford University Press, 1961, 95–122.

Makdisi, Saree, 'Versions of the East: Byron, Shelley, and the Orient', in Alan Richardson and Sonia Hofkosh (Eds.), in *Romanticism, Race, and Imperial Culture, 1780–1834,* Bloomington, Indiana University Press, 1996, 203–36.

Makdisi, Ussama, 'Mapping the Orient: Non-Western Modernization, Imperialism, and the End of Romanticism', in Helena Michie and Ronald Thomas (Eds.), *Nineteenth-Century Geographies: The Transformation of Space from the Victorian Age to the American Century*, New Brunswick, NJ, Rutgers University Press, 2003, 40–54.

Maleckova, Jitka, 'European Travel Books about the Ottoman Empire in the Late Eighteenth and Early Nineteenth Centuries as Historical Sources', *Archiv Orientalni*, 60, 1992, 147–56.

Malieckal, Bindu, '*"Bondslaves and Pagans Shall Our Statesmen Be": Moors, Turks, and Venetians in Othello*', Shakespeare Association of America, San Francisco, California, April 1999.

Malieckal, Bindu, '"Hell's Perfect Character": The Black Woman as the Islamic Other in Fletcher's *The Knight of Malta*', *Essays in Art and Sciences*, 28, 1999, 53–68.

Malieckal, Bindu, '"Turkish Women in Early Modern Drama", Presented at the 'Modern Language Association Convention', New Orleans, December 2001.

Malieckal, Bindu, '"Wanton Irreligious Madness": Conversion and Castration in Massinger's *The Renegado*', *Essays in Arts and Sciences*, 31, 2002, 25–43.

Malieckal, Bindu, '"O Treason of the Blood": Moors and Miscegenation in Shakespeare', Presented at the 'South Atlantic Modern Language Association Conference', Savannah, Georgia, November 1996.

Manganaro, Elise Salem, 'Voicing the Arab: Multivocality and Ideology' in Leon Uris' *The Haj*', *Melus*, 15:4, 1988, 3–13.

Manning, Peter J., 'Tales and Politics: The *Corsair*, *Lara* and *The White Doe of Rylstone*', in Peter J. Manning, *Reading Romantics*, New York, 1990, 195–215.

Manning, Peter J., 'The Home-ing of Byron's *Corsair*' in Peter J. Manning, *Reading Romantics*, New York, 1990, 216–237.

Mannsaker, Frances, 'Elegancy and Wilderness: Reflections of the East in the Eighteenth-Century Imagination', in G.S. Rousseau and Roy Porter (Eds.), *Exoticism in the Enlightenment*, Manchester, Manchester University Press, 1990, 175–95.

Manzalaoui, Mahmoud, 'Pseudo-Orientalism in Transition: the Age of *Vathek*' in Fatma Mahmoud Moussa (Ed.), *William Beckford of Fonthill 1760–1844*', 1960, 123–50.

Manzalaoui, Mahmoud, 'Swooning Lovers: A Theme in Arab and European Romance', *Comparative Criticism*, 8, 1986, 71–90.

Manzalaoui, Mahmoud, 'Mouths of the Sevenfold Nile: Modern Egypt in English Fiction', in D. Hopwood (Ed.), *Studies in Arab History: The Antonius Lectures, 1978–87*, London, 1990, 131–50.

Marandi, Seyed Mohammed, 'Byron's Infidel and The Muslim Fisherman', *Keats-Shelley Review*, 20, 2006, 133–55.

Marandi, Seyed Mohammed, 'The Bride of The East', in Peter Cochran (Ed.), *Byron and Orientalism*, Cambridge, Cambridge Scholars, 2006, 215–31.

Marez, Curts, 'The Other Addict: Reflections on Colonialism and Oscar Wilde's Opium Smoke Screen', *ELH*, 64:1, 1997, 257–87.

Marle, Hans van, 'Conrad and Richard Burton on Islam', *Conradiana*, 17:2, 1985, 137–42.

Marshall, W.H., 'The Accretive Structure of Byron's *The Giaour*', *Modern Language Notes*, 76, 1961, 502–9.

Martin, Joe, 'Doris Lessing's Alchemy: Fusing Sufism and Fiction', *Sufi*, 39, 1998, 38–49.

Matar, Nabil, 'Renaissance England and the Turban', in David Banks, (Ed.) *Images of the Other: Europe and the Muslim World before 1700, Cairo Papers in Social Science*, 1996, 39–55.

Matar, Nabil, '"The Taming of the Turk" in Seventeenth-Century England', Paper presented at San Antonio, Texas, 1993.

Matar, Nabil, 'Anglo-Islamic Relations in the Early Modern Period', Paper presented at University of Kent, 2006.

Matar, Nabil, 'Before Orientalism: The Allure of Islam in Renaissance England', Paper presented at Modern Language Association, Chicago, 1995.

Matar, Nabil, 'Britons, Muslims and American Indians: Gender and Power', Paper presented at South Central Renaissance Conference, Waco, Texas, 2–4 April 1998.

Matar, Nabil, 'Conversion to Islam in English Renaissance Thought', Paper presented at National Social Science Association, Memphis, Tennessee, 1991.

Matar, Nabil, 'England and Islam in the Seventeenth Century', Paper presented at American University in Cairo, 1996.

Matar, Nabil, 'English Accounts of Captivity in North Africa and the Middle East: 1577–1625', *Renaissance Quarterly*, 54:2, 2001, 553–72.

Matar, Nabil, 'Islam in Interregnum and Restoration England', *The Seventeenth Century*, 6, 1991, 57–71.

Matar, Nabil, 'Moors on the English Stage, 1589–1604', Paper presented at University of Wisconsin, Madison, 2005.

Matar, Nabil, 'Muslims in Early Modern England', Paper presented at University of Delaware, 1996.

Matar, Nabil, 'Muslims in Seventeenth-Century England', *Journal of Islamic Studies*, 8, 1997, 63–82.

Matar, Nabil, 'Perceptions of the Other among Early Modern Christians and Muslims', Paper presented at University of Lancaster, 2005.

Matar, Nabil, 'The First Turks and Moors in England', in Randolph Vigne and Charles Littleton (Eds.),

From Strangers to Citizens, Brighton, Portland, The Huguenot Society of Great Britain and Ireland, 2001, 261–8.

Matar, Nabil, 'The Renegade in English Seventeenth-Century Imagination', *Studies in English Literature,* 33, 1993, 489–505.

Matar, Nabil, 'The Representation of Muslim Women in Renaissance England', *Muslim World,* 86:1, 1996, 50–61.

Matar, Nabil, 'The Tolerance of Muslims in Renaissance England: Practice and Theory', in John C. Laursen (Ed.), *Religious Toleration 'The Variety of Rites' from Cyrus to Defoe,* London, St. Martin's Press, 1999, 127–46.

Matar, Nabil, 'The Traveller as Captive: Renaissance England and the Allure of Islam', *LIT,* 7:2/3, 1996, 187–96.

Matar, Nabil and Stoeckel, Rudolph, 'Europe's Mediterranean Frontier: The Moor', in Andrew Hadfield and Paul Hammond (Eds.), *Shakespeare and Renaissance Europe,* London, Arden Shakespeare, 2004, 220–52.

Matinuddin, Abu Rushd, 'Shakespeare and the East', in Syed Sajjad Hussain (Ed.), *Homage to Shakespeare,* Dacca, Bangladesh, Department of English Dacca University, 1965, 29–39.

McBratney, John, 'Images of Women in Rudyard Kipling: A Case of Doubling Discourse', *Inscriptions,* 3–4, 1988, 28–56.

McBratney, John, 'Rebuilding Akbar's 'Fane': Tenneyson's Reclamation of the East', *Victorian Poetry*, 32:4, 1993, 411–7.

McColl, Robert, '"Best Success were Sacrilege": Investigating Antitheses in *The Siege*', in Peter Cochran (Ed.), *Byron and Orientalism*, Cambridge, Cambridge Scholars, 2006, 232–45.

McJannet, Linda, 'Mapping the Ottomans on the Renaissance Stage', *Journal of Theatre and Drama*, 2, 1996, 9–34.

Meachen, Edward, 'History and Transcendence in Robert Southey's Epic Poems', *Studies in English Literature*, 19, 1979, 589–608.

Mead, Jenna, 'Reading by Said's Lantern: Orientalism and Chaucer's *Treatise on the Astralobe*', *Medieval Encounters: Jewish, Christian and Muslim Dialogues and Culture*, 5: 3, 2000, 350–7.

Meisami, Julie Scott, 'Arabic Culture and Medieval European Literature', *Journal of the American Oriental Society*, 111:2, April-June 1991, 343–51.

Mellor, Anne K., 'Romantic Orientalism Begins at Home: Elizabeth Hamilton's Translations of the Letters of a Hindoo Rajah', *Studies in Romanticism*, 44:2, 2005, 151–64.

Menocal, Maria Rosa, 'Pride and Prejudice in Medieval Studies: European and Oriental', *Hispanic Review*, 53: 1, 1985, 61–78.

Menon, Nivedita, 'Orientalism and After', *Public Culture*, 6:1, 1993, 65–76.

Merrett, Robert, 'Daniel Defoe and Islam', *Lumen*, 24, 2005, 19–34.

Meyer, Eric, '"I Know Thee Not, I Loath Thy Race": Romantic Orientalism in the Eye of the Other', *ELH*, 58, 1991, 657–99.

Meyer, Susan L., 'Colonialism and the Figurative Strategy of *Jane Eyre*', *Victorian Studies*, 33:2, 1990, 247–68.

Meyers, J., 'The Politics of *A Passage to India*', *Journal of Modern Literature*, 1:3, 1971.

Millar-Heggie, Bonnie, 'Sanctity, Savagery and Saracens in *Capystranus:* Fifteenth Century Christian-Ottoman Relations', *Al-Masaq*, Abingdon, UK, 14:2, 2002, 113–21.

Milligan, Barry, 'Opium smoking and the Oriental infection of British identity', in Sue Vice (Ed), *Beyond the Pleasure Dome: Writing and Addiction from the Romantics*, Sheffield, Sheffield Academic Press, 1994, 93–100.

Miloetich, John S., 'Muslim Oral Epic and Medieval Epic', *Modern Language Review*, 83: 4, 1988, 911–24.

Mirrer, Louise, 'Representing "Other" Men: Muslims, Jews, and Masculine Ideals in Medieval Castilian Epic and Ballad', in Clare Lees (Ed.), *Medieval Masculinities*, Minneapolis, University of Minnesota Press, 1994, 169–86.

Mohanty, S.P., 'Kipling's Children and the Colour Line', *Race and Class*, 31, 1989, 16–22.

Mohd, Jamal A.I., 'Image of Islam and Muslims in British Fiction' in A.R.Kidwai, (Ed.), *Stranger than*

Fiction: Images of Islam and Muslims in English Fiction, Delhi, A.P.H., 2000, 1–14.

Mojumder, Abu Taher, 'Orientalism and Sir William Jones', *Journal of the Asiatic Society*, Calcutta, India, 36:3, 1994, 123–6.

Momma, Haruko, 'A Man on the Cusp: Sir William Jones's 'Philology' and 'Oriental Studies'', *Texas Studies in Literature and Language*, 41:2, 1999, 160–79.

Monés, Mona H., 'Limitations in Vision: The Egyptian People in Lawrence Durrell's *The Alexandria Quartet*', *Parergon*, 8:2, 81–95.

Monticelli, Rita, 'The Return of the Repressed: Utopian Orients in the Nineteenth- and Early Twentieth-Century British Travel Literature on the Near and Middle East', in Raffaella Baccolini (Ed.), *Viaggi in Utopia*, Ravenna, Longo, 1996, 327–34.

Moore, John S., 'Who was "Mahumet"? Arabs in Angevin England', *Prosopon Newsletter*, 11, July 2000, 1–7.

Morse, Ruth, 'Orientalism: Edward Said's Imperialism as Culture', *Cambridge Review*, 114, 1993, 115–9.

Most, Glenn W., 'Wordsworth's "Dream of the Arab" and Cervantes', *English Language Notes*, 22:3, 1985, 52–8.

Mousa al-, Nidal, 'A Comparative Study of Hardy's *Tess of the d'Urbervilles* and Haykal's Zainab', *Arab Journal for the Humanities*, 9:34, 1989, 277–94.

Moussa, Mahmoud Fatma, 'Beckford, *Vathek* and The Oriental Tale', in Fatima Mahmoud Moussa (Ed.), *William Beckford of Fonthill 1760–1844*, 1960, 63–121.

Moussa, Mahmoud Fatma, 'Orientals in Picaresque: A Chapter in the History of the Oriental Tale in England', *Cairo Studies in English*, 1961–2, 145–88.

Msiska, Mpalive, 'The Concept of the Other in Said's Orientalism', in Isobel Armstrong (Ed.), *Critical Dialogues: Current Issues in English Studies in Germany and Great Britain*, Tübingen, Narr, 1995, 158–68.

Mueller, Roger Chester, 'Transcendental Periodicals and the Orient', *Emerson Society Quarterly*, IV Quarter, 57, 1969, 52–7.

Mula, Stefano, 'Muhammad and the Saints: The History of the Prophet in the *Golden Legend*', *Modern Philology*, 2003, 175–88.

Munro, D.C., 'The Western Attitude toward Islam During the Period of the Crusades', *Speculum*, 6, 1931, 329–43.

Murphey, R., 'Bigots or Informed Observers? A Periodization of Pre-Colonial English and European Writing on the Middle East', *Journal of the American Oriental Society*, 110, 1990, 291–303.

Murphy, Clare M., 'Ottoman Analogs to *Utopia*', *Moreana*, 18, 1981, 65–75.

Murray, E.B., '"Elective Affinity" in *The Revolt of Islam*', *Journal of English and Germanic Philology*, 1968, 570–85.

Musawi, Muhsin J., 'Beckford's *Vathek*, as an Arabian Tale', *Orientalism*, 3, 1989, 3–16.

Musawi, Muhsin J., 'On the Literary Significance of English Travel Books About the Near East, 1750–1850', in Muhsin J. Al-Musawi (Ed.), *Orientalism*, Baghdad, Cultural Affairs, 2, 1987, 16–61.

Musawi, Muhsin J., 'Possible Arabic Sources for Imlac's Poetics in Johnson's *Rasselas*', *Orientalism*, 1, January 1987, 5–34.

Musawi, Muhsin J., 'The Arabic Context of Johnson's *Rasselas*', *Orientalism*, 2 February 1987, 5–61.

Musawi, Muhsin J., 'Waiting for the 'Liberal Saints': An Assessment of Matthew Arnold's Last Political Essays', *Arab Journal for the Humanities*, 9:35, 1989, 321–37.

Mutalib, Hussin, 'Beyond Pride and Prejudice: Western Perceptions of Islam and the Muslims', in Z. Ansari and J. Esposito (Eds.), *Muslims and the West: Encounter and Dialogue*, Islamabad, Pakistan, Islamic Research Institute, 2001, 87–102.

Nafissi, M.R., 'Reframing Orientalism: Weber and Islam', *Economy and Society*, London, 27:1, 1998, 97–118.

Neill, Michael, ''Mulattos', 'Blacks', and 'Indian Moors': Othello and Early Modern Constructions of

Human Difference', *Shakespeare Quarterly*, 49:4, 1998, 361–74.

Newall, V., 'The Turkish Knight in English Traditional Drama', *Folklore*, 92, 1981, 196–202.

Nguyen-vo, Thu-huong, 'Orientalism: Entrances and Exits', *Amerasia Journal*, 31:1, 2005, 51–4.

Niebrzydowski, Sue, 'The Sultana and Her Sisters: Black Women in the British Isles before 1530', *Women's History Review*, 10: 2, 2001, 187–210.

Noble, Peters. 'Saracen Heroes in Adenet le Roi', in Hans-Erich Keller (Ed.), *Romance Epic: Essays on a Medieval Literary Genre*, Kalamazoo, Medieval Institute Publications, 1987.

Nochlin, Linda, 'The Imaginary Orient', in Linda Nochlin (Ed.), *The Politics of Vision: Essays on the Nineteenth Century Arts and Society*, New York, Harper & Row, 1989, 33–59.

Nodelman, Perry, 'The Other: Orientalism, Colonialism, and Children's Literature', *Children's Literature Association*, 17:1, 1992, 29–35.

Nourallah, M.Riad Atif, 'Sorcerer, Straight Swords and Scimitars (Image of Arab-Islamic East in the West)', *International Journal of Islamic and Arabic Studies*, 7: 2, 1990, 1–14.

Nunokawa, Jeff, 'Oscar Wilde in Japan: Aestheticism, Orientalism and the Derealization of the Homosexual', in Jonathan Freedman (Ed.), *Oscar Wilde: A Collection of Critical Essays*, New Jersey, Prentice Hall, 153–7.

Nussbaum, Felicity, '"An Affectionate and Voluntary Sacrifice": Sati, Rape, and Marriage in British Narratives of the East', *Nineteenth-Century Contexts*, 19:4, 1996, 347–71.

O'Connor, John J., 'A Jacobean Allusion to the Turkish Mahomet and Hiren the Fair Greek', *Philological Quarterly*, 35, 1956, 427–9.

Obeidat, Marwan M., 'A Reflection on and Analysis of Western Literary Sources on Islam', *International Journal of Islamic and Arabic Studies*, 2:1, 1985, 47–67.

Obeidat, Marwan M., 'In Search of the Orient: The Muslim East on the Contemporary American Literary Scene', *International Journal of Islamic and Arabic Studies*, 3:1, 1986, 43–9.

Obediat, Marwan and Mumaiz, Ibrahim, 'Anglo-American Literary Sources on the Muslim Orient', *Journal of American Studies of Turkey*, 13, 2001, 47–72.

Ober, W.U., '"Muhammad": The Outline of a Proposed Poem by Coleridge and Southey', *Notes and Queries*, New Series, 5, 1958, 448.

Ogden, Daryl, 'The Architecture of Empire: "Oriental" Gothic and the Problem of British Identity in Ruskin's Venice', *Victorian Literature and Culture*, 25:1, 1997, 109–20.

Ogle, Robert B., 'The Metamorphosis of Selim: Ovidian Myth in *The Bride of Abydos*', *Studies in Romanticism*, 20, 1981, 21–31.

Omar, Irfan A., 'Representation and Appropriation of the "Muslim Woman" in the European Literary Imagination: From Medieval to the Romantic Period', *The Muslim World*, 90:3–4, 2000, 479–87.

Orel, Harold, 'Shelley's *The Revolt of Islam:* The Last Great Poem of the English Enlightenment?', *Studies on Voltaire and the Eighteenth Century*, 89, 1972, 187–207.

Orfalae, Gregory, 'Literary Devolution: The Arab in the Post-World War II Novel in English', *Journal of Palestine Studies*, 17:2, 1988, 109–28.

Orr, John C., 'When East Meets West: Rethinking the Domestic Heroine and the Western in Dorothy Scarborough's *The Wind*', *Pacific Coast Philology*, 31:1, 1996, 107–19.

Osborne, Edna, 'Oriental Diction and Theme in English Verse, 1740–1840', *Bulletin of the University of Kansas Humanistic Studies*, 2 May 1916, 8–141.

Oueijan, Naji B., '*Byron and Sufism: His Concept of Selfless Love,* The 25th International Byron Conference in Messilonghi, Athens, in Marios Byron Raizis (Ed.), *Byron: A Poet for all Seasons*, Athens, The Messolonghi Byron Society, 2000, 258–67.

Oueijan, Naji B., 'Byron's Eastern Literary Portraits', in M.B. Raizis (Ed.), *Byron and the Mediterranean World*, Athens, Hellenic Byron Society, 1995, 93–103.

Oueijan, Naji B., 'Echoes from the Orient in Romantic Visions, The 10th International Symposium of the German Society of English Romanticism, University of Regensburg', in Christophe Bode and Katharina Rennhak (Eds.), *Romantic Voices, Romantic Poetics*, Trier, Wisssenschchaftlicher Verlag Trier, 2005, 177–85.

Oueijan, Naji B., 'Futile Encounters between East and West: Islam and Christianity in Byron's *The Giaour*, The 28th International Byron Conference-Kyoto, Japan, in Reiko Aiura (et. al.) (Eds.), *Byron the Traveller*, Kyoto, The Japanese Byron Society, 2003, 193–208.

Oueijan, Naji B., 'Orientalism', in Virgil Nemoianu (Ed.), *The Romantic's Added Dimension: Romanticism in its Modern Aspects*. Wilmington, Council on National Literatures, 1998, 37–50.

Oueijan, Naji B., 'Perceptions and Misconceptions: Islam in Nineteenth-Century Art and Literature, in Edward Allam (Ed.), *God in Multicultural Society*, Beirut, Notre Dame University, 2006, 85–98.

Oueijan, Naji B., 'Sexualizing the Orient', *Prism(s), Essays in Romanticism*,14, 2006, 7–25.

Oueijan, Naji B., 'Sufism, Christian Mysticism and Romanticism', *Palma Journal*, Beirut, Notre Dame University Press, 7, 2001, 9–22.

Oueijan, Naji B., 'The Orient in Dr. Johnson's Rasselas', *Dirasat*, 22, 1987, 41–8.

Oueijan, Naji B., 'The Romantic Selflessness: Sufism in Romanticism', *International Journal of Arabic-English Studies-IJASE*, 2:1&2, 2001, 43–54.

Oueijan, Naji B., 'Western Exoticism and Byron's Orientalism', *Prism(s): Essays in Romanticism*, 6, 1998, 27–39.

Oueijan, Naji B., *'Byron's Eastern Bride,* The 7th International Conference of the Society for English Romanticism in the University of Duisburg, Germany, *in* Petra Bridzum and Frank Erik Pointer (Eds.), *Byron as Reader*, Essen, Die Blaue Eule, 2000, 100–8.

Oueijan, Naji B., Byron, 'Delacroix and the Oriental Sublime', *Revue de l'Université de Moncton*, Numéro hors série, 2005, 115–25.

Oueijan, Naji B., *Byron's Eastern Quests: A Liberation of the Spirit, Palma Journal,* Beirut: Notre Dame University Press (8), 2002, 83–96.

Palit, Chittabrata, 'Orientalism, William Jones and Oriental Studies', *Journal of the Asiatic Society*, Calcutta, India, 36:3, 1994, 131–40.

Parker, Gerald D., 'The Moor's Progress: A Study of Edward Young's Tragedy, *'The Revenge''*, *Theatre Research International*, 6, 1981, 172–95.

Parker, Patricia, 'Black Hamlet: Battening on the Moor', *Shakespeare Studies*, 31, 2003, 127–64.

Parker, Patricia, 'Fantasies of "Race" and "Gender": Africa, Othello and Bringing to Light', in Margo Hendricks and Patricia Parker (Eds.), *Women,*

Race, and Writing in the Early Modern Period, London, Routledge, 1994, 84–100.

Parreaux, A., 'The Caliph and the Swinish Multitude' in Fatma Moussa Mahmoud (Ed.), *William Beckford of Fonthill, 1760–1844*, Cairo, Dar al-Marifah, 1960.

Parry, Benita, 'The Contents and Discontents of Kipling's Imperialism', *New Formations*, 6, 1988, 49–63.

Passmann, Dirk F., 'The Dean and the Turk: Jonathan Swift, "Mahometanism", and Religious Controversy Before the "Discourse Concerning the Mechanical Operation of the Spirit"', *Swift Studies*, 22, 2007, 113–45.

Pathak, Zakia (et al.), 'The Prisonhouse of Orientalism', *Textual Practice*, 5:2, 1991, 195–218.

Patrick, J. Max, 'Hawk Versus Dove: Francis Bacon's Advocacy of a Holy War by James I against the Turks', *Studies in Literary Imagination*, 4, 1971, 159–73.

Patrides, C., 'The Bloody and Cruell Turke: The Background of a Renaissance Commonplace', *Studies in the Renaissance*, 10, 1963, 126–35.

Paull, Michael Ray, 'Mahomet and the Conversion of the Heathen in *Piers Plowman*', *English Language Notes*, 10:1, 1972, 1–8.

Peers, Douglas M., '"There is Nothing More Poetical Than War": Romanticism, Orientalism, and Militarism in J. W. Kaye's *Narratives of the Conquest of India*', in Julie F. Codell (Ed.),

Imperial Co-Histories: National Identities and the British and Colonial Press, London, Assoc. University Presses, 2003, 273–99.

Pelckmans, Paul, 'Walter Scott's Orient: *The Talisman*' in C.C. Barfoot and Theo D'haen (Eds.), *Oriental Prospects: Western Literature and the Lure of the East,* Amsterdam, Rodopi, 1998, 97–109.

Perna, Floriana, 'Between Orient and Occident: T. S. Eliot's Encounter with Alterity', in Agostino Lombardo (Ed.), *Presenza di T. S. Eliot,* Rome, Bulzoni, 2001, 71–82.

Peternel, Joan, 'Laurel Sicks, Rag Words, and James Joyce: Crossroads of East and West', *James Joyce Quarterly,* 34:1/2, 1996/97, 135–43.

Pettit, Henry, 'Coleridge's Mount Abora', *MLN,* 54, 1941, 376.

Phialas, Peter G., 'The Source of Massinger's *Emperour of the East*', *Publications of Modern Language Association,* 65: 4, 1950, 473–82.

Phillips, K.J., 'Hindu Avatars, Moslem Martyrs, and Primitive Dying Gods in E.M. Forster's *A Passage to India*', *Journal of Modern Literature,* 15:1, Summer 1988, 121–40.

Piazza, Elio di, 'Narrating the Arab in Kinglake's Travel-diary', in Jalal Uddin Khan and Adrian E. Hare (Eds.), *English and Islam: Creative Encounters 96,* Kuala Lumpur, Malaysia, International Islamic University, 1996, 259–68.

Pionke, Albert D., 'Beyond "The Hero as Prophet": A Survey of Images of Islam in Carlyle's Works', *Literature and Belief*, 25:1/2, 2005, 496–511.

Pirbhai, Mariam, 'Against the Oriental(ist) Current: Homosexuality and Empire in E. M. Forster's *The Other Boat*', *Dalhousie Review*, 86:3, 2006, 345–58.

Pitcher, E. W., 'Franklin's Ephemera in Oriental (Cross-Over?) Guise', *Notes and Queries*, 44:2, 1997, 236–8.

Pitt, A.S., 'The Sources, Significance and Date of Franklin's *An Arabian Tale*', *PMLA*, 57, 1942, 155–68.

Platt, Jas, 'Pronunciation of "Giaour"', *Notes and Queries*, 8th Series, 9 May 1896, 368.

Pope, Arthur Upham, 'Persia and the Holy Grail', *Literary Review*, 1: 1, 1957, 57–71.

Porter, Dennis, '*Orientalism* and Its Problems', in Francis Barker (et al.), (Eds.), *The Politics of Theory*, Colchester, UK, University of Essex, 1983, 179–211.

Potter, Lois, 'Pirates and Turning Turk in Renaissance Drama', in Jean-Pierre Maquerlot and Michele Willems (Eds.), *Travel and Drama in Shakespeare's Time*, New York, Cambridge University Press, 1996, 14–31.

Power, Henriette Lazaridis, 'Shahrazade, Turko the Terrible, and Shem: The Reader as Voyeur in *Finnegans Wake*', in Morris Beja and Shari Benstock (Eds.), *Coping with Joyce: Essays from the Copenhagen Symposium*, Columbus, Ohio State University Press, 1989, 248-61.

Power, Stephen S., 'Through the Lens of Orientalism: Samuel Johnson's *Rasselas*', *West Virginia University Philological Papers*, 40, 1994, 6–10.

Qian, Zhaoming, 'Late Stevens, Nothingness, and the Orient', *Wallace Stevens Journal*, 25:2, 2001, 164–72.

Ragussis, Michael, 'Language and Metamorphosis in Wordsworth's Arab Dream', *Modern Language Quarterly*, 36, 1975, 148–65.

Rahimieh, Nasrin, 'Orientalism Revised', *Canadian Review of Comparative Literature*, 16:1/2, March-June 1989, 155–60.

Rahman, Shazia, 'Orientalism, Deconstruction, and Relationality: Sara Suleri's *Meatless Days*', *LIT*, 15:4, 2004, 347–62.

Raizada, Harish, 'T.S. Eliot and the Wisdom of the East' in Harish Raizada, *Literary Studies*, Aligarh, India, Three Men's Publications, 1968, 81–158.

Ramakrishnan, A.K., 'The Gaze of Orientalism: Reflections on Linking Postcolonialism and International Relations', *International Studies*, New Delhi, India, 36:2, 1999, 129–63.

Ramey, Lynn Tarte, 'Le Jeu de Saint Nicolas: Saracens and Dramatic Genre', Presented at Southeastern Medieval Association Conference. New Orleans, LA, 18–20 October 2001.

Ramey, Lynn Tarte, 'The Imaginary and Symbolic Saracen', Presented at Modern Language Association Convention, Washington, DC, 27-30 December 2000.

Ramey, Lynn Tarte, 'Imagining the Route: Getting to the Orient in Medieval Romances', Presented at the Conference on 'La Géographie dans les romans médiévaux', Saint-Valery-sur-Somme, France, 28–31 March 1996.

Rapf, Joanna, 'The Byronic Heroine: Incest and the Creative Process', *Studies in English Literature*, 21, 1918, 637–45.

Raw, Laurence, 'T. E. Lawrence, the Turks, and the Arab Revolt in the Cinema: Anglo-American and Turkish Representations', *Literature/Film Quarterly*, 47:2, 2004, 252–61.

Rawi Al-, Ahmed Khalid, 'Manipulating Muslims in John Buchan's *Greenmantle* and A. J. Quinnell's *The Mahdi*: A Pattern of Consistency', *John Buchan Journal*, 36, 2007, 18–32.

Reid, Brian Holden, 'The Experience of the Arab Revolt as Interpreted in T. E. Lawrence's *Seven Pillars of Wisdom*', *Journal of the T. E. Lawrence Society*, 4:2, 1995, 36–49.

Reisinger, Deborah Streifford, 'The Other and the Same: The Ambiguous Role of the Saracen in *La chanson de Roland*', *Romance Languages Annual*, 9, 1997, 94–7.

Relihan, Constance C., 'Suppressing Islam: The Geography of Sidney's Arcadian Landscape', Paper read at the MLAS Conference, Chicago, December 1995.

Rendall, Jane, 'Scottish Orientalism from Robertson to James Mill, *The Historical Journal,* 25:1, 1982, 43–69.

Repplier, Agnes, 'When Lalla Rookh was Young', *Atlantic Monthly*, 100, 1907, 807–12.

Ribner, Irving, 'The Idea of History in Marlowe's *Tamburlaine*', in, R.J. Kaufmann (Ed.), *Elizabethan Drama: Modern Essays in Criticism,* New York, Oxford University Press, 1961, 81–94.

Rice, Warner G., 'A Principal Source of *The Battle of Alcazar*', *Modern Language Notes,* 58, 1943, 428–31.

Rice, Warner G., 'Early English Travelers to Greece and the Levant', *University of Michigan Publications*, 10, 1933, 205–6.

Rice, Warner G., 'The Sources of Massinger's *"The Renegado"*', *Philological Quarterly,* 11, 1932, 65–75.

Rice, Warner G., 'To Turn Turk' *Modern Language Notes,* 46, 1931, 153–4.

Richardson, Alan, 'Astarte: Byron's *Manfred* and Montesquieu's *Letters Persanes*', *Keats-Shelley Journal*, 40, 1991, 19–22.

Richardson, Alan, 'Epic Ambivalence: Imperial Politics and Romantic Deflection in Williams's *Peru* and Landor's *Gebir*', in Alan Richardson and Sonia Hofkosh (Eds.), *Romanticism, Race and Imperial Culture, 1780–1834*, Bloomington, Indiana University Press, 1996, 265–82.

Richardson, Alan, 'Escape from the Seraglio: Cultural Transvestism in *Don Juan*', in Alice Levine and Robert N. Keane (Eds.), *Rereading Byron: Essays Selected from Hofstra University's Byron Bicentennial Conference*, New York, Garland, 1993, 175–85.

Richon, Olivier, 'Representation, the Harem and the Despot', *Block*, 10, 1985, 34–41.

Rishmawi, G.K., 'Islam and Muslims in Byron's *The Corsair*', *International Journal of Arabic-English Studies*, 1:2, 2000, 299–312.

Rishmawi, G.K., 'The Muslim East in Byron's *Don Juan*', *Papers on Language & Literature*, 35:3, 1999, 227–43.

Rizvi, Simi, 'Muslim Characters in E.M.Forster's *A Passage to India*', in A.R. Kidwai, (Ed.), *Stranger than Fiction: Images of Islam and Muslims in English Fiction*, Delhi, A.P.H., 2000, 49–85.

Roberts, Mary, 'Contested Terrains: Women Orientalists and the Colonial Harem', in Jill Beaulieu and Mary Roberts (Eds.), *Orientalism's Interlocutors: Paintings, Architecture, Photographs*, Durham, NC, Duke University Press, 2002, 179–204.

Robinson, Benedict, '"Strange Commodities": Commerce and Conversion in *The Renegado*', Paper presented at the Conference '1453 to 1699: Cultural Encounters between East and West', Institute of English Studies, London, 5–7 December 2002.

Robinson, Julian, 'The Impact of the Orient on European Thought, 1770–1850', *Renaissance and Modern Studies*, 31, 1987, 102–33.

Rodgers, Terence, 'Restless Desire: Rider Haggard, Orientalism and the New Woman', *Women: A Cultural Review*, 10:i, 1999, 35–46.

Rodinson, Maxime, 'The Western Image and Western Studies of Islam', in Joseph Schacht and C.E. Bosworth (Eds.), *The Legacy of Islam*, Oxford, Oxford University Press, 1979, 10–62.

Rosen, Alan, 'The Rhetoric of Exclusion: Jew, Moor and the Boundaries of Discourse', in Joyce Green MacDonald, (Eds.), *The Merchant of Venice'* in *Race, Ethnicity, and Power in the Renaissance*, NJ, Madison, Farleigh Dickinson University Press, 1997, 67–79.

Rosenthal, Melinda M., 'Burton's Literary Uroburos: *The Arabian Nights* as Self-Reflexive Narrative', *Pacific Coast Philology*, 25:1–2, 1990, 116–25.

Ross, Lawrence J., '"Marble", "Crocodile", and "Turban'd Turk" in "Othello"', *Philological Quarterly*, 40, October 1961, 476–84.

Rossington, Michael, 'Shelley and the Orient', *Keats-Shelley Review*, 6, Autumn 1995, 18–36.

Rouse, Robert, 'Expectation vs. Experience: Encountering the Saracen Other in Middle English Romance', *SELIM: Journal of the Spanish Society for Medieval English Language and Literature*, 10, 2000, 125–40.

Rowse, A.L., 'Welsh Orientalist: Sir William Jones', *History Today,* 21, 1971, 57–64.

Roy, Parama, 'Oriental Exhibits: Englishmen and Natives in Burton's *Personal Narrative of a Pilgrimage to al-Madinah & Meccah*', *Boundary,* 2, 22:1, 1995, 186–210.

Rozen, M., 'Pedigree Remembered, Reconstructed, Invented: Benjamin Disraeli between East and West' in M. Kramer (Ed.), *The Jewish Discovery of Islam: Studies in Honor of Bernard Lewis,* Tel Aviv University 1999, 49–75.

Rudd, Andrew, '"Oriental" and "Orientalist" Poetry: The Debate in Literary Criticism in the Romantic Period', *Romanticism,* 13:1, 2007, 53–62.

Rushdy, Rashad, 'English Writings on Egypt', *Cairo Studies,* 1963–6, 78–96.

Rushdy, Rashad, 'The English Travel Book (1780–1850) – A Popular Literary Form', *Bulletin of the Faculty of Arts, University of Cairo,* 15 May 1953, 159–79.

Saglia, Diego, 'Orientalism', in Ferber, Michael (Ed.), *A Companion to European Romanticism,* Oxford, Blackwell, 2005, 467–85.

Saglia, Diego, 'William Beckford's "Sparks of Orientalism" and the Material-Discursive Orient of British Romanticism', *Textual Practice,* 16:1, 2002, 75–92.

Saglia, Diego, 'Words and Things: Southey's East and the Materiality of Oriental Discourse', in Lynda Pratt (Ed.), *Robert Southey and the Contexts of*

English Romanticism, Aldershot, UK, Ashgate, 2006, 167–86.

Sahas, Daniel J., 'Saracens and Arabs in the *Leimon* of John Moschos', *Byzantiaka,* 17, 1997, 123–38.

Sahas, Daniel J., 'Saracens and the Syrians in the Byzantine Anti-Islamic Literature and Before', *Orientalia Christiana Analecta,* 256, 1998, 387–408.

Sahni, Chaman L., 'E.M. Forster's *A Passage to India*: The Islamic Dimension', *Cahiers Victoriens Et edouardiens,* 17 April 1983, 73–88.

Said, Edward, '"*Kim*": The Pleasures of Imperialism', *Raritan,* 2, 1987, 20–30.

Said, Edward, 'Orientalism Reconsidered', in Francis Baker (Ed.), *Europe and Its Others: Proceedings of the Essex Conference on the Sociology of Literature,* Essex, 1984, 14–27.

Salami, Mahmoud, 'The Archaeological Representation of the Orient in John Fowles's *Daniel Martin*', *Ariel,* 29:3, 1998, 143–68.

Sallam, Mona Hamed, 'The Different Attitudes Toward Women in the East and the West in the Late 19th Century and the Early 20th Century: A Comparative Study with Special Emphasis on Hilton Hill's novel, '*His Egyptian Wife*'.' *The Proceedings of the International Conference: Comparative Literature in the Arab World,* Cairo, Egyptian Society of Comparative Literature (ESCL), 1998, 209–16.

Salt, J., 'Fact and Fiction in the Middle Eastern Novels of Leon Uris', *Journal of Palestine Studies*, 14:3, 1985, 54–63.

Sanok, Catherine, 'Almoravides at Thebes: Islam and European Identity in *Roman de Thebes*', *Modern Language Quarterly*, 64: 3, 2003, 277–98.

Sanok, Catherine, 'East of England: "Orientalism" in Middle English Virgin Martyr Legends', Presented at the Conference 'Between Empires: "Orientalism" Before 1600', Cambridge, 12–15 July 2001.

Scaglione, Aldo, 'The Mediterranean's Three Spiritual Shores, Images of the Self between Christianity and Islam in the later Middle Ages' in A. Leigh and Rochester Arrathoon, (Eds.), *The Craft of Fiction: Essays in Medieval Poetics*, MI, Solaris Press, 1984, 453–74.

Scherwatzky, Steven, 'Johson, *Rasselas* and the Politics of Empire', *Eighteenth-Century Life*, 16, 1992, 103–13.

Schibanoff, Susan, 'Worlds Apart: Orientalism, Antifeminism, and Heresy in Chaucer's *Man of Law's Tale*', *Exemplaria*, 8: 1, 1996, 59–96.

Schiffer, Reinhold, 'The Romanticized Orient: Varieties of Cultural Description in English Travel Books of the Early 19th Century', in Kaluza, Irena (Ed.), *Proceedings of the Second April Conference of University Teachers of English, Cracow*, 1984, 215–25.

Schildgen, Brenda Deen, 'Heathenesse in the *Canterbury Tales*: Christian versus Islamic and Pagan Space in the *Man of Law's Tale*', in Brenda Deen Schildgen, *Pagans, Tartars, Moslems and Jews in Chaucer's Canterbury Tales*, Gainsville, FL, University Press of Florida, 2001, 48–68.

Schmitt, Cannon, 'Mother Dracula: Orientalism, Degeneration, and Anglo-Irish National Subjectivity at the Fin de Siècle', *Bucknell Review*, 38:1, 1994, 25–43.

Schmuck, Stephan, 'From Sermon to Play: Literary Representations of "Turks" in Renaissance England 1550–1625', *Literature Compass*, 2, 156, 2006, 1–29.

Schneider, Jeffrey L., 'Secret Sins of the Orient: Creating a (Homo)textual Context for Reading Byron's *The Giaour*', *College English*, 65:1, 2002, 81–95.

Schoeck, Richard, 'Thomas More's "Dialogue of Comfort" and the Problem of the Real Grand Turk', *English Miscellany*, Rome, 20, 1969, 23–37.

Schouppe, William, 'Orientalist Visions and Revisions: Edward Said's *Orientalism* and Representations of the Orient in Paul Bowles' in C.C. Barfoot and Theo D'haen (Eds.), *Oriental Prospects: Western Literature and the Lure of the East*, Amsterdam, Rodopi, 1998, 54–63.

Schueller, Malini Johar, 'Harems, Orientalist Subversions, and the Crisis of Nationalism: The Case of Edgar Allan Poe and "Ligeia"', *Criticism*, 37, 1995, 601–23.

Schwarz, D., 'Disraeli Abroad: The Making of a "Continental Mind" 1830–1876', in M. Cotsell (Ed.), *Creditable Warriors*, London, Ashfield Press, 1990, 53–66.

Schwoebel, Robert, 'Coexistence, Conversion, and the Crusade Against the Turks', *Studies in the Renaissance*, 12, 1965, 164–87.

Seed, David, '"Disjointed Fragments" Concealment and Revelation in *The Giaour*', *Byron Journal*, 18, 1990, 14–27.

Sergheni, El Habib Benrahal, 'William Beckford's Symbolic Appropriation of the Oriental Context', in C.C. Barfoot and Theo D'haen (Eds.), *Oriental Prospects: Western Literature and the Lure of the East*, Amsterdam, Rodopi, 1998, 43–64.

Shaffer, E.S., 'The Oriental Idyll', in E.S. Shaffer, *'Kubla Khan' and the Fall of Jerusalem: The Mythological School in Biblical Criticism and Secular Literature, 1770–1880*, Cambridge, Cambridge University Press, 1975, 96–144.

Shaheen, J., 'The Hollywood Arab', *Journal of Popular Film and Television*, 14:4, 148–57.

Shaheen, Mohammad, 'Forester's Salute to Egypt', *Twentieth Century Literature*, 39, 1993, 32–47.

Shaheen, Mohammad, 'Forster's *Alexandria*, The Transitional Journey', in G.K. Das and John Beer (Eds.), *E.M. Forster: A Human Exploration: Centenary Essays*, New York, New York University Press, 1979, 78–89.

Shaheen, Mohammad, 'Forster's Orientalism', *Arab Journal for the Humanities,* 6:24, 1986, 324–45.

Shatto, Susan, 'The Strange Charm of "Far, Far Away": Tennyson, the Continent, and the Empire', in Michael Cotsell (Ed.), *Creditable Warriors, 1830–1876,* London, Ashfield, 1990, 119–29.

Shaw, Marion, 'Tennyson's Dark Continent', *Victorian Poetry* 32:2, 1994, 157–69.

Shaw, Sheila G., 'Early English Editions of the *Arabian Nights*: Their Value to the Eighteenth Century Literary Scholarship', *Muslim World,* 49, 1959, 232–8.

Sheeran, P. F., 'Wilfred Scawen Blunt - A Tourist of the Revolutions', in W. Zach & H. Kosoked (Eds.), *Literary Interrelations: Ireland, England and The World, 3: National Images and Stereotypes,* Tübingen, Narr, 1987, 153–60.

Shepherd, Simon. 'Turks and Fathers', in Simon Shepherd, *Marlowe and the Politics of Elizabethan Theatre,* New York, St. Martin's Press, 1986, 142–77.

Sherwani, Sherin, 'Muslim Characters in Beckford's *Vathek*' in A.R. Kidwai (Ed.), *Stranger Than Fiction: Images of Islam and Muslims in English Fiction,* Delhi, A.P.H., 2000, 15–48.

Shetawi al-, Mahmoud F., 'The Oriental in Shakespeare', *Arab Journal for the Humanities,* 17:68, 1999, 310–30.

Shloss, Carol Loeb, ''Behind the Veil': James Joyce and the Colonial Harem', *James Joyce Quarterly,* 35, 1998, 333–47.

Shloss, Carol Loeb, 'Joyce in the Context of Irish Orientalism', *James Joyce Quarterly*, 35:2/3, 1998, 264–71.

Shurbutt, Sylvia Bailey, 'The Poetry of Matthew Arnold: Nature and the Oriental Wisdom', *University of Dayton Review*, 13:3, 1985–6, 41–8.

Siddiqui, M. N., 'Milton and the Orient', *Osmania Journal of English Studies*, 2, 1962, 37–47.

Siddiqui, Mohd Asim, 'Imperial Attitudes in W. Somersel Maugham's *Up at the Villa, Aligarh Journal of English Studies*, 27:1–2, 2005, 61–72.

Siegrist, Mary, 'A Poet of the Orient, J.E. Flecker', *New York Times Book Review*, 30 July 1922, 8–24.

Silverstein, Theodore, 'Andreas, Plato and the Arabs: Remarks on Some Recent Accounts of Courtly Love', *Modern Philology*, 47: 2, 1949, 117–26.

Simmons, Clare A., '"Useful and Wasteful Both": Southey's *Thalaba the Destroyer* and the Function of Annotation in the Romantic Oriental Poem', *Genre*, 27:1/2, 1994, 83–104.

Simon, Daniel, 'Translating Ruskin: Marcel Proust's Orient of Devotion', *Comparative Literature Studies*, 38:2, 2001, 142–68.

Sipple, James B., 'Endgame: Beckett's Oriental Subtext and the Prison of Consciousness', *Analecta Husserliana*, 56, 1998, 229–35.

Sitwell, Osbert, 'The Sole Arabian Tree', *Times Literary Supplement*, 1941, 199.

Skura, Meredith Anne, 'Discourse and the Individual: The Case of Colonialism in *The Tempest*', *Shakespeare Quarterly*, 40, 1989, 42–69.

Soguk, Nevzat, 'Reflections on the 'Orientalized Orientals'', *Alternatives*, 18:3, 1993, 361–84.

Somers, Leonard H., 'Islam and Creation Myths: A Reading of Page Five of *Finnegans Wake*', in Gottlib Gaiser (Ed.), *International Perspectives of James Joyce*, New York, Whitston, 1986, 153–60.

Spector, Sheila A., 'Orientalism in Disraeli's *Alroy*', in Diane Long Hoeveler and Jeffrey Cass (Eds.), *Interrogating Orientalism: Contextual Approaches and Pedagogical Perspectives*, Columbus, Ohio State University Press, 2006, 121–36.

Speed, Diane, 'The Saracens of *King Horn*', *Speculum*, 65:3, 1990, 564–95.

Spencer, T., 'Turks and Trojans in the Renaissance', *Modern Language Review*, 47, 1952, 330–3.

Sperry, Stuart, 'The Sexual Theme in Shelley's *The Revolt of Islam*', *Journal of English and Germanic Philology*, 82:1, 1983, 32–49.

Srigley, Michael, '"Heavy-Headed Revel East and West": Hamlet and Christian IV of Denmark', in Gunnar Sorelius (Ed.), *Shakespeare and Scandinavia: A Collection of Nordic Studies*, London, Associated University Presses, 2002, 168–92.

Srivastava, R.K., 'Indianness of Southey's *Curse of Kehama*', *Aligarh Journal of English Studies*, 22:1, 2000, 67–80.

Stauffer, Andrew, 'The Hero in the Harem: Byron's Debt to Medieval Romance in *Don Juan*', *European Romantic Review*, 10:1, Winter 1999, 84–97.

Stevens, Paul and Sapra, Rahul, 'Akbar's Dream: Moghul Toleration and English/British Orientalism', *Modern Philology*, 104:3, 2007, 379–411.

Stotesbury, J.A., 'Genre and Islam in Recent Anglophone Romantic Fiction', in Susan Onega and Christian Gutleban (Eds.), *Refractoring the Canon in Contemporary British Literature and Film*, Amsterdam, Rodopi, 2004, 69–82.

Suleiman, M. Yasir, 'The Arabs are Different from You and I', *Archiv Orientálni*, 61:iii, 1993, 241–60.

Suleri, Sara, 'Forster's Imperial Erotic', in Sara Suleri, *The Rhetoric of English India*, Chicago, University of Chicago Press, 1992, 132–48.

Suleri, Sara, 'The Adolescence of Kim' in Sara Suleri, *The Rhetoric of English India*, Chicago, University of Chicago Press, 1992, 111–13.

Suyoufie, Fadia, 'The Representation of Oriental Women in Nineteenth-Century Women's Poetry', *Abhath al-Yarmouk (Literature & Linguistics)*, 11:1, 1993, 9–25.

Sunne Conklin Akbari, 'From Due East to True North: Orientalism and Orientation', in The Postcolonial Middle Ages, 2000.

Svilpis, J.E., 'Orientalism, Fantasy, and *Vathek*', in Kenneth W. Graham (Ed.), *Vathek and the Escape from Time: Bicentenary Revaluations*, New York, AMS, 1990, 49–72.

Takaki, Ronald, '*The Tempest* in the Wilderness: The Racialization of Savagery', *Journal of American History*, 79, 1992, 892–912.

Tarawreh, Yousef, 'Islamic Reflection: Revisionist Portrayals of Arab Civilization with Particular Reference to Wordsworth, Pope, Cervantes, and Dante', *International Journal of Islamic and Arabic Studies*, 4, 1987, 55–74.

Taylor, Jessica, 'And You Can Be My Sheikh: Gender, Race, and Orientalism in Contemporary Romance Novels', *Journal of Popular Culture*, 40:6, 2007, 1032–51.

Taylor, Susan, 'Orientalism in the Romantic Era', *Literature Compass*, 1:1, 2003–4.

Thomas, Donald, 'Samuel Johnson's Arabia', *Journal of English*, 15, 1987, 1–14.

Thomas, Gordon K., 'Finest Orientalism, Western Sentimentalism, Proto-Zionism: The Muses of Byron's *Hebrew Melodies*', *Prism(s)*, 1, 1993, 51–66.

Thomas, Susie, 'This Thing of Darkness I Acknowledge Mine: Aphra Behn's *Abdelazer; or, The Moor's Revenge*', *Restoration*, 22:1, 1998, 18–39.

Thompson, K.F., 'Beckford and Henley', *Etudes Anglaises*, 41, July-September 1961, 225–8.

Thompson, K.F., 'Henley's Share in *Vathek*', *Philological Quarterly*, 31, 1952, 75–80.

Thomson, Rodney M., 'William of Malmesbury and Some Other Western writers on Islam', *Medievalia et Humanistica*, 6, 1975, 179–87.

Thumboo, Edwin, 'E.M. Forster's *A Passage to India*: from Caves to Court', *Southern Review*, 10:4, 1978.

Thundy, Zacharias P., 'The Dragon in Beowulf: Cain's Seed, Heresy, and Islam', in Loren C. Gruber, Meredith Crellin Grueber and Gregory K. Jember (Eds.), *Essays on Old, Middle, Modern English and Old Icelandic in Honor of Raymond P. Tripp, Jr.*, Lewiston, NY, Edwin Mellen Press, 2000, 201–30.

Thurston, Bonnie, 'Thomas Merton's Interest in Islam: The Example of *Dhikr*', *American Benedictine Review*, 45:2, 1994, 131–41.

Tidrick, Kathryn, 'Richard Burton', in Kathryn Tidrick, *Heart Beguiling Araby: The English Romance with Arabia*, London, I.B. Tauris, 1989, 57–83.

Tillotson, Geoffrey, '*Rasselas* and the Persian Tales', *Times Literary Supplement*, 29 August 1935.

Tintner, A.R., 'Fire of the Heart in "Al Aaraaf": Beckford and Byron as Source', *Poe Studies*, 22 December 1989, 47–8.

Tóibín, Colm, 'Avoid the Orient', *London Review of Books*, 29:1, 2007, 30–4.

Trivedi, Harish, 'T.S. Eliot, English Literature and India', in Harish Trivedi, *Colonial Transaction: English Literature and India*, Manchester, Manchester University Press, 1993, 15–22.

Tolan, John Victor, 'Looking East Before 1453. The Saracen in the Medieval European Imagination', Presented at the Conference '1453 to 1699: Cultural Encounters between East and

West', Institute of English Studies, London, 5-7 December 2002.

Trumpener, Katie, 'Rewriting Roxanne: Orientalism and Intertextuality in Montesquieu's *Lettres Persanes* and Defoe's *The Fortunate Mistress*', *Stanford French Review*, 11, 1987, 177-91.

Twitchell-Waas, Jeffrey, 'Seaward: H.D's *Halen in Egypt* as a Response to Pound's Cantos', *Twentieth Century Literature*, 44, 1998, 464-84.

Tyquin, Michael, 'The Image of the Turk at Gallipoli: Turkish Soldier in 1915 in Australian Literature and Historiography', in Hasan Celâl Güzel, C.Cem Oðuz and Osman Karatay (Eds.), *The Turks*, 4: Ottomans, Ankara, Yeni Türkiye, 2002, 432-8.

van Teeffelen, Toine, 'Argumentation and the Arab Voice in Western Bestsellers', *Text*, Berlin, 11:2, 1991, 241-66.

Vaughan, Virginia Mason. 'Global Discourse: Turks and Venetians', in Mason Virginia (Ed.), *Othello: A Contextual History*, Cambridge, Cambridge University Press, 1994, 13-34.

Versluis, Arthur, 'From Transcendentalism to Universal Religion: Samuel Johnson's Orientalism', *American Transcendental Quarterly*, 5:2, 1991, 109-14.

Viguers, Susan T., 'Peele's *The Battle of Alcazar*', *Explicator*, 43, 1985, 9-12.

Vitale, Marina, 'The Domesticated Heroine in Byron's *Corsair* and William Hone's Prose

Adaptation', *Literature and History*, 10, Spring 1984, 72–94.

Vitkus, Daniel, 'Adventuring Heroes in the Mediterranean: Mapping the Boundaries of Anglo-Islamic Exchange on the Early Modern Stage', *The Journal of Medieval and Early Modern Studies*, 37:1, 2007.

Vitkus, Daniel, 'Turks and Jews in Marlowe's *The Jew of Malta*', in Sullivan, Garrett A., Jr. (et al.) (Eds.), *Early Modern English Drama: A Critical Companion*, Oxford, Oxford University Press, 2006, 61–72.

Vitkus, Daniel, 'Turning Turk in *Othello*: The Conversion and Damnation of the Moor', *Shakespeare Quarterly*, 48, 1997, 145–76.

Vitkus, Daniel, 'Early Modern Orientalism: Representations of Islam in Sixteenth and Seventeenth-Century Europe', in David R. Blanks and Michael Frassetto (Eds.), *Western Views of Islam in Medieval and Early Modern Europe: Perception of Other*, New York, St. Martin's, 1999, 207–30.

Vitkus, Daniel, 'Trafficking with the Turk: English Travelers in the Ottoman Empire During the Early Seventeenth Century', in Jyotsna G. Singh and Ivo Kamps (Eds.), *Travel Knowledge: European Discoveries in the Early Modern Period*, New York, St. Martin's Press, 2000, 35–52.

Vitoux, Pierre, '*Gebir* as an Heroic Poem', *Wordsworth Circle*, 7:1, 1976, 51–7.

Wahab, Amar, 'Mapping West Indian Orientalism: Race, Gender and Representations of Indentured Coolies in the Nineteenth-Century British West Indies', *Journal of Asian American Studies*, 10:3, 2007, 283–311.

Wahba, M., 'Beckford, Portugal and "Childish Error"' in Fatma Moussa Mahmoud (Ed.), *William Beckford of Fonthill, 1760–1844*, Cairo, 1960.

Waith, Eugene M., 'Tamburlaine', in Clifford Leech (Ed.), *Marlowe: A Collection of Critical Essays*, New Jersey, Prentice-Hall, Inc., 1964, 68–91.

Walker, Warren S., 'Extant Analogues of "Franklin's Tale" in Turkish Oral Tradition', *The Chaucer Review*, 33: 4, 1999, 432–8.

Waltz, James Calvin, 'Muhammad and the Muslims in St. Thomas Aquinas', *Muslim World*, 66, 1976, 81–95.

Waltz, James Calvin, 'Carolingian Attitudes Regarding Muslims', *Studies in Medieval Culture*, 5, 1975, 33–40.

Wang, N., 'Orientalism Versus Occidentalism?' *New Literary History*, Baltimore, MD, 28:1, 1997, 57–8.

Wann, Louis, 'The Oriental in Elizabethan Drama', *Modern Philology*, 12 January 1915, 163–87.

Ward, Adrienne, 'Eastern Others on Western Pages: Eighteenth-Century Literary Orientalism', *Literature Compass*, 1:1, 2003/4.

Ward, Geoff, 'Orientalism' in Geoff Ward (Ed.), *Bloomsbury Guide to English Literature: Romantic Literature*', London, Bloomsbury, 1993, 184–5.

Warden, J.S., '*Siege of Corinth*', *Notes and Queries*, 5, June, 1852, 534.

Warren, F. W., 'The Enamored Muslim Princess in Orderic Vital and the French Epic', *PMLA*, 29, 1914, 314–58.

Warren, Michelle R., '*La Chanson de Roland* between France and the East Indies', Presented at the Conference 'Between Empires: "Orientalism" Before 1600', Cambridge, 12–15 July 2001.

Wassil, Gregory, 'Keats' Orientalism', *Studies in Romanticism*, 39:3, 2000, 419–47.

Wasti, Syed Munir, 'A Study of Sir Burton's [Sic] English "Kasidah"' *Ariel (A Research Journal of English Language and Literature)*, 18, 1992–93, 49–53.

Wasti, Syed Munir, 'Eastern Elements in the Works of Leigh Hunt', *Ariel (A Research Journal of English Language and Literature)*, 19, 1993–94, 72–6.

Wasti, Syed Munir, 'The Exotic East in the Poetry of Walter Savage Landor', *Ariel (A Research Journal of English Language and Literature)*, 39–46.

Waterman, David F., 'Byron's Reflexive Orientalism in Cantos V and VI of *Don Juan*', *Etudes Anglaises*, 49:1, Winter 1996, 29–39.

Watkins, D.P., 'Social Relations in Byron's *The Giaour*', *Journal of English Literary History*, 52, Winter 1985, 873–92.

Watson, J.R., 'Orientalism', in J. Raimond and J.R. Watson (Eds.), *A Handbook to English Romanticism*, New York, St. Martin's Press, 1992, 192–5.

Watson, Geoff, 'Representations of Central Asian Ethnicities in British Literature c.1830–1914', *Asian Ethnicity*, 3:ii, 2002, 137–51.

Watt, James, 'Scott, the Scottish Enlightenment, and Romantic Orientalism', in Leith Davis (et al.) (Eds.), *Scotland and the Borders of Romanticism*, Cambridge, Cambridge University Press, 2004, 94–119.

Watt, Montgomery, 'Carlyle on Muhammed', *Hibbert Journal*, 53, 1954–55, 247–54.

Watt, Montgomery, 'Muhammad in the Eyes of the West', *Boston University Journal*, 22:3, 1974, 61–9.

Wazzan, Adnan M., '*The Arabian Nights* in Western Literature: A Discourse Analysis', *Islamic Studies*, Islamabad, Pakistan, 32:1, 1993, 61–71.

Weitzman, A.J., 'More Light on *Rasselas*: The Background of the Egyptian Episodes', *Philological Quarterly*, 48, 1969, 42–58.

Weitzman, Arthur J., 'The Oriental Tale in the Eighteenth Century: A Reconsideration', *Studies on Voltaire in the Eighteenth Century*, 58, 1967, 1389–455.

Weitzman, Arthur J., 'Voyeurism and Aesthetics in the Turkish Bath: Lady Mary's School of Female Beauty', *Comparative Literature Studies*, 39:iv, 2002, 347–59.

Wenner, Manfred W., 'The Arab/Muslim Presence in Medieval Central Europe', *International Journal of Middle East Studies,* 12, 1980, 59–79.

Weryho, Jan, 'Under Eastern Eyes: The Relevance of Edward Said's Study of Joseph Conrad to His Critique of Orientalism', *Conradiana,* 1992, 57–65.

Whale, John, 'Indian Jugglers: Hazlitt, Romantic Orientalism and the Difference of View', in Fulford, Tim (Eds.), *Romanticism and Colonialism: Writing and Empire, 1780–1830,* Cambridge, Cambridge University Press, 1998, 206–20.

Whelan, Frederick G., 'Burke, India, and Orientalism', in Ian Crowe (Ed.), *An Imaginative Whig: Reassessing the Life and Thought of Edmund Burke,* Columbia, Missouri University Press, 2005, 127–57.

Whitney, Lois, 'Did Shakespeare Know "Leo Africanus"?' *Publication of Modern Language Association,* 37, 1922, 470–83.

Wickens, G.M., '*Lalla Rookh* and the Romantic Tradition of Islamic Literature in English', *Year Book of Comparative and General Literature,* 20, 1971, 61–6.

Wiener, H.S.L., 'Byron and the East: Literary Sources of the "*Turkish Tales*"', in Herbert John Davis (Ed.), *Nineteenth Century Studies in Honour of C.S. Northup,* New York, 1968, 89–128.

Wilcox, Rebecca, 'Romancing the East: Greeks and Saracens in Guy of Warwick', in Nicola,

McDonald (Ed.), *Pulp Fictions of Medieval England: Essays in Popular Romance*, Manchester, Manchester University Press, 2004, 217–40.

Williams, Gwyn, 'Durrell in Egypt', *Twentieth Century Literature*, 33, 1987, 298–302.

Wilson, Diana de Armas, 'Turning Turk: Cervantes, Shakespeare and Ottomite Islam', 50th Anniversary Cervantes Lecture, Fordham University, 11 April 2002.

Wilson, Richard, 'Voyage to Tunis: New History and the Old World of *The Tempest*', *English Literary History*, 64, 1997, 333–57.

Wolfson, S.J., 'Couplets, Self and *The Corsair*', *Studies in Romanticism*, 27, 1988, 491–513.

Wood, A.C., 'The English Embassy at Constantinople: 1660–1762', *English Historical Review*, 40: 160, 1925, 533–61.

Wood, A.G., 'Murder in the Seraglio: Orientalism in Seventeeth Century Tragedy', *Papers on 17th Century French Literature*, 12, 1979–80, 91–107.

Wood, Marjorie Elizabeth, 'The Sultaness, Donegild, and Fourteenth Century Female Merchants: Intersecting Discourses of Gender, Economy, and Orientalism in Chaucer's *Man of Law's Tale*', *Comitatus*, 37, 2006, 65–85.

Woodford, 'The Sick King in Bokhara: Arnold and the Sublime of Suffering', in Robert Giddings (Ed.), *Matthew Arnold: Between Two Worlds*, London, Vision, 1986, 100–20.

Woods, Samuel H., 'Images of the Orient: Goldsmith and the Philosophers', *Studies in Eighteenth-Century Culture,* 15, 1986, 257–70.

Wright, Glenn, 'Convention and Conversion: The Saracen Ending of the *Taill of Rauf Coilzear, Al-Masâq: Islam and the Medieval Mediterranean,* 14:ii, 2002, 101–12.

Wu, Ya-Feng, '*The Assassins*: Shelley's Appropriation of History', *Keats-Shelley Review,* 9, Spring 1995, 51–62.

Wunder, Amanda, 'Western Travelers, Eastern Antiquities, and the Image of the Turk in Early Modern Europe', *Journal of Early Modern History,* 7: 1-2, 2003, 89–119.

Yaeger, Patricia, 'Southern Orientalism: Flannery O'Connor's Cosmopolis', *Mississippi Quarterly,* 56:4, 2003, 491–510.

Yaghmour, Fakhry, 'Renegades in Heroic Plays', *Dirasat,* Amman, Jordan, 12: 3, 1985, 39–55.

Yamazaki, Hiroyuki, 'Yeats and Orientalism', in Toshi Furomoto (et al.) (Eds.), *International Aspects of Irish Literature,* Gerrards Cross, Smythe, 1996, 82–92.

Yared, Aida, '"In the Name of Annah": Islam and Salam in Joyce's *Finnegans Wake*', *James Joyce Quarterly,* 35:2/3, 1998, 401–38.

Yegenoglu, Meyda, 'Supplementing the Orientalist Lack: European Ladies in the Harem', in Mahmut

Mutman and Meyda Yegenoglu (Eds.), *Orientalism and Cultural Differences*, Santa Cruz, University of California at Santa Cruz, 1992, 45–80.

Yohannan, John D., 'The Persian Poetry Fad in England 1770–1825', *Comparative Literature*, 4, Spring 1952, 137–160.

Youngkin, Molly, '"Into the Woof, a Little Thibet Wool": Orientalism and Representing "Reality" in Walter Scott's *The Surgeon's Daughter*', *Scottish Studies Review*, 3:1, 2003, 33–57.

Youssef, Loubna A., 'The Image of Nineteenth-Century Cairo as a Medieval City in Kinglake's *Eôthen*', in Paul and Janet Starkey (Eds.), *Interpreting the Orient: Travellers in Egypt and the Near East*, Reading, Ithaca, 2001, 123–37.

Zahlan, Anne Ricketson, 'The Destruction of the Imperial Self in Lawrence Durrell's *The Alexandria Quartet*', *Perspective on Contemporary Literature: Self and Other*, 12, 1986, 3–12.

Zahrawi, Samar, 'The Millionairess: Islam and Capitalism: A Shavian Fantasy About Internationalism', *Tishreen University Journal*, 7, 1994, 99–109.

Zhijian, Tao, 'Citizen of Whose World? Goldsmith's Orientalism', *Comparative Literature Studies*, 33:1, 1996, 15–34.

Zhou, Xiaoyi, 'Oscar Wilde's Orientalism and Late Nineteenth-Century European Consumer Culture', *Ariel*, 28:4, 1997, 49–71.

Ziolkowski, E. J., 'Waking up from Akbar's Dream: The Literary Prefiguration of Chicago's 1893 World's Parliament of Religions', *Journal of Religion*, 73:i, 1993, 42–60.

Zonana, Joyce, 'The Sultan and the Slave: Feminist Orientalism and the Structure of *Jane Eyre*', *Signs*, 18:3, 1993, 592–617.

4

Doctoral Dissertations on Literary Orientalism

Abd el-Hamid, M.S., 'A Study of Warburton's *The Crescent and the Cross* in Relation to the Literary Interest in the Near East shown by English Romantic Writers in the Eighteenth and Earlier Nineteenth Centuries', M.A., University of Bristol, 1948.

Abd el-Hamid, M.S., 'Oriental Satanism in English Literature, with Special Reference to the Romantic Movement', University of London, 1958–9.

Abdelwahed, Said Ibrahim, 'Orientalism and Romanticism; A Historical Dialectical Relationship', Duquesne University, 1992.

Abdullah, A.M., 'The Arabian Nights in English Literature to 1900', University of Cambridge, 1962–3.

Abood, Paula, 'The Arab as Spectacle: Race, Gender and Representation in Australian Popular Culture', University of New South Wales, 2007.

Abu Baker, Mohamed Hassan, 'Representations of Islam and Muslims in Early Modern English Drama from Marlowe to Massinger', University of Glasgow, 1997.

Abu Hilal, Fatin A., 'The Construction of Woman in the Colonial Text: Reorienting Colonial Discourse Analysis Theory', Indiana University of Pennsylvania, 2002.

Abunasser, Rima Jamil, 'Corporate Christians and Terrible Turks: Aesthetics, Economics, and Empire in the Early British Travel Narrative, 1630–1780', University of North Texas, 2003.

Ackerman, Jan Condra Bryant, 'The Education of a Poet: A Study of Shelley's *The Revolt of Islam*', University of Arizona, 1976.

Adams, Valerie Denise, 'The Use of Orientalism in the Drama of Elizabeth Inchbald', University of Mississippi, 1990.

Adipurwawidjana, Ari Jogaiswara, 'The Orient in America: A Post-Colonialist Study of Orientalism in the Writings of Ralph Waldo Emerson', University of Kentucky, 1995.

Agzenay, A., 'Theoretical Approaches to the "Other" of Europe: Between "Fact" and "Fiction"', Notingham University, 1989.

Ahmad, M., 'Oriental Influence in English Poetry of the Romantic Period', University of Birmingham, 1959–60.

Ahmed, Abdel Aziz, L.N., 'The Works of Edward William Lane and Ideas of the Near East in England, 1800–1850: The Transformation of an Image', University of Cambridge, 1970–1.

Ahmed, Saad Noah, 'Desert Quest: French and British Writers in Arabia and North Africa, 1850–1950', University of Illinois at Urbana-Champaign, 1983.

Aksoy, Yildiz, 'The Turks in Eighteenth Century English Theatre', Ataturk University, 1970.

Alaki, A., 'The Sublime and the Arabesque: *The Thousand and One Nights* and its Gothic Re-Writings', University of East Anglia, 2001.

Alcalay, Ammiel, 'Re:Orienting/Writing the Mediterranean', City University of New York, 1989.

Ali, Muhsin Jassim, [Musawi, Muhsin Jasim], 'Nineteenth-Century English Criticism of the "Arabian Nights"', Dalhousie University, Canada, 1978.

Ali, Zahra Ahmed Hussein, 'Between Shahrazad and Marcel Proust: Narrative Techniques in *The Alexandria Quartet*', Brown University, 1985.

Allen, Malcolm Dennis, 'The Medievalism of T.E. Lawrence', Pennsylvania State University, 1983.

Almansour, Ahmed Nidal, 'The Middle East in Antebellum America: The Cases of Ralph Waldo Emerson', Nathaniel Hawthorne, and Edgar Allan Poe', Ohio State University, 2005.

Aloni, Gila, 'Islamic Ideology in Chaucer's *Man of Law's Tale*', University of Paris, 2008.

Ambastha, K. P., 'Traces of Oriental Mysticism in the Poetry of the English Romantic Revival', University of Edingburgh, 1955–6.

Apple, Max Issac, 'Arabism, Hermeticism and the Form of the *Anatomy of Melancholy* of Robert Burton', University of Michigan, 1970.

Archer, Frederick, 'Orientalism in Browning', University of North Carolina at Chapel Hill, 1904.

Artemel, S.S., 'The Idea of Turkey in the Elizabethan Period and in the Early Seventeenth Century, with Special Reference to Drama', University of Durham, 1965–6.

Arthur, James, 'Ex Oriente Lux: American Transcendentalism and the Orient Versluis', University of Michigan, 1990.

Asfour, Mohammad Hassan, 'The Crescent and the Cross: Islam and the Muslims in English Literature from Johnson to Byron', Indiana University, 1973.

Askari Al-, Ghida Tarik, 'Dante and al-Ma'arri's "*Risalat al-Ghufran*": A Reconsideration of Islamic Sources of the "*Divina Commedia*"', The Catholic University of America, 1994.

Assad, Thomas J., 'The Near East and the Late Victorians: An Approach to Sir Richard Francis Burton, Wilfrid Scawen Blunt, and Charles Montagu Doughty', University of Wisconsin-Madison, 1954.

Avery, Elizabeth Christina, 'The Oriental Tale in England and France: With Special Reference to Dr. Johnson and Voltaire', State University of New York at Buffalo, 1932.

Azouqa, Aida O., 'Sir Walter Scott and British Orientalism: 1800–1825', University of Chicago, 1993.

Baeshen, Lamia Mohamed Saleh, '*Robinson Crusoe* and *Hayy Bin Yaqzan*: A Comparative Study', The University of Arizona, 1986.

Bagabas, Omar Abdullah, 'Byron's Representation of the Orient in *Childe Harold's Pilgrimage, Don Juan* and *The Oriental Tales*', University of Essex, 1993.

Bahous, Abbes, 'The Novel and Moorish Culture: Cide Hamete, Author of *Don Quixote*', University of Essex, 1990.

Bak, Greg, 'English Representations of Islam at the Turn of the Century: Islam Imagined and Islam Experienced', Dalhousie University, 2000.

Bakhsh, Jalauddein Khuda, 'Melville and Islam', Florida State University, 1988.

Bancroft, Nicholas M., 'Constructing the Self and the Other: An Analysis of Joseph Conrad's *Heart of Darkness*', Northern Michigan University, 2003.

Bangura, Ahmed Sheikh, 'The Politics of Representation: Islam and the Sub-Saharan African Novel', University of Alberta, Canada, 1994.

Baragona, Alan, 'The Depiction of Paganism and Islam in the Fourteenth-Century English Romances of Charlemagne, Troy and Elexander', University of North Carolina, Chapel Hill, 1989.

Barker, C., 'The Stone and the Shell: The Image of the Arab and the Romantic Sublime in the Poetry of Wordsworth and Coleridge', University of Exeter, 2006.

Barthelemy, Anthony Gerard, 'The Representation of Moors in English Drama: 1589–1695', Yale University, 1984.

Basu, Sriparna, 'Overlapping Terrains: Orientalism, Indian Nationalism and the Erotics of Cross-Cultural Contact', University of Illinois at Urbana-Champaign, 1999.

Bazei al-, Saad Abdulrahman, 'Literary Orientalism in Nineteenth-Century Anglo-American Literature: Its Formation and Continuity', Purdue University, 1983.

Behdad, Ali, 'Split Orientalism: The Micropolitics of Modern Representations of Europe's Other (England, France)', University of Michigan, 1990.

Benrahhal-Serghini, el-Habib, 'The Road to Istakhar: A Critical Study of the Text and Context of William Beckford's *Vathek* and the *Episodes*, 1760–1844', Universitaire Instelling Antwerpen, Belgium, 1994.

Beratlis, Stella Stavrula, 'Re-imaging the East : Orientalism, Resistance, and the Travel Essays of Paul Bowles', Arizona State University, 1995.

Beshti el-, Bashir Mahmud, 'The Displacement Towards the East: The Oriental in English Renaissance Literature and Culture', University of California, Berkeley, 1989.

Birchwood, M., 'Dramatic Representations of Islam in England 1640–1685', University of London, 2002.

Bisaha, Nancy, 'Renaissance Humanists and the Ottoman Turks', Cornell University, 1997.

Bishop, Schoen J. and Newman, John R., 'Deconstructing Indian History: Orientalism's Creation and Use of India's Past', New College, 1994.

Bishti, Tarek Malmoud, 'Orientalism and Nineteenth Century English Travellers to the Middle East', University College Dublin, 1990.

Bluck, R.N., 'Oriental and Christian religion in the work of T.S. Eliot, up to "Ash-Wednesday"', University of Leeds, 1983.

Bly, Siobhain Montserrat, 'Stereotypical Saracens, the Auchinleck Manuscript, and the Problems of Imagining Englishness in the Early Fourteenth Century', University of Notre Dame, 2002.

Boerth, Robert John, 'Disorientations: The Matter of the East in English Renaissance Drama', University of California, Irvine, 1995.

Bolton, Jonathan William, 'Personal Landscape: British Poets in Egypt During the Second World War', University of Maryland College Park, 1996.

Bouagada, Habib, 'Orientalism in Translation: *The One Thousand and One Nights* in 18th Century France and 19th Century England', University of Ottawa, 2005.

Bouanani, Ali, 'The Kasbah in the American Imaginary: A Study of the Representation of Morocco in American Travel Narratives, Fiction and Film', University of Toledo, 1996.

Bourara, Hassan, 'Paul Bowles: An 'Invisible Spectator'', University of Minnesota, 1966.

Brocking, M. Elisabeth, 'Common sympathies': Shelley's *Revolt of Islam*', Rice University, 1985.

Broughton, E.S., 'Orientalism in English Poetry', M.A., University of London, 1919.

Brown, Malcolm David, 'The Construction of Muslim Identities in the United Kingdom and France: A Contribution to the Critique of Orientalism', University of Glasgow, 1999.

Brown, Margaret June, 'Henry Adams and the Orient', Tulane University, 1976.

Brown, Wallace C., 'The Near East as Theme and Background in English Literature, 1775–1825, with Special Emphasis on the Literature of Travel', University of Michigan, 1935.

Brown-Haysom, Ryan, '"What deuyl is þis?": Saracens and the Problems of "Sameness" in Middle-English verse Romance', University of Otago, 2007.

Brunson, James Edward, 'The Moor's Last Sigh : Boabdil and the Black Image in American Orientalism, 1816–1893', University of Chicago, 2006.

Burns, J. R., 'William Lithgow's *Total Discourse* (1632) and His 'Science of the World': A Seventeenth-Century Protestant Traveller's View of Europe and the Near East', University of Oxford, 1997.

Burton, Jonathan, '"Turn'd Turk": Islam and English Drama, 1579–1624', City University of New York, 1999.

Cannon, Garland Hampton, 'Oriental Jones: A Biography', University of Texas at Austin, 1955.

Carrasco, Maria Soledad, 'The Moor of Granada in Spanish Literature of the Eighteenth and Nineteenth Centuries', Columbia University, 1954.

Chamrawi El-, A.A.W., 'Some Eastern and Esoteric Aspects in the Works of W.B. Yeats', University of Exeter, 1977.

Chang, Ming-Chu, 'William Butler Yeats and the Orient', University of Colorado, 1949.

Charry, Brinda, 'Representations of Islam in Early Modern England', Syracuse University, 2002.

Chin, Cherry Ying, 'Orientalism in Eighteenth-Century England', State University of New York at Buffalo, 1975.

Choudhry, Z.A., 'Some Eastern Aspects of *Finnegans Wake*', University of Reading, 1994.

Christy, Arthur, 'The Orient in American Transcendentalism: A Study of Emerson, Thoreau, and Alcott', Columbia University, 1978.

Chubbuck, K., 'Empire of the Spirit: the East, Religion and Romanticism in the Works of Some Nineteenth-Century Travel Writers', Oxford University, 1998.

Colon, David A., 'Embodying the Ideogram: Orientalism and the Visual Aesthetic in Modernist Poetry', Greene Roland University, 2004.

Comfort, William Wistar, 'The Development of the Character Types in the French *Chansons de Geste*', Harvard University, 1902.

Conant, Martha Pike, 'Oriental Tale in England in the Eighteenth Century', Columbia University, 1908.

Cordery, Leona F., 'The Picture of the Saracens in Middle English Literature', University of Innsbruck, 1993.

Corwin, Joan, 'Identity in the Victorian Travel Narrative', Indiana University, 1987.

Couling, Scott, 'Constructions of the Orient/Constructions of Self: A Select Study of Contemporary Travel Literature', University of Guelph, 1992.

Coyle, R.D., 'Commerce and Exchange in Eighteenth-Century English and French Oriental Fiction', University London, Royal Holloway, 2006.

Cummins, Rodney John Travers, 'Australian Perceptions of the Orient 1880–1910', Deakin University, Victoria, 2001.

Dagel, Gena Emily, 'Paul Bowles: Manufactured Savage', The University of Texas at Austin, 1984.

Daimiani, Anita, 'British Travel Attitudes to the Near East in the Eighteenth and Nineteenth Centuries', University of Edinburgh, 1977.

Dale, Joshua Paul, 'The Complicity of a Lateral Gaze: From Fantasies of the 'Orient' to an Ethics of Alterity in Cross-Cultural Encounters', University of New York at Buffalo, 2002.

Davies, Robert, 'Warriors and Gentlemen: The Occidental Context of the Arabian Travel Narratives of Burton, Blunt and Lawrence', University of Technology, Loughborough, 1991.

Dean, Tessa, 'The Hookah, Orientalism, and Colonialism in Eighteenth-Century India: An Analysis of Colonel Polier Watching a Nautch', University of North Carolina at Chapel Hill, 2004.

Deen El-, Ahmed Alam, 'A Critical Edition of Thomas Goffe's *The Raging Tyrke, or, Baiazet the Second (1631)*', West Virginia University, 1984.

Degabriele, Maria, 'PostOrientalism: Orientalism since Orientalism', Murdoch University, 1997.

Degenhardt, Jane Hwang, 'Faith, Embodiment and Turning Turk: Islamic Conversion on the Early Modern Stage and the Production of Religious and Racial Identity', University of Pennsylvania, 2005.

Dharmaraj, Glory Ebhenezer, 'Rewriting the East in Old and Middle English Texts: A Study in the Problem of Alterity and the Representation of the Third World Feminine', Loyola University of Chicago, 1992.

Dhesi, Nirmal Singh, 'The Paynims and Saracens of Spenser's *The Faerie Queene*' Michigan State University, 1968.

Diboll, M., 'A Disciple has Crossed Over by Water': An Analysis of Lawrence Durrell's *Alexandria Quartet*', University of Leicester, 2000.

Dixon, John Spencer, 'Representations of the East in English and French Travel Writing 1798–1882 with Particular Reference to Egypt', University of Warwick, 1991.

Dobie, Madeleine Louise, 'Foreign Bodies: The Figure of Oriental Women in Eighteenth- and Nineteenth-Century French and British Literature', Yale University, 1994.

Doll, Robert, G., 'From Alexandria to Aziz: Sources of E.M. Forster's Eastern Protagonist', University of California, San Diego, 1992.

Dow, William E., 'Thoreau's Orientalism: His Eastern Influences and Sources in Walden', Clark University.

Dubey, Mandakini, 'Esotericism and Orientalism: Nineteenth-Century Narrative Initiations', Duke University, 2003.

Duffy, John Dennis, 'Arabia in Literature: Four Visions of the East, 1855–1926', University of Toronto, Canada, 1964.

Durdana, Benazir, 'Muslim India in Anglo-Indian Fiction', Ohio State University, 1997.

Eggers, Marilyn K., 'Orientalism in Wallace Stevens: A Study of the Early Poems and Three Travelers Watch a Sunrise', California State University, 1973.

Einboden, J. M., 'Ralph Waldo Emerson, Persian Poetry and the German Critical Tradition', Cambridge University, 2005.

Ekhtiar, Rochelle Suzette, 'Fictions of Enlightenment: the Oriental Tale in Eighteenth-Century England', Brandeis University, 1985.

Elshqeirat, W., 'Representations of Arabia and North Africa in Selected Prose and Novels in English: 1949–1983', University of Central England, 2005.

Epelde, Kathleen R., 'Travel Guidebooks to India: A Century and a Half of Orientalism', University of Wollongong, 2004.

Esplin, Bruce Willard, 'A Good Westerner Gone Wrong: Asia-Pacific Identity in Pearl Buck's Writing and Activism', Utah State University, 2006.

Evenson, Jennie Malika, 'Judaism, Islam, and English Reformation Literature', University of Michigan, 2005.

Fakahani, Suzan Jamil, 'Irving's *The Alhambra*: Background, Sources, and Motifs', Florida State University, 1988.

Fallon, Gretchen Kidd, 'British Travel-Books from the Middle East, 1890–1914: Conventions of the Genre and Three Unconventional Examples', University of Maryland College Park, 1981.

Farag, F.F., 'Oriental Mysticism in W. B. Yeats', University of Edinburgh, 1959–60.

Farhan, I.H., 'Traces of Averroistic Influence on Christopher Marlowe', M.Litt., University of Strathclyde, 1978.

Farsy al-, Layla Abed al-Salam, 'Washington Irving's *Mahomet*: A Study of the Sources', University of Wisconsin–Milwaukee, 1983.

Fattouh, Essam, 'Ca…Ca… Caliban: Cultural Constructions of Otherness in English Renaissance Drama', State University of New York at Stony Brook, 1993.

Ferguson, Philip R., 'Us and Them : Orientalism and the Evolution of Robert Olen Butler's Fiction', Radford University, 2007.

Ferrantello, Donna, '"The Symphony" in *Moby Dick*: the Chinese Eye in Melville's Storm. The Influence of the China Trade, Oriental Thought and Universalism on Melville's Romanticism', Drew University, 1993.

Fielding, A.T., 'The Image of the Mongols in Western European Imagination (1220–1500)', Cambridge University, 2005.

Finkelstein, Dorothee Metltzky, 'Melville and the Near East', Yale University, 1957.

Flanagan, Kathleen Theresa, 'The Orient as Pretext for Aesthetic Revolution in Modern Poetry in English', University of North Carolina at Chapel Hill, 1987.

Florschuetz, Timothy Jon, 'An Examination of the Nile River in Samuel Johnson's *The History of Rasselas, Prince of Abyssinia*', Arizona State University, 1991.

Forbes, W., 'Aspects of Orientalism in Eighteenth-Century English Literature', Queen Mary and Westfield College, 1991.

Frawley, Maria Barton Hinkle, 'A Wider Range: Travel Writing by Women in Victorian England', University of Delaware, 1991.

Friedman, Jack E., 'A Critical Study of George Sandys' *Relation of His Journey to the Levant*', New York University, 1972.

Frost, Kevin, 'Revisioning Enlightenment: A Critique of Classical Orientalism', La Trobe University, 2001.

Furuhata, Yuriko, 'Looking for the East: Cinematic Orientalism in Popular Film', University of New Mexico, 2001.

Galin, Muge N., 'The Path of Love: Sufism in the Novels of Doris Lessing', Ohio State University, 1992.

Ganguly, A.P., 'E.M. Forster's *A Passage to India*: A Detailed Study of his Treatment of India's Landscape, History, Social Anthropology and Religion', University of London, 1984.

Gendron, Charisse, '"A Sadly Long Strain About Self": The British Literary Travel Book, 1766–1937', The University of Connecticut, 1984.

Georgis, Dina, 'The Feminization of the East: An Historical Look at the Impact of Western Patriarchy on Orientalism', University of Toronto, 1995.

Georgoudaki, Ekaterini, 'Melville's Artistic Use of His Journeys to Europe and the Near East', Arizona State University, 1980.

Ghazi, Saeed, 'V.S. Naipaul, Post Colonial Orientalism and Islam', University of Toledo.

Gibson, Suzanne, 'The Eighteenth-Century Oriental Tales of Eliza Haywood, Frances Sheridan and Ellis Cornelia Knight', McMaster University, 1996.

Goh, Gillian Hui Lynn, 'Influences of Orientalism and the Orient Within Imagism', University of Western Australia, 2001.

Goldsmith, Elizabeth N. Fisher, 'Lifting the Veil: Images of the Exotic in Judith Gautier's Novels (1845–1917)', Brandeis University, 1995.

Grant, B. J., 'Burton/Empire: Strategies of Appropria-tion', University of Kent, 2005.

Haddad, Emily Anne, 'Orientalist Poetics: The Islamic Middle East in Nineteenth-Century English and French Poetry', Harvard University, 1997.

Haddawy, Husain Fareed Ali, 'English Arabesque: The Oriental Mode in Eighteenth-Century English Literature', Cornell University, 1962.

Hage el-, George Nicolas, 'William Blake and Kahlil Gibran: Poets of Prophetic Vision', State University of New York at Binghamton, 1981.

Halaby, Raouf Jamil, 'Arabic Influences on Chaucer: Speculative Essay on a Study of a Literary Relationship', East Texas State University, 1973.

Hamilton, John Alexander, 'Epics of the Lone Will: A Study of *Travels in Arabia Deserta* and *Seven Pillars of Wisdom*', Harvard University, 1979.

Harrington, M. J., 'Representations of Otherness in the 17th Century *récit de voyage* to the Orient', University of Dublin, 2005.

Hartley, Robert Arnold, 'Images of Change in *The Revolt of Islam*', Columbia University, 1971.

Hasan, H. M., 'Jewels of Blood: An Arab Perspective on R. S. Thomas', University of Wales, Aberystwyth, 1985.

Hassan Al-, Naser Yousef, 'Heroism in Old English and Classical Arabic Poetry: a Comparative Study of Four Battle Poems', Indiana University, 1982.

Hassan, Kaied Filfil, '*Arabian Nights*: Its Background, Its Development as an Original Play, and the Influence of the *Nights* on English Literature and Drama', Texas Tech University, 1991.

Hawari, R., 'The Arabian Background of Tennyson, Thomson and Meredith', B.Litt., University of Oxford, 1962–3.

Hawari, R., 'A Study of the 'Exotic' East in the Works of Thackeray, with Reference to the Cult of the Oriental in Eighteenth and Nineteenth Century', London, Birckbeck College, 1966–7.

Haynes, Jonathan Marshall, 'George Sandys' *Relation of a Journey Begun an.Dom., 1610*': The Humanist as Traveller', Yale University, 1980.

Hejazi al-, Ali Ahmad Ali, 'Arabo-Islamic Mythology in English Poetry, 1755–1825, University of Wisconsin-Milwaukee, 1979.

Hellal, Arida, 'Emerson's Knowledge and Use of Islamic Literature', University of Houston, 1971.

Hildreth, Ethan Joe David, 'Writing an Imperial Narrative: Treatment of the Arab Image in Nineteenth-Century British Literature', Georgia State University, 1997.

Hout, Syrine Chafic, 'Viewing Europe from the Outside: Cultural Encounters and European Culture Critiques in the Eighteenth-Century Pseudo-Oriental Travelogue and the Nineteenth-Century Voyage en Orient', Columbia University, 1994.

Howell, Margaret J., 'Oriental Influences in Chaucer's *Squire's Tale*', Indiana University, 1970.

Humoud al-, Sana Ahmad, 'Changing Attitudes in Literary Relations between the Islamic East and Christian West with Primary Emphasis Upon the Nineteenth Century', University of Denver, 1987.

Hurley, James Luke, 'Orientalism in Johnson and Goldsmith', DePaul University, 1939.

Husain, I., 'The Oriental Elements in English Poetry (1784–1859)', University of Edinburgh, 1934.

Hussein, Hassan Soleiman, 'The Koran and Courtly Love: A Study of the Koran and Its Influence on the Development of Divine and Courtly Love', University of Southern California, 1971.

Isani, Mukhtar Ali, 'The Oriental Tale in America Through 1865: A Study of American Fiction', Princeton University, 1962.

Ismael, Abed Mahmmoud, 'Wallace Stevens: A Sufi Supreme Fiction', New York University, 1995.

Issa, W., 'Aspects of Orientalism: Four English Writers; Burton, Blunt, Flecker and T.E. Lawrence', University of Reading, 1986.

Jankiewicz, Stephen R., 'The Intimate Orient: British Cross-Cultural Encounters, 1850–1950', Rutgers State University, 2005.

Javadi-Tabrizi, H., 'The Idea of Persian Literary Influence in English Literature, with Special Reference to the Nineteenth Century', University of Cambridge, 1964–5.

Jeffreys, Peter G., 'Hellenism and Orientalism in the Works of E.M. Forster and Constantine Cavafy: A Parallel Reading', University of Toronto, 1999.

Johanpur, F., 'Oriental Influences on the Works of Ralph Waldo Emerson', MA, University of Hull, 1964–5.

Johnson, Maya Ayana, 'Harem Fantasies and Music Videos: Contemporary Orientalist Representation', College of William and Mary, 2007.

Jubouri Al-, D.A.H., 'The Medieval Idea of the Saracen, as Illustrated in English Literature, Spectacle and Sport', University of Leicester, 1971–2.

Kadi Al-, Thaer T., '"Here is my Space": Shakespeare's Treatment of the Orient in *Othello, Antony and Cleopatra* and the *Tempest*', Indiana University of Pennsylvania, 2000.

Kahf, Mohja, 'The Muslim Woman in Western Literature from Romance to Romanticism', Rutgers State University of New Jersey, New Bruswick, 1994.

Kaiser, Timothy David, '"Orientalism" in Auden and Isherwood's Journey to a War', University of Hong Kong, 1997.

Kanaan, F., 'Shakespeare on the Arab Page and Stage', University of Manchester, 1998.

Kang, Nae Heui, 'The Renaissance Representation of the Other: Travel Literature, Spenser, Shakespeare, and Milton', Marquette University, 1986.

Kararah, A. M.A.H., 'Simon Ockley: His Contribution to Arabic Studies and Influence on Western Thought', Cambridge University, 1955.

Kaufman, Ester, 'The Use of Oriental Material by James Thomson, Oscar Wilde, and Rudyard Kipling', Cornell University, 1947.

Keller, Kathleen E., 'The Development of Western European Men's "At-Home" Caps from Mid-Sixteenth Century to Mid-Eighteenth Century and their Relationship to the Parallel Development of Luxury, Orientalism and Undress', Fashion Institute of Technology, Program in Museum Studies, 1996.

Kenna, Christopher, 'Rural Crime, Banditry and Colonial Control: Thags, Dakaits and "Bureacratic" Orientalism in India c. 1790–1863', University of Sydney, 1987.

Kenton, William G., 'English Liberty and Turkish Tyranny: The Symbolic Function of the East in Milton's Poetry and Prose', New York University, 2005.

Khair-Ullah, F.S., 'Orientalism in the Romantics', University of Edinburgh, 1952–3.

Khan, A.B., 'The Indian Vision of E.M. Forster', Oxford University, 1982.

Khan, H.A., 'A Study of the Relationship Between the Sensuous and the Mystical in Wordsworth, with Some Oriental Parallels'.

Khatib al-, Issam, 'The Orientalism of Alfred Lord Tennyson', Case Western Reserve University, 1967.

Khatib al-, Waddah, 'Trends in the Evolution of Romantic Orientalism', University of Virginia, 1999.

Kidwai, A. R., '"Samples of the Finest Orientalism": A Study of the Orient in Lord Byron's "*Turkish Tales*"', University of Leicester, 1993.

Klein, Christina, 'Cold War Orientalism: Musicals, Travel Narratives, and Middlebrow Culture in Postwar America', Yale University, 1997.

Kleitz, Dorsey Rodney, 'Orientalism and the American Romantic Imagination: The Middle East in the Works of Irving, Poe, Emerson, and Melville', University of New Hampshire, 1988.

Knipp, Charles Christopher, 'Types of Orientalism in Eighteenth-Century England', University of California at Berkeley, 1974.

Kobor, Kelli Michele, 'Orientalism, the Construction of Race, and the Politics of Identity in British India, 1800–1930', Duke University, 1998.

Kopf, David, 'Orientalism and the Genesis of the Bengal Renaissance, 1800–1830', University of Chicago, 1964.

Lall, Ann Joyce M., 'Gendering the Orient: Women and the Imagined India', California State University, Long Beach, 2006.

Lasater, Alice Elizabeth, 'Hispano-Arabic Relationships to the Works of the "Gawain"-Poet', University of Tennessee, 1971.

Lee, Katherine H., 'North American Orientalism: The Career and Works of Winnifred Eaton (1875–1954)', University of Missouri-Columbia, 2001.

Leesch, Agnieszka E., 'A Woman of the Orient', University of South Dakota, 2001.

Lekesizalin, Ferma, 'Cultural Encounters, Difference, and Reconstruction of History: Islam and the West', University of Southern Mississippi, 2006.

Lennon, Joseph Allen, 'The Celt and the Oriental: The Narratives of Irish Orientalism', University of Connecticut, 2001.

Leo, Kwang-lin, 'Orientalism as a type of Discourse', University of Singapore, 1986.

Lew, Joseph William, 'The Deceptive Other: English Writing and the Orient, 1717–1820', Stanford University, 1990.

Lewis, A.D., 'Oriental Influence in English Literature from 1800 to 1850', M.A., University of Wales, 1953–4.

Liassis, N., 'Lord Byron's Attitudes to the Near East in the Oriental Tales', University of Reading, 1997.

Lindores, E.A., 'The Oriental Tale in English Prose Fiction from 1740 to 1839', M.A., University of Manchester, 1924.

Lo, F. R., 'Orientalism, Empire and Revolution, 1785–1810', University of Sussex, 1997.

Lockwood, Anne M., 'Voyagers Out of the Harem Within: British Women Travel Writers in the Middle East', University of North Carolina at Greenshboro, 1997.

Lonnquist, Barbara Christian, 'James Joyce and Virginia Woolf, Two-Tongue Common Readers: Egypt and the Rites of Allusion in *Finnegans Wake* and *Between the Acts*', University of Pennsylvania, 1995.

Low, Sharon, 'Domestic Orientations: Travel Writing and Romantic Fiction on the Middle East', University of Melbourne, 2005.

Ma'at, Y.S., 'Sir Richard Burton; A Study of His Literary Works Relating to the Arab World and Islam', University of St. Andrews, 1978.

MacKnight, Annette Bassford, 'Orientalism in English Poetry of the Nineteenth Century', Tufts College, 1918.

MacNeill, Jennie E., 'The Orient in Matthew Arnold's Poetry', University of Toronto, 1935.

Majeed, Javed, 'Orientalism, Utalitarianism and British India James Mill's *The History of British India* and the Romantic Orient', University of Oxford, 1988.

Maktabi, Anas, 'The Representation of Islam and Muslims in Eighteenth-Century British Fiction', Indiana University of Pennsylvania, 2001.

Maner, Selin, 'Narrating the Orient; Orient-ing the Narrative', Cornell University, 1999.

Marandi, Seyed Mohammed, 'Lord Byron, His Critics and Orientalism', University of Birmingham, 2003.

Marr, Timothy Worthington, 'Imagining Ishmael: Studies of Islamic Orientalism in America from the Puritans to Melville', Yale University, 1997.

Martinez, Alicia, 'The Hero and Heroine of Shelley's *The Revolt of Islam*', Columbia University, 1974.

Mattar, O. M. S., 'Themes in the Early Tales of Joseph Conrad and their Presentation to Arab Students', University of London, Institute of Education, 1975.

Maynard, T.G.J., 'The Literary Relevance of the Enclosed Garden as an Image in the Oriental Tale', 1704–1820, University of London, 1969–70.

Mayo Lopez, Jose, 'The Tragedy of Being a Moor, or Racialism in Shakespeare's *Othello*', Salamanca University, 1972.

Mcalister, Melani Lynn, 'Staging the American Century: Race, Gender, and Nation in United States Representations of the Middle East, 1945–1992', Brown University, 1996.

McCormick, A.M., 'The Origins and Development of the Style of Charles M., Doughty's *Arabia Deserta*', University of London, 1951–2.

Meagher, Shelley, 'Islam in Irish Poetry', University of Oxford, 2006.

Meester, Marie E., 'Oriental Influences in the English Literature of the Nineteenth Century', University of Heidelberg, Germany, 1915.

Melikian, Anahid, 'Byron and the Near East', University of Wisconsin-Madison, 1954.

Melissinos, Joyce Mitchell, 'The Stuff of Fable: Accounts of Embassies from England and Russia to the Middle East and the Far East in the Eighteenth Century: An Overlooked Dimension of Voyage and Travel Literature', University of Rochester, 1995.

Meloccaro, Lynne, 'Orientalism and the Oriental Tale: Gender, Genre, and Cultural Identity in Eighteenth-Century England', Rutgers University, 1992.

Menocal, Maria Rosa, 'The Singers of Love: Al-Andalus and the Origins of Troubadour Poetry', University of Pennsylvania, 1979.

Menon, Sridevi, 'Discursive Realms and Colonial Practice: Contrapuntal Studies of Race in Colonial India and the United States', University of Hawaii at Manoa, 2000.

Merghelani, Abdul-Rahman Amin, 'Saracenism on the British Stage 1580–1642: A Formula for Distance', University of Colorado at Boulder, 1982.

Mesina, Editha G., 'Partial Truth: Orientalism, Anthropology and the Other', Rutgers University, 1991.

Metwalli, Ahmed Mohamed, 'The Lure of the Levant. The American Literary Experience in Egypt and the Holy Land: A Study in the Literature of Travel, 1800–1865', State University of New York at Albany, 1971.

Middleton, Kimberly S., '"You Gotta Chink It Up!": Asian American Performativity in the New Orientalism', University of Notre Dame, 2003.

Milligan, Barry, 'Pleasures and Pains: Opium and the Orient in Nineteenth-Century English Culture', Duke University, 1992.

Minikes, Madeline, 'The Contribution of Sir William Jones's Orientalism to Nineteenth Century Occidental Thought', Sarah Lawrence College, 1965.

Mohamad, M. Haj, 'Ezra Pound and Ibn Hazem: Modernist and Arabic Culture', University of Keele, 1992.

Mohamed, Donna Fahimah, 'Western Biographies of Muhammad and the Question of Orientalism', University of North Carolina at Chapel Hill, 1994.

Mohd, Jamal A.I., 'A Critical Study of Richard F. Burton's Tales from 1001 *Arabian Nights*', Aligarh Muslim University, Aligarh, India, 1999.

Moss, E.V., 'The Poetics of Alterity: Representatives of the Oriental in Insular and Related Literatures 1066–1453', Belfast, Queen's University, 2004.

Mowafy El-, M.I., 'Arabia in English Literature: 1650–1750', University of Wales, 1961.

Moussa, F.M., 'The Oriental Tale in England in the Early Nineteenth Century (1786–1824)', University of London, 1957–58.

Mueller, Roger Chester, 'The Orient in American Transcendental Periodicals, 1835–1886', University of Minnesota, 1968.

Mugawar, Fahd M.T.S., 'The Oriental Element in the Elizabethan Drama with Special Reference to Marlowe, Shakespeare and Ben Jonson', Aligarh Muslim University, Aligarh, India, 2004.

Musa, Mohammed Ali, 'The Subterranean Caverns: The East and its Progeny in Eighteenth-Century English and French Literature', University of Arkansas, 1981.

Mutman, Mahmut, 'Under the Sign of Orientalism', University of California, Santa Cruz, 1992.

Naddaff, Sandra Ann, 'Arabesque: Narrative Structure and the Aesthetics of Repetition in the "*1001 Nights*" Cycle of "The Porter and the Three Ladies of Baghdad"', Harvard University, 1983.

Naimi, Mohammed Nour, 'T.E. Lawrence and the Orientalist Tradition', University of Essex , 1991.

Nasir, Sari Jamil, 'The Image of the Arab in American Popular Culture', University of Illinois at Urbana-Champaign, 1962.

Nasralla, Abderrahim Ali, 'The Enemy Perceived: Christian and Muslim Views of Each Other During the Crusades', New York University, 1980.

Nassir, Ghazi Q., 'A History and Criticism of Samuel Johnson's Oriental Tales', The Florida State University, 1989.

Neal, Shirley Winifred Zwoyer, 'Family Relationships in *The Revolt of Islam*, University of Illinois at Urbana-Champaign, 1973.

Nechamkin, Judith, 'Edward Said's Orientalism: Discourse of Power', McGill University, 1994.

Nichols, Pamela Catherine, 'Force and Charm in the Desert: Manly Adventure and Gentlemanly Behaviour in the Middle Eastern Travel Writings of Richard and Isabel Burton and Wilfrid Scawen and Anne Blunt', New York University, 1994.

Nusair, L., Gender Writing: Representations of Arab Women in Postcolonial Literature', University of Edinburgh, 2005.

Obaid, Thoraya Ahmed, 'The Moor Figure in English Renaissance Drama', Wayne State University, 1974.

Obeidat, Marwan Mohammad, 'The Muslim East in American Literature: The Formation of an Image', Indiana University, 1985.

O'Brien, Amy, 'Border Crossing: Gender, Transvestism and Orientalism in M. Butterfly', Simmons College, 2004.

O'Dwyer, Carolyn, 'Pacific Orientalisms: South Seas Discourse and Colonial Cultures', University of Melbourne, 2002.

Orachoonwongse, Somtawil, 'A Study of Selected Symbols Through Poetry: the Orient and the West', Oklahoma State University, 1976.

Orman, Thomas Joseph, '"Something Which Is Not Us": Self, Place, and Otherness in Byron's Poetry', University of Toronto, 1992.

Orr, Bridget Erica, 'Theatrical Voyages and Conquests: The Colonial Discourse of Restoration Drama, 1660–1696', Cornell University, 1995.

Osborne, Edna Pearle, 'The Orientalism of Byron', University of Kansas, 1914.

Oueijan, Naji Boulos, 'A Compendium of Eastern Elements in Byron's Oriental Tales', Baylor University, 1985.

Pandit, Pallavi, 'Orientalist Discourse and Its Literary Representations in the Works of Four British Travel Writers: James Morier, Alexander Kinglake, Richard Burton, and Gertrude Bell', Pennsylvania State University, 1990.

Parreiras-Horta, Luis Paulo, 'Mirrors of Ink and Wonderful Lamps: The *Arabian Nights* in Victorian and Postmodern Literature', University of Toronto, 2004.

Paull, Michael Ray, 'The Figure of Mahomet in Middle English Literature', University of North Carolina at Chapel Hill, 1969.

Pease, Raymond Burnette, 'The Saracen in English Literature', University of Wisconsin-Madison, 1922.

Peernajmodin, H., 'Orientalist Representations of Persia in the Works of Spenser, Marlowe, Milton, Moore and Morier', University of Birmingham, 2002.

Pinault, David, 'Stylistic Features in Selected Tales from *The Thousand and One Nights*', University of Pennsylvania, 1986.

Plowright, P.S., 'The Influence of Oriental Theatrical Techniques on the Theory and Practice of Western Drama', University of London, 1976.

Poe, Angela Chia-yi, 'The Orient of the Boulevards: The Representation of the Middle East in Nineteenth Century French Popular Theatre', University of California, 1989.

Ponseti, Joseph, 'Representing the Other: The Orientalism of Arminius Vambery', University of New Orleans, 1987.

Porter, John C., 'The Definition and Redefinition of West African Muslims in Tudor Drama', University of Missouri-Columbia, 2005.

Powell, Kathryn E., 'The Anglo-Saxon Imaginary of the East: A Psychoanalytic Exploration of the Image of the East in Old English Literature', University of Notre Dame, 2001.

Power, Carla, 'The Reception of Persian Classical Poetry in England, 1770–1835: A Study in Orientalism', 1991.

Power, Henriette Lazaridis, 'Shahrazade's Wake: The *Arabian Nights* and the Narrative Dynamics of Charles Dickens and James Joyce', University of Pennsylvania, 1988.

Price, Jessamine W., 'British Tourism in Egypt: Orientalism and Spatial Change, 1869–1914', University of Oxford, 2000.

Price, Jessamine, 'Women in an Antique Land: Travel, Gender, and the Orient in Nineteenth Century Britain', Drew University, 1996.

Pruitt, Lisa Joy, '"A Looking-Glass for Ladies": American Protestant Women and the Orient in the Nineteenth Century', Vanderbilt University, 1998.

Qazi, Munir Ahmad, 'Three Eastern Folktales and Shakespeare's *Romeo and Juliet*: A Comparison in Themes, Motifs, and Modes of Transference', University of Toledo, 1982.

Rahal, I., 'A Critical Apparatus for an Edition of James Elroy Flecker's *Hassan*', M.A., University of Leicester, 1978.

Rahman, Shazia, 'Resisting Women: Orientalism, Diaspora, and Gender', University of Alberta, 2002.

Rais, Mahmoud, 'The Representation of the Turk in English Renaissance Drama', Cornell University, 1973.

Ram, Harsha, 'Geographies of Empire: The Poetics of Orientalism in Europe and Russia', Yale University, 1995.

Raman, Shankar, 'Looking East: 'India' and the Renaissance', Stanford University, 1995.

Ramaswami, Shankar, 'The Imperialist Rules: Orientalism and Conceptions of Development', Harvard University, 1989.

Ramey, Lynn Tarte, 'Christians and Saracens: Imagination and Cultural Interaction in the French Middle Ages', Harvard University, 1997.

Rawashdeh, Moh'd, 'England in Disguise: The Orient on Restoration and Eighteenth-Century Stage', Purdue University, 2001.

Ray, Amit, 'Negotiating the Modern : Orientalism and 'Indianess' in the Anglophone World', University of Michigan, 2004.

Raz, Ronen, 'The Transparent Mirror: Arab Intellectuals and Orientalism, 1798–1950', Princeton University, 1997.

Reany, Daniel P., 'Social Orientalism', American University in Cairo, 2002.

Rezai Ghassemi, A.A., 'Major Oriental Influences upon English Literature During the Late 18th and Early 19th Centuries, with Special Reference to Persia', London, King's College, 1980.

Rice, Warner G., 'Turk, Moor, and Persian in English Literature from 1550 to 1660, with Particular Reference to the Drama', University of Harvard, 1931.

Richon, O., 'Exoticism and Representation', Polytechnic of Central London, 1988.

Rideout, Christian Ernest, 'The Orient of the Imagination: Intertextuality, Orientalism and satire in Montesquieu's *Lettres Persanes*', Mills College, 2002.

Rishmawi, George K., 'Oriental Element in English Romantic Poetry: Shelley and Byron', State University of New York at Buffalo, 1983.

Rizvi, Simi, 'The Oriental Content and Context in E.M. Forster's Novels and Essays', Aligarh Muslim University, Aligarh, India, 2001.

Robinson, Benedict, 'The Romance of the East: Islam and English Literature after the Reformation (Edmund Spenser, William Shakespeare, John Milton)', Columbia University, 2002.

Robinson-Dunn, Diane Liga, 'Imperial Identities: Anglo-Muslim Relations and the Politics of Orientalism in British-occupied Egypt and Victorian England, 1870–1900', State University of New York at Stony Brook, 1999.

Rockwell, Kenneth Guy, 'The Orient in American Poetry, 1900–1933', University of Kansas, 1933.

Rogers, William Norris, 'Arabian Involvement: A Study of Five Victorian Travel Narratives', University of California, Berkeley, 1972.

Rompkey, Ronald G., 'A Study of Orientalism in English Literature, 1707–1824', Memorial University of Newfoundland, 1968.

Rooney, Jeannette L., 'Constructing a Fantasy: "Orientalism" and the Native American in

Charles M. Russell's *Waiting and Mad'*, Indiana University, 2007.

Rose, Dallen J., 'A Classical Orient : Orientalism and Greece in John Cam Hobhouse's *A Journey Through Albania – During the Years 1809 and 1810'*, Washington State University, 2004.

Ruff, James Lynn, 'Image, Theme and Structure in *The Revolt of Islam'*, Northwestern University, 1968.

Rushdy, M.R., 'English Travelers in Egypt during the Reign of Mohamed Ali (1850–1847): A Study in Literary Form', University of Leeds, 1950.

Russell, S., 'Home and Empire: Domesticity and Imperialism in some Mid-Nineteenth Century Fiction', Oxford University, 1998.

Saab, H., 'Restoration Orientalism: The Representation of the Turk in Serious Drama', University of Swansea, 1999.

Safady, Issam, 'Attempt and Attainment: A Study of Some Literary Aspects of Doughty's *Arabia Deserta* as the Culmination of Late-Victorian Anglo-American Travel Books to the Levant', University of Kentucky, 1968.

Sahaj Pal, T. R., 'Oriental Influence in the Poetry of P. B. Shelley', MA, University of Belfast, 1964–5.

Saigh, E. J. S., 'Eastern Influences in Chaucer with Special Reference to the Arabs', University of London, 1946.

Saleh, T.A., 'The Foreign Milieu in E.M. Forster's Works', M.A., University of Exeter, 1964–5.

Salem, Mahmoud Mohamed Mahmoud, 'Egypt as Represented in Two Twentieth-Century Trilogies', University of South Carolina, 1989.

Sampson, Kathryn Ann, 'The Romantic Literary Pilgrimage to the Orient: Byron, Scott, and Burton', University of Texas at Austin, 1999.

Sandeman, C., 'The Orient in Spanish Literature and Thought, 1830–1930', University of Bristol, 1982.

Sapra, Rahul, 'The Limits of Orientalism: Seventeenth-Century Representations of India', Queen's University, 2004.

Sawda al-, Mahel, 'The Rise and Transformation of Courtly Love: A Study in European Thought of Love', University of Essex , 1993.

Scarfe Beckett, K., 'Anglo-Saxon Perceptions of the Arabs, Ismaelites and Saracens', Cambridge University, 1999.

Scott, A., 'Representation of the Barbarian in the Early Medieval West, c.800–1100', Oxford University, 1998.

Seminario, Lee Anne Durham, 'The Black, the Moor and the Jew in the 'Comedia' of Lope De Vega (1609–1625)', Florida State University, 1974.

Sh'aban, Fuad, 'The Mohemmedan World in English Literature, c.1580–1642: Illustrated by a text of *The Travailes of Three English Brothers*', Duke University, 1965.

Shamma, Mohammed S., 'The Virtual Orient', University of Texas at Austin, 1997.

Sharafuddin, M. A., 'Islam and Romanticism: A Study of Orientalism in English Verse Narrative, 1798–1817', University of York, 1988.

Shaw, Sheila G., 'The Influence of the *Arabian Nights* on Early Eighteenth Century English Literature, with Special Reference to *Robinson Crusoe* and *Gulliver's Travels*', Bryn Mawr College, 1959.

Sheltag, Hussein Abdul-Azim, 'The Influence of the *Arabian Nights* Upon Nineteenth Century English Fiction', University of Exeter, 1989.

Shervani, Shirin, 'A Critical Study of William Beckford's *Vathek*: *An Arabian Tale* (1786)', Aligarh Muslim University, Aligarh, India, 2000.

Shirazi, Zeinab Abdel-Mohsen Ahmed, 'Eastern Themes in the Fiction of D.H. Lawrence', University of Exeter , 1987.

Siddiqui, Shahzad Ahmad, 'The Oriental Content and Context in Byron's *Don Juan*', Aligarh Muslim University, Aligarh, India, 2008.

Shoukany, Muhammed Nasser, 'Orientalism and the Arab Literary Responses: Studies in Ahmad Faris Al-Shidyaq, Charles M. Doughty, Joseph Conrad, Jabra I. Jabra and Tawfiq Yusuf Awwad', University of Texas at Austin, 1990.

Skidmore, Mark, 'The Moral Traits of Christian and Saracen as Portrayed by the *Chansons de Geste*', Columbia University, 1935.

Smith, Byron Porter, 'Islam in English Literature', Columbia University, 1939.

Smith, Martha L., 'Creating the Exotic East : Romantic Literature, Orientalist Scholarship, and the Colonial Construction of the East', Southwest Missouri State University, 2005.

Smith, Patricia Clark, 'Novel Conceptions, Unusual Combinations: The Arabesque in Poe', Yale University, 1970.

Stavrou, Stavros, 'Seeking the Exotic Romantic Orientalism in Keats, Shelley, and Byron', Dalhousie University, 1991.

Sulaiman, J.Y., 'Victorian Travellers' Attitudes to the Arab World', University of Wales, Bangor, 1991.

Sultana, Fehmida, 'Romantic Orientalism and Islam: Southey, Shelley, Moore, and Byron', Tufts University, 1989.

Sun, Dongming, 'Orientalism in Imagist Poetics', City College of New York, 1989.

Suratgar, M.L.K., 'Traces of Persian Influence upon English Literature During the Fifteenth and Sixteenth Centuries', University of London, 1939.

Sweet, Nanora Louise Ziebold, 'The Bowl of Liberty: Felicia Hemans and the Romantic Mediterranean', University of Michigan, 1993.

Tageldin, Shaden M., ''Mahomet's Bride' and the 'Moral North': The Poetic Politics of European Spatial, Social, and Sexual 'Orient-ation' in *Don Juan's* Byronic Near East', Harvard University, 1992.

Taha Al-, M., 'The Orient and Three Victorian Travellers: Kinglake, Burton and Palgrave', University of Leicester, 1989.

Taipei, 'Chang, Tom Tung-p'ing, 'Dialectic of Reason and Imagination in William Beckford's *Vathek, An Arabian Tale*', Tamkang University, 1993.

Takahashi, I., 'From Palestine to India: Bishop Heber's Poetic Pilgrimage', Cambridge University, 2004.

Tansley, Tangea, 'Writing from the Shadowlands: How Cross-Cultural Literature Negotiates the Legacy of Edward Said', Murdoch University, 2004.

Taseer, M.D., 'India and the Near East in English Literature', University of Cambridge, 1936.

Tavalaie, Mohammad, 'The Orientalist Construction of Persia', University of New South Wales, 1998.

Taylor, S.E., 'The Saracen Princess in the Medieval *Chanson de geste*', University of Sheffield, 1982.

Taylor, Susan Beth, 'Ruining Oppositions: Orientalism and the Constructions of Empire in British Romanticism', Brown University, 1993.

Tezla, Albert, 'Byron's Oriental Tales: A Critical Study', University of Chicago, 1952.

Thacker, Christopher John Charles, 'Attitudes of European Travellers in the Levant (1696–1811)', Indiana University, 1963.

Thiessen, Jacob Gregg Ann, 'Orientalism and the East India Company, 1773–1858', Arbor, Mich. Johns Hopkins University, 1992.

Toler, Pamela D., 'Building the Orient of the Imagination: Excess, Confusion, and Violence in Orientalist Painting and Literature', University of Chicago, 2003.

Tong, S., 'Discourse and Colonial Encounter: Situating Robert Louis Stevenson's South Seas Fiction', University of Edinburgh, 2001.

Tounsi, Mohamed Mohamed, 'Shakespeare in Arabic: A Study of the Translation, Reception, and Influence of Shakespeare's Drama in the Arab World', University of Northern Colorado, 1989.

Towey, P., 'The New Orientalism': Representations of Islam and its Effects in Ireland, Dublin University College, 2004.

Turk, Jo Audrey Mastrud, 'E.M. Forster's Double Vision: The Split in *A Passage to India*', University of Florida, 1977.

Twaij, Mohammed Baqir, 'Shakespeare in the Arab World', Northwestern University, 1973.

Uebel, Michael David, 'Locating utopia: the Orient and the Cultural Imaginary of the Middle Ages', University of Virginia, 1997.

Van de Bilt, Eduardus Franciscus, 'Proximity and Distance: American Travellers to the Middle East, 1819–1918', Cornell University, 1985.

Versluis, Arthur James, 'Ex Oriente Lux: American Transcendentalism and the Orient', University of Michigan, 1990.

Voelz, Glenn James, 'Savages of the Sea : Orientalism, Indians and the Cultural Construction of non-European Diplomacy During the Barbary Conflict', University of Virginia, 2001.

Walker, J. F. H., 'The Perception of the Orient in Romantic Literature', University of Oxford, 1990.

Walker, J.M., 'The Saracens in the Thirteenth-Century *Chansons de Geste* and Romances', M.A., University of London, 1961–2.

Wang, Li, 'The Orient in Henry David Thoreau', Ohio University, 1949.

Warner Grenelle, 'Turk, Moor and Persian in English Literature from 1550 to 1660, with Particular Reference to the Drama', Harvard University, 1926.

Warren, Mary Keith, 'Orientalism in Browning', Boston University, 1930.

Washburn, Benjamin Earle, 'Orientalism: or, the Influence of the *Arabian Nights* on English Literature', University of North Carolina at Chapel Hill, 1906.

Washington, Lynette, 'Orientalism in Australia: Gender and Race Representation in Australian Cinema', University of South Australia, 2001.

Watson, Nessim John, 'Action Movie Arabs and the American Call to Endless War: The Role of

American Orientalism in Organizing the U.S. 'Response' to the 9/11 Attacks', University of Massachusetts, Amherst, 2005.

Webb, Jennifer, 'Inscribing the Other: Colonialist Discourses and Some Stories of Difference', Central Queensland University, 1994.

Weber, Charlotte Esther, 'Unveiling Sheherezade: The Intersection of Feminism and Orientalism within the International Women's Movement, 1911–1950', Ohio State University, 1996

Weitzman, A.J., 'The Influence of Middle East on English Prose Fiction 1600–1725: An Eighteenth-Century Perspective', New York University, 1964.

White, Deborah Elise, 'Action, Suffering, and Allegory: Shelley's *Revolt of Islam*', Yale University, 1993.

White, Samantha, 'The Representation of the "Orient" in "Occidental" Theatre', Murdoch University, 1992.

Whitelock, J., 'The Seven Sages of Rome and Orientalism in Middle English Literature, with an Edition of the Poem from Cambridge, University Library', University of Cambridge, 1997.

Wiener, Harold S.L., 'The Eastern Background of Byron's Turkish Tales', Yale University, 1938.

Willson, Jennifer F., 'Building Borders with New Orientalism: Cultural Appreciation, Appropriation, and Representation', Georgetown University, 2004.

Workman, Nancy Victoria, 'A Victorian *Arabian Nights'* Adventure: A Study in Intertextuality', Loyola University of Chicago, 1989.

Yaghmour, F.E., 'Some Oriental Elements in Restoration Tragedy', University of Sheffield, 1977.

Yamasaki, Nobuko, 'Melville's Orientalism in Type: Race, Sexuality, and Christianity', Cornell University, 2003.

Yang, Chi-ming, 'Forging the Orient: Virtue and Exoticism in Eighteenth-Century England, 1660–1760', Cornell University, 2003.

Yaqub, Huma, 'A Critical Study of Thomas Moore's *Lalla Rookh*, "The Loves of the Angels" and "Ghazals"', Aligarh Muslim University, Aligarh, India, 2000.

Yegenoglu-Mutman, Meyda, 'Veiled Fantasies: Towards a Feminist Reading of Orientalism', University of California, Santa Cruz, 1993.

Yong, John L., 'The Journey to the Orient', Mankato State University, 1991.

Yoshihara, Mari, 'Women's Asia: American Women and the Gendering of American Orientalism, 1870s-WWII', Brown University, 1997.

Youssef, Lamia Ben, 'The Production of the Muslim Women in Western Gnosis, Feminist Theory, Maghrebian Nationalism and Literature', Michigan State University, 2002.

Yu, Su-lin, 'Fantasizing the Oriental Other: Race, Gender, and Western Female Subjectivity', Northern Illinois University, 2001.

Zaidi, Syed Faiz, 'Image of the Orient in Victorian Poetry with Special Reference to Tennyson, Browning and Arnold', Aligarh Muslim University, Aligarh, India, 2003.

Zane, Kathleen J.C., 'Paradigms of Place in Travel Literature: The Oriental Voyages of Nerval, Burton, Kinglake, and Chateaubriand', City University of New York, 1984.

Zubaydi Al-, S.J., 'Dryden's *Almanzor and Almahide* or *the Conquest of Granada*: A Study of Its Sources and Meaning', M.A. University of Birmingham, 1974–5.

Zughoul, Mohammed Siad, 'A Comparative Study of Islamic Allusions in Lord Byron's Poetry and Prose', Indiana University of Pennsylvania, 1992.

5

Role of the *Arabian Nights* in the Development of Literary Orientalism

Books

Ali, Muhsin J., *Scheherazade in England: A Study of Nineteenth-Century English Criticism of the Arabian Nights*, Washington DC, Three Continents Press, 1981.

Bettleheim, Bruno, *The Frame Story of Thousand and One Nights, The Uses of Enchantment: The Meaning and Importance of Fairy Tales*, New York, Knopf, 1976.

Campbell, Kay Hardy (et al.), *'1001 Nights: Critical Essays and Annotated Bibliography*, Cambridge, MA, Dar Mahjar, 1985.

Caracciolo, Peter L. (Ed.), *The Arabian Nights in English Literature: Studies in the Reception of The Thousand and One Nights into British Culture*, London, Macmillan, 1988.

Ghazoul, Ferial, *Nocturnal Poetics: The Arabian Nights in Comparative Context*, Cairo, The American University in Cairo Press, 1996.

Naddaff, Sandra, *Arabesque: Narrative Structure and the Aesthetics of Repetition in 1001 Nights*,

Evanston, IL, Northwestern University Press, 1991.

Pinault, David, *Stylistic Features in Selected Tales from The Thousand and One Nights*, University of Pennsylvania, 1986.

Power, Henriette Lazaridis, *Shahrazade's Wake: The Arabian Nights and the Narrative Dynamics of Charles Dickens and James Joyce*, University of Pennsylvania, 1988.

Yamanaka, Yuriko and Nishio, Tetsuo (Eds.), *The Arabian Nights and Orientalism: Perspectives from East and West*, London; New York: Tauris, 2006.

Article/s

Abdul-Razzak, Fakhir, 'The *Arabian Nights* in America: A General Survey', in Muhsin Al-Musawi (Ed.), *Orientalism*, 3, Baghdad, Cultural Affairs, 1989, 28–42.

Ali, Muhsin Jassim, 'The Growth of Scholarly Interests in the *Arabian Nights*', *Muslim World*, 70, 3–4, 1980, 196–212.

Ali, Muhsin Jassim, '*The Arabian Nights* in Eighteenth-Century English Criticism', *Muslim World*, 67, 1977, 12–32.

Bagehot, Walter, 'The People of the *Arabian Nights*', *National Review*, IX, July 1859, 44–71.

Bennett, J.O., 'Book of the Thousand and One Nights', in James O Dennell Bennet, *Much Loved Books:*

Best Sellers of the Ages, New York, Boni and Liveright, 1927, 154–9.

Cannon, Garland, '"The Lady of Shallot" and "*The Arabian Nights" Tales*', *Victorian Poetry*, 8, 1970, 344–6.

Da'mi Al-, Muhammed A., 'Mistaking the *Arabian Nights* for Socio-Historical Document', *al-Ma'thurat al-Sha'biyyah*, Doha, Qatar, 49, January 1998, 7–19.

Da'mi Al-, Muhammed A., 'Some Aspects of the *Arabian Nights'* Impact on Nineteenth-Century American Culture', *Al-Ma'thurat al-Sha'biyyah*, 31, 1993, 7–16.

Denuccio, Jerome D., 'Fact, Fiction, Fatality: Poe's 'The Thousand-and-Second Tale of Scheherazade', *Studies in Short Fiction*, 27, 1990, 365–70.

Geddes, Sharon S., 'The Middle English Poem of Floriz and Blauncheflur and the *Arabian Nights* Tale of 'Ni'amah and Naomi': A Study in Parallels.' *Emporia*, 19:1, 1970, 14–21 and 23–4.

Ghazoul, Ferial, '*The Arabian Nights in* Shakespearean Comedy: "The Sleeper Awakened" and *The Taming of the Shrew'*, in Ferial Ghazoul, *Nocturnal Poetics: The Arabian Nights in Comparative Context*, Cairo, The American University in Cairo, 1996, 58–70.

Haddad, Emily A., 'Grounding a Poetics in the *1001 Nights*: Tennyson', in Emily A. Haddad, *Oriental Poetics*, Aldershot, UK, Ashgate, 2002, 183–6.

Hamori, Andras, 'The Magian and the Whore: Readings of Qamar al-Zaman'' in Kay Hardy Campbell (et al.), '*1001 Nights: Critical Essays and Annotated Bibliography*, Cambridge, MA, Dar Mahjar, 1985, 25–40.

Hampson, Robert G., 'Conrad, Guthrie, and "*The Arabian Nights*"', *Conradiana: A Journal of Joseph Conrad Studies*, 18, 1986, 141–3.

John, Brian, 'Tennyson's 'Recollections of the *Arabian Nights*' and the Individuation Process', *Victorian Poetry*, 4, 1966, 275–9.

Johnson, Rebecca Carol (et al.), '*The Arabian Nights*, Arab-European Literary Influence, and the Lineages of the Novel', *Modern Language Quarterly*, 68:2, 2007, 243–79.

Macdonald, Duncan B., 'A Bibliographical and Literary Study of the First Appearance of the *Arabian Nights* in Europe', *Library Quarterly*, 2, 1932, 387–420.

Mew, James, 'The *Arabian Nights*', *Cornhill Magazine*, 32, December 1875, 711–31.

Plotz, Juidth, 'In the Footsteps of Aladdin: De Quincy's *Arabian Nights*', *Wordsworth Circle*, 29:2, 1988, 120–6.

Power, Henriette Lazaridis, 'Shahrazade, Turko the Terrible, and Shem: The Reader as Voyeur in *Finnegans Wake*', in Morris Beja and Shari Benstock (Eds.), *Coping with Joyce: Essays from the Copenhagen Symposium*, Columbus, Ohio State University Press, 1989, 248–61.

Shaw, Sheila G. 'Early English Editions of the *Arabian Nights*: Their Value to Eighteenth Century Literary Scholarship', *Muslim World*, 49, 1959, 232–8.

Stephens, G.A. '*Arabian Nights* and Arthurian Romances', *Comparative Literature Studies*, 20, 1946, 11–15.

Wazzan, Adnan M., '*The Arabian Nights* in Western Literature: A Discourse Analysis', *Islamic Studies*, Islamabad, Pakistan, 32:1, 1993, 61–71.

Workman, Nancy V., 'Schederazade at Thornfield: Mythic Elements in *Jane Eyre*', *Essays in Literature*, 15, 1988, 177–92.

Doctoral Dissertaion/s

Abdullah, A.M., 'The *Arabian Nights* in English Literature to 1900', University of Cambridge, 1962–3.

Alaka, Madeleine Shireen, '*The Thousand and One Nights* in Translation: Its influence on Some Pre-Romantic English Writers', University of Redlands, 1951.

Alaki, A., 'The Sublime and the Arabesque: *The Thousand and One Nights* and its Gothic Re-Writings', University of East Anglia, 2001.

Ali, Muhsin Jassim, 'Nineteenth-Century English Criticism of the "*Arabian Nights*"', Dalhousie University, Canada, 1978.

Ali, Zahra Ahmed Hussein, 'Between Shahrazad and Marcel Proust: Narrative Techniques in 'The *Alexandria Quartet*'', Brown University, 1985.

Annan, Margaret Cecilia, '*The Arabian Nights* in Victorian Literature', Northwestern University, 1945.

Bouagada, Habib, 'Orientalism in Translation: *The One Thousand and One Nights* in 18th Century France and 19th Century England', University of Ottawa, 2005.

Brant, Nataliya Borisovna, 'Profiling Chagall: an Analysis of *Arabian Nights*', University of Georgia, 2000.

Coppinger, Kristyn Nicole, 'The *Arabian Nights* in British Romantic Children's Literature', Florida State University, 2006.

Ghazoul, Ferial Jabouri, 'Nocturnal Poetics: Towards a Diacritical Reading of the *Arabian Nights*', Columbia University, 1978.

Goldstein, Harry, 'A Radio Adaptation and Production Manual of Four Stories from the *Arabian Nights*', Wayne University, 1938.

Hassan, Kaied Filfil, '*Arabian Nights*: Its Background, Its Development as an Original Play, and the Influence of the *Nights* on English Literature and Drama', Texas Tech University, 1991.

Jamal Al-, Huda, 'Shahrazad's Daughters: Examining Female Roles in the *Thousand and One Nights*', Dominican College of San Rafael, 1999.

Morsy, Faten I., 'The Frame-Narrative and Short Fiction: A Continuum from 'One Thousand and One Nights' to Borges', University of Essex, 1989.

Naddaff, Sandra Ann, 'Arabesque: Narrative Structure and the Aesthetics of Repetition in the '1001 Nights' Cycle of 'The Porter and the Three Ladies of Baghdad'', Harvard University, 1983.

Parreiras-Horta, Luis Paulo, 'Mirrors of Ink and Wonderful Lamps: The "*Arabian Nights*" in Victorian and Postmodern Literature', University of Toronto, 2004.

Pinault, David, 'Stylistic Features in Selected Tales from *The Thousand and One Nights*', University of Pennsylvania, 1986.

Pollak, Marian, 'The *Arabian Nights* in English', City College of New York, 1967.

Power, Henriette Lazaridis, 'Shahrazade's Wake: The *Arabian Nights* and the Narrative Dynamics of Charles Dickens and James Joyce', University of Pennsylvania, 1988.

Sallis, E. K., 'Identity in Diversity: *The Thousand and One Nights* in English', University of Adelaide, 1997.

Schacker-Mill, Jennifer, 'Otherness and Otherworldliness: Edward W. Lane's Ethnographic Treatment of The *Arabian Nights*', Indiana University, 1995.

Shaheen, Mohammad, 'The *Arabian Nights*: Its History and Introduction in English Literature', University of Colorado, 1964.

Shaw, Sheila Goldstein, 'The Influence of the *Arabian Nights* on Early Eighteenth Century English Literature: With Special Reference to *Robinson Crusoe* and *Gulliver's Travels*', Bryn Mawr College, 1959.

Sheltag, Hussein Abdul-Azim, 'The Influence of the *Arabian Nights* upon Nineteenth-Century English Fiction', University of Exeter, 1989.

Shiber, Cornelia Scheider, 'Echoes of *Alf Layla wa-Layla* in E.T.A. Hoffmann's Märchen...', Tulane University of Louisiana, 1967.

Washburn, Benjamin Earle, 'Orientalism: or, The influence of the *Arabian Nights* on English literature', University of North Carolina at Chapel Hill, 1906.

Wassef, Nadia R, '(De)construction of Patriarchal Gendering in the *Arabian Nights*: John Barth's *Dunyazadiad* and Salwa Bakr's *The Golden Chariot*', American University in Cairo, 1996.

Workman, Nancy Victoria, 'A Victorian *Arabian Nights* Adventure: A Study in Intertextuality', Loyola University of Chicago, 1989.

Zimmerman, Mary Alice, 'The Archaeology of Performance: A Study of Ensemble Process and Development in the Looking Glass Theatre Production of The *Arabian Nights*', Northwestern University, 1994.

6

Role of the Oriental Tales in the Development of Literary Orientalism

Book/s

Conant, M.P., *The Oriental Tale in the Eighteenth Century*, New York, 1908.

Mack, R.L. (Ed.), *Oriental Tales*, Oxford, Oxford University Press, 1992.

Richardson, Alan (Ed.), '*Three Oriental Tales: Complete Texts with Introduction, Historical Contexts, Critical Essays*,' Boston, MA: Houghton Mifflin, 2002.

Article/s

Aravamudan, Srinivas, 'In the Wake of the Novel: The Oriental Tale as National Allegory,' *Novel*, 33:1, 1999, 5–31.

Ascari, Maurizio, 'The Role of Addison's Dream Visions and Oriental Tales in the Nascent Poetics of Short Fiction,' *Textus*, 18:1, 2005, 11–23.

Baker, Ernest, 'The Oriental Tale from *Rasselas* to *Vathek*', in Ernest Baker (Ed.), *History of English Novel*, 5, 55–76.

David, Alun, 'The Story of Semiramis: an Oriental tale in Elizabeth Rowe's *The History of Joseph*,' *Women's Writing*, 4:1, 1997, 91–101.

Grenby, M. O., 'Orientalism and Propaganda: The Oriental Tale and Popular Politics in Late Eighteenth-Century Britain,' *Eighteenth Century Novel*, 2, 2002, 215–37.

Jones, Russell, 'Leigh Hunt's Oriental Motifs – 'Abou Ben Adhem', *Journal of the Royal Asiatic Society*, 7:iii, 1997, 389–97.

Kamrath, Mark, 'An 'Inconceivable Pleasure' and the Philadelphia Minerva: Erotic Liberalism, Oriental Tales, and the Female Subject in Periodicals of the Early Republic,' *American Periodicals*, 14:1, 2004, 3–34.

Moussa, Mahmoud Fatma, 'Beckford, *Vathek* and The Oriental Tale', in Fatma Mahmoud Moussa (Ed.), *William Beckford of Fonthill 1760–1844*, 1960, 63–121.

Weitzman, Arthur, 'The Oriental Tale in the Eighteenth Century: A Reconsideration', *Studies on Voltaire in the Eighteenth Century*, 58, 1967, 1389–455.

Doctoral Dissertation/s

Avery, Elizabeth Christina, 'The Oriental Tale in England and France: With Special Reference to Dr. Johnson and Voltaire', State University of New York at Buffalo, 1932.

Conant, Martha Pike, 'The Oriental Tale in England in the Eighteenth Century', Columbia University, 1908.

Ekhtiar, Rochelle Suzette, 'Fictions of Enlightenment: The Oriental Tale in Eighteenth-Century England, Brandeis University, 1985.

Gibson, Suzanne, 'The Eighteenth-Century Oriental Tales of Eliza Haywood, Frances Sheridan and Ellis Cornelia Knight,' McMaster University, 1996.

Hout, Syrine Chafic, 'Viewing Europe from the Outside: Cultural Encounters and European Culture Critiques in the Eighteenth-Century Pseudo-Oriental Travelogue and the Nineteenth-Century "Voyage En Orient"', Columbia University, 1994.

Isani, Mukhtar Ali, 'The Oriental Tale in America Through 1865: A Study in American Fiction', Princeton University, 1962.

Lindores, E.A., 'The Oriental Tale in English Prose Fiction from 1740 to 1839', M.A., University of Manchester, 1924.

Moussa, F.M., 'The Oriental Tale in England in the Early Nineteenth Century (1786–1824)', University of London, 1957–8.

Maynard, T.G.J., 'The Literary Relevance of the Enclosed Garden as an Image in the Oriental Tale', 1704–1820, University of London, 1969–70.

Meloccaro, Lynne, 'Orientalism and the Oriental Tale: Gender, Genre, and Cultural Identity in Eighteenth-Century England', Rutgers State University of New Jersey-New Brunswick, 1992.

Nassir, Ghazi Q., 'A History and Criticism of Samuel Johnson's Oriental Tales', The Florida State University, 1989.